QUALITATIVE CHANGE IN HUMAN GEOGRAPHY

Other Titles of Interest

QUALITATIVE CHANGE IN HUMAN GEOGRAPHY

Edited by

S. S. DUNCAN
The London School of Economics & Political Science

PERGAMON PRESS
Oxford · New York · Toronto · Sydney · Paris · Frankfurt

U.K.	Pergamon Press Ltd., Headington Hill Hall, Oxford OX3 0BW, England
U.S.A.	Pergamon Press Inc., Maxwell House, Fairview Park, Elmsford, New York 10523, U.S.A.
CANADA	Pergamon of Canada, Suite 104, 150 Consumers Road, Willowdale, Ontario M2J 1P9, Canada
AUSTRALIA	Pergamon Press (Aust.) Pty. Ltd., P.O. Box 544, Potts Point, N.S.W. 2011, Australia
FRANCE	Pergamon Press SARL, 24 rue des Ecoles, 75240 Paris, Cedex 05, France
FEDERAL REPUBLIC OF GERMANY	Pergamon Press GmbH, 6242 Kronberg-Taunus, Hammerweg 6, Federal Republic of Germany

British Library Cataloguing in Publication Data

Qualitative change in human geography.
1. Anthropo-geography
I. Duncan, S S
909   GF41   80-49925
ISBN 0-08-025222-2 ✓

First published 1979 as a special issue of the journal *Geoforum*, Volume 10, Number 1 and supplied to subscribers as part of their subscription.

Reissued 1981

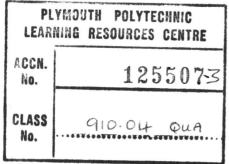
Printed in Great Britain by A. Wheaton & Co. Ltd., Exeter

Contents

Geoforum, Vol. 10, pp.1-4, 1979.
Pergamon Press Ltd. Printed in Great Britain.

Qualitative Change in Human Geography — An Introduction

S.S. DUNCAN, *London, U.K.

Change in Geography

The context of this issue of *Geoforum* is the current disarray of geography with the decay of quantitative geography as the dominant mode of explanation. Declining interest in quantitative geography has gone hand in hand with a realisation of its inability to solve empirical or explanatory problems. It is just this disarray, however, which is currently so fruitful in creating impulses for innovation and development after a period when geography's scope and potential seemed to have narrowed considerably. Of course, we should deny the tendency to write off quantitative geography completely. The quantitative revolution was important in forcing geography into a position where it had to be reconciled with the changes and advances achieved in other social science. In turn this meant breaking down geography's earlier, and somewhat petty, isolation. But, I suggest, this potential was restricted by the type of theory employed by quantitative geography, especially its treatment of space relations as a separate object of study. Potential could only be realised, therefore, by the breakdown of quantitative geography as the dominating method of analysis.

The particular purpose of this issue is to provide an introduction to, and illustration of, one of the more coherent and developed departures from the ruins of quantitative geography — what has become called (probably unfortunately) 'radical geography'. A more informative label might be 'social geography', if this had not already been appropriated and so imbued with connations of the isolation of the 'social' from the 'economic'. For the concern of 'radical geography' is with the interaction between social structures and social change (which include spatial form and change) as people create and transform their relationships, and thus create and transform space. Unlike quantitative geography, people are seen as active social agents, who nevertheless act in and under specific social forms and structures which have been produced in the past. The concern lies with social theory rather than with deterministic, asocial explanations where space remains independent of people. Social analysis replaces spatial analysis.

Re-erecting the status of people to that of active social beings — instead of passive objects — also means that explanation becomes historical. Society, including space as part of society, is created by people and therefore, presumably, changed by them. In this way, social and spatial forms are historically produced and so the actions of people are subsequently constrained by their own historical products. In contrast, under the quantitative revolution, even much of historical geography became ahistorical. History became little more than a static objectified data source, and all that marched through it were abstracted spatial processes purged of social meaning.

Again unlike quantitative geography, historical and social explanation implies that geography can be a critical social science. That is, explanation can expose the nature of the social world rather than merely reflecting or reproducing its patterns. A social and historical explanation of how space is created and transformed implies an evaluation of present arrangements. Their development in social historical processes is exposed and it becomes possible to conceive of alternatives. And, founded in the attempt to understand histor-

*Department of Geography, London School of Economics.

ical reality, these alternatives are likely to be superior to the idealistic 'scenario-building'; the inspired (or less-inspired) guesses, simulations and projections based on static and deterministic model fitting which is all that can be offered by truly quantitative geography. (Luckily, perhaps, for geography, some of the more inspired quantitative georaphers have been ready to throw away their quantification when it came to the pinch and to rely on an intuitive or immediate historical analysis.)[1]

Lest it is not already abundantly clear, let me point out that this should not be read as an appeal for geography to become sociology or economics. Just as geography has its spatial 'fetishism' so these subjects have theirs. Geography's fetishism has been described as "the clinging to the notion of some asocial, ahistorical purely spatial effect", where "the spatial expression of social processes can be described by some mysterious mathematical or geometrical laws that have an identical impact, irrespective of these social processes" (SAYER, 1977). But orthodox sociology tends to define the social so as to exclude economic and even political relations, and to remove any historical rationale for social behaviour. An extreme might be small group sociology, or voluntaristic but essentially deterministic social psychology based around replicating experiments on rats. At these extremes sociology becomes asocial. Even 'radical sociology', appealing to Weberian and Marxist themes, often remains resolutely 'sociological' in the sense of excluding economic social relations. Thus Castells' *The Urban Question* (CASTELLS, 1972), which has had an important influence on studies into the political economy of urbanism. tends to demote its subject into an urban and political sociology. Political change outside the city, and economic relations are largely excluded. The city becomes sociologically defined as just the site of the reproduction of labour power, where "the heart of the sociological analysis of the urban question is the study of urban politics" (*Ibid*., p.244 Engl. Trans).[2] On the other side of the coin to sociology, neoclassical economics doggedly excludes political or cultural relationships, and, in its ability to exclude the real world, has become notorious as a self-indulgent theoretical pastime.

In this sense geography remains a valuable and interesting discipline if only because of its scope and eclecticism (despite the attempt to pare geography down to a supposedly scientific spatial analysis that might better fulfill the positivist ideal of a scientific mass production line). In this way geography retains opportunities, often lacking in other disciplines, for synthesising and original research An economist interested in the urban question for example, and not convinced by urban microeconomics, might well be better off migrating to geography. And more fundamentally, while geographers have studied space in isolation from process, sociologists and economists have usually studied process abstracted from space. True, in replacing spatial analysis, social and historical analysis will shift geography to the concerns of Marx, Ricardo and Weber — we might almost say, to the concerns of Park, de la Blanche and Sauer. The latter may have developed somewhat inadequate and limited explanations of social change, but at least their theories and investigations were about social and historical processes. They contained the seeds of their own obscelescence in a way that could have led to advances in social understanding. But these concerns are not the self-isolating and fragmented investigations of empiricist social science. [3]

The need for such a demonstration or introduction to 'radical' or 'social' geography seems twofold. First of all, despite the thorough re-arrangement of social science as a whole under the impact of phenomenology, Weberian conflict theory, and Marxist political economy human geography, remains essentially unchanged in some important ways. Thus the changes following the decay of quantitative geography have affected research much more than teaching; the normal progression between the two seems almost blocked by a defininition of these changes as socially marginal. So too an acceptance of 'different paradigms' or 'personal ideology' is taken to remove the need for critical analysis of the relative validity of alternative methodologies, or the usefulness of the research they lead to. If everyone can do their thing, then the same old thing can go on unchanged. How many 'methods' courses are still based on *Explanation in Geography*, in disregard of *Social Justice and the City* where the same author

(HARVEY, 1969; 1973) rejects or severely qualifies the arguments of the earlier book? Similarly how can a book like *Locational Analysis in Human Geography* (HAGGETT *et al.*, 1978) be reissued as though most of what had happened since 1965 was the refining of yet more techniques? The authors of the new Locational Analysis now realise that "geographical writing inevitably reflects the assumptions and experience of the authors.[5] But having said that it is deemed adequate to deal with possible alternatives – the complete re-arrangement of the social sciences – in two pages, before getting down to more of the same.

Secondly, much current radical research takes place outside geography as a departmental discipline, and so many geographers may remain unaware of developments. In Britain, for instance, a good deal of research on the political economy of cities and regions, on the links between economic development, political conflict and spatial change (the very stuff of human geography) has been carried out by the Community Development Projects, the Political Economy of Housing Workshop, or the Conference of Socialist Economists Regionalism group. In realising the potential in the decay of disciplinary boundaries the remaining departmental discipline itself seems to have fallen behind.

It is important also to point out some of the limitations of 'radical' research. Some has become over-theoretical, somewhat self-indulgent or even jargonistic (academic diseases not, of course, confined to neoclassical economics of the *New Left Review*). A good example might be some of the papers in the recent *Captive Cities: Studies in the Political Economy of Cities and Regions* (ed. HARLOE, 1977). Despite the editor's gallant introduction and some notable exceptions among the papers, it includes several examples of the reduction or research to the assertion and counter-assertion of abstract debate. The *Captive Cities* themselves disappear. In the new reductionism of 'Grand Theory' assertion itself becomes the subject of research, and rigid and formal abstract theory allows little critical engagement with historical practice.[6] Research attempts to connect general social processes with specific forms without establishing the casual relationships linking one with the other. As is now well known much of this new reductionism can be traced to the limiting effects of Althusserian inspired structuralism. As SAYER (1978) has it, it is a pity that urban and regional political economy had to begin its life accompanied by a diversion. Of course, these criticisms do not remove the need for abstraction and therefore also for a technical language – if it is properly supported by theoretical development (see GRAY and DUNCAN, 1978). Some concepts are likely to remain difficult to grasp, and to require hard thinking, although of course this is no excuse for bad writing. It is also necessary to point out that the empirical research presented in this issue is not completely successful in integrating the abstract and the concrete, in causally relating general social processes to particular social changes, and so in explaining the creation of geographical forms. The point is rather that this research sees this as its objective; it does not isolate space outside social and historical change.

The papers in this volume can be broken down into three groups. First, Asheim and Sayer provide an epistemological discussion of qualitative change in human geography. Asheim gives a general overview of the issues raised so briefly in this introduction in asking what social practices research in geography leads to, or might lead to. Sayer focusses on the concepts of people, society and nature in social science and geography. In so doing he outlines stage by stage a justification for a historical materialist treatment of these concepts and, most usefully, his justification demands engagement with corresponding epistemological positions in positivist and 'humanist' social science.

The next group of papers follow through empirically many of the issues identified by Asheim and Sayer. Cromar shows how the interaction of economic and political forces explains the creation of spatial structure, in this case the changing geography of the Tyneside coal industry in the late eighteenth century. The following two papers continue the theme of the centrality of social relations of production and political conflict in the creation and transformation geographical differences, and both develop this in the context of traditional areas of geographical research. Santos and Sayer attempt to understand the spatial organisation of land reform in Chile, between 1965 and 1973, while Dunford tries to explain the formation of recent changes in employment patterns in France. The final two papers in the issue develop from the analysis of changing geographies to a more direct examination of eplanatory theories and ideologies. Forrest, Lloyd, Williams and Rogers deal with the current obsession with the inner-city on the part of policy-makers and state organisations – an obsession partly expressed through spatial determinism. Gray and Boddy continue this theme by looking in detail at one particular interpenetration of academic theory with state policy making –filtering theory. This issue ends by answering Asheim's question with one instance of what political practice research in geography *has* led to.

I do not want to continue, however, in any attempt to provide some synthesis of change in geography. That would merely be an inferior version of the papers to follow, and in any case some useful accounts already exist.[7] It is time to let the papers speak for themselves.

Notes

1. Examples which come to mind, although there are others, are Torsten Hägerstrand's historical work leading up to *Innovations förloppet ur korologisk synpunkt* (HÄGERSTRAND, 1953) or the detailed descriptive and historical studies in *The Containment of Urban England* (HALL *et al.*, 1973).

2. Castells' erstwhile reliance on Althusserian structuralism, which conceives of society as a number of distinct and relatively autonomous levels, encourages his fragmentation of historical change. Similarly, the early influence of Althusserian structuralism on radical sociology as a whole has allowed the subject to remain 'sociological'. This is not to deny the seminal advances of Castells' work, however. Most importantly he argued that "there is no theory of space that is not an integral part of a general social theory" and against the ideological concept of urban society as a specific form of social organisation, and hence an object of study. See the review of *The Urban Question* by BODDY (1978).

3. See C. WRIGHT-MILLS (1970) for an early, but still very useful and readable demonstration of the inadequacies of empiricism.
4. There are now many useful amounts of recent changes in social science. Good examples are BLACKBURN (1972); HOLLIS and NELL(1975); KEAT and URRY (1975).
5. HAGGET *et al.*, (1978) p.1.
6. See the comments on the 'new reductionism' of over-theoretical marxism in WILLIAMS (1976).
7. See HARLOE (1977); PEET (1977) and GREGORY (1978).

References

BODDY M. (1978) Review of Castells M. 'The Urban Question' *Envir. Plann.* A**10**, 735-743.
BLACKBURN R. (Ed.) (1972) *Ideology in social science: readings in critical social theory,* London.
CASTELLS M. (1972) *La Question Urbaine.* Paris, trans. 1977, London.
GRAY F. and DUNCAN S.S. (1978) Etymology mystification and urban geography, *Area* **10**, 4.
GREGORY D. (1978) *Science, Ideology and Human Geography.* London.
HÄGERSTRAND T. (1953) *Innovationsförloppet ur korologisk synpunkt,* trans as Innovation diffusion as a spatial process (1967).
HALL P. *et al.* (1973) *The Containment of Urban England.* London.
HAGGET P., CLIFF A. and FREY A.(1978) *Locational Analysis in Human Geography.* London.
HARLOE M. (1977) Introduction to his (Ed.) *Captive Cities: Studies in the Political Economy of Cities and Regions,* London.
HARVEY D.W. (1969) *Explanation in Geography,* London.
HARVEY D.W. (1973) *Social Justice and the City.* London.
HOLLIS M. and NELL E. (1975) *Rational Economic Man: A Philosophical Critique of Neo-classical Economics,* London.
KEAT R. and URRY P. (1975) *Social Theory as Science.* London.
PEET R. (Ed.) (1977) The development of radical geography in the United States in (Ed.) *Radical Geography: Alternative Viewpoints on Contemporary Social Issues,* Chicago.
SAYER R.A. (1977) Gravity models and spatial autocorrelations or atrophy in urban and regional modelling, *Area* **9**, 3.
SAYER R.A. (1978) Review of Harloe (Ed.) 'Captive cities', *Tn. Plann. Rev.*
WILLIAMS R. (1976) Developments in the sociology of culture, *Sociology* **10**, 3.
WRIGHT-MILLS C. (1970) *The Sociological Imagination.* Harmondsworth.

Geoforum, Vol. 10, pp.5-18, 1979.
Pergamon Press Ltd. Printed in Great Britain.

Social Geography — Welfare State Ideology or Critical Social Science?

B.T. ASHEIM Aarhus and Roskilde, Denmark*

Abstract: The theme of the paper is the question of whether social geography has an ideological or a critical function in society. This question is approached from four different perspectives: (i) the history of ideas, (ii) the philosophy of science, (iii) the development of theory, and (iv) the view of practice.

Having identified the two main directions of social geography as being a liberal (positivist) and a radical (marxist) approach, they are subjected to a brief epistemological examination.

The development of theory of the liberal and marxist directions differ in three ways. These are the positioning of production *vis-à-vis* distribution, the conception of the relationship between the individual and society, and the understanding of space. The concept of relative space, making geography the science of space (chorology), is criticized. An alternative conceptualization of space, where space is not separated from and understood independent of the object under study, is formulated. Space is here considered as a *property* of the object (society), which totally integrates space and object.

In the last section of the paper it is pointed out that the liberal approach represents either 'counter-revolutionary' or 'status-quo' theories, while the radical approach is 'revolutionary'. The concept of space as the property of the object makes social geography more politically relevant, in that the actors in the political struggle became more precisely identified as groups in regional social structures.

Introduction

The theme of the paper is the function of social geography in society; that is the question of what social practices the theories and empirical results of social geography will (or might) lead to.

This question *ought* to be a basic problem for all who have taken issue with the uncritical acceptance of those 'ideals' of positivism, the supposed objectivity of science and the neutrality of values, and come to realise that research in science does not take place in a social vacuum separate from social processes

and their contradictions. More specifically, this imples that the social scientist in undertaking research, does not only disclose — or obscure — conditions and relations in society. The researcher is simultaneously and actively influencing those relations (s)he is researching. The question is not, therefore, *whether* the social scientist influences social relations, but *in what way*. If the influence is to confuse our understanding of reality by portraying a part of reality as reality itself, and so conceal the relationship between the parts and the whole, then research has a clear ideological effect. On the other hand social science can realise a critical potential in going beyond existing self-understanding, and so raise awareness and initiate action. The aim of research becomes that of revealing contradictions.

* Geographical Institutes of the University of Aarhus and Roskilde University Centre, Denmark.

It seems necessary to approach this question from four different perspectives. These are, in order:

(i)   the history of ideas,
(ii) the philosophy of science,
(iii) the development of theory, and, finally,
(iv) the view of practice.

The Historical Analysis of Geographical Thought

The history of thought in any one subject can be written in a number of ways. Up to now the most widespread have been varieties of an idealistic approach, where the development of a subject is seen as a result of the independent development of ideas in isolation. Such an idealistic method of writing the history of a subject might easily lead to a view of science as being completely divorced from society as a whole. Accordingly, the development of ideas is seen to depend on purely scientific relationships alone.

Alternatively, the history of ideas can be approached from a historical materialist point of view, which stresses the importance of examining the relations linking science to the rest of society. This is the approach I follow here, where the relations between science and society are considered to be dialectical. That is, science and society influence each other mutually and dynamically. In the end, however, it is the material conditions of society that will provide limits on what ideas, and what type of research, is possible or at least acceptable. Nonetheless, in this view, science develops an important relative autonomy from its basis in society, and it is important to keep this in mind if we are not to end up with a mechanisitic analysis of their interrelationships.

So as to examine the history of social geography, in terms of the development of ideas, it therefore seems most appropriate to concentrate on three dialectically-interrelated factors. These are, in order of importance:

(i)   general social relations and conditions,
(ii) specific intrascientific relations, either within the subject of study or bettween that subject and other related disciplines,
(iii) the influence of pioneers.

Towards the end of the 1960's there seems to have been a marked theoretical break in the development and direction of social geography and its leading ideas. Before this social geography was little more than a version of traditional regional geography, and was separated from it more by the choice of subject matter, rather than the development of particular theories or methods. Even the choice of supposed 'social' subjects remained untheorised. The most important field of study during this period was the description of community life patterns and activities, with a strong prediliction for studying rural communities and avoiding those political and economic issues important to industrial urbanism. To some extent this was complemented by the study of different cultural and ethnic groups, usually minority groups where the examination of the dominant culture itself was neglected. The development from an ideographic descriptive geography to nomothetic analytic geography moved more slowly, however, than in economic geography for instance. However, with a certain time-lag in relation to other specialisations social geography gradually changed towards more systematic studies using the methodology of model building, especially those taken from urban geography and perception geography (JONES, 1975).

At the end of the 1960's the demand for 'social relevance' in human geography came to have an important influence on the development of ideas in social geography. The origin and background for this demand has to be sought partly in the internal relations of geography and partly in external conditions.

Internal to geography, positivism's myth of the possibility and desirability for 'value-free' science put an effective stop to normative research, with any active social engagement. This lack was reinforced by the increasing gap between advanced statistical methods and techniques, as used during quantitative geography's heyday, and this geography's potential to come up with explanations of growing and acute social problems. Harvey's work is the most well-known in expressing dissatisfaction with this state of affairs, and in seeking alternatives (HARVEY, 1973). As Robson says:

". . . the novelty of social geography is that it is associated with a more aggressive stance on the question of values, it has a more direct involvement with social policy and has a greater interest in the political processes which mould the world as it is, rather than the more descriptive and traditional geographical concern with the environment and spatial patterns" (ROBSON, 1977: 481).

This internal development took place in a period of growing conflict both within late capitalist societies and in their external relations, and these conflicts contributed to a radicalisation of younger geographers. Among the more external conflicts the most important were those resulting from neo-colonialism and the independence struggles in the Third World, (especially the Vietnam war). Within capitalist society conflict arose partly over the manifestations of the costs of economic growth (regional imbalance, pollution, resource depletion, etc.), partly as a consequence of supposedly 'new', less material social problems (such as the feeling of increasing powerlessness and alienation), and partly reflected the survival of 'old' but unsolved, more material welfare problems. Despite many years of welfare politics, rapid economic growth, and a supposedly more even distribution of income, there were obviously many marginal groups in society (both socially and regionally) who appeared not to have received a just share of the growing wealth.

The rise of the 'new' social problems, together with the continuing existence of the old ones, implied that the late capitalist state needed more knowledge and insight about micro-level social processes, as well as information on environmental problems and at a macro (system) level. These different needs became reflected in the division of labour within human geography, and by the early 1970's we can distinguish the following pattern: (i) First of all, a *meta-process geography*. This used systems theory to find optimum locations, and to study decision-making processes on the macro-level in complex 'spatial' systems. (BERRY, 1973).
(ii) Secondly, the renaissance of *geography as human ecology*. Systems analysis, combined with ecological theory, was used to study the connection between nature and society and thus find ways of solving the many ecological

problems of modern society (CHORLEY, 1973).
(iii) And finally, *social geography* looking at 'geographical' welfare problems on the individual level, using explanatory theories from psychology, sociology and economics (SMITH, 1977).

This development of ideas within social geography was far from uniform, and little conscensus emerged concerning the choice of theories and methods. According to Robson:

"The question of value has been at the core of recent changes in social geography . . . . This more conscious interest in theory and in the value systems underlying research has meant that the old hegemony of a 'value-free' approach based on the natural sciences has been replaced, and replaced not by one but by a variety of philosophical positions. The argument now in social geography is no longer about the empirical facts of society, but about the interpretations put upon those data . . . . The facts of deprivation are not in dispute; what is debated are the underlying mechanisms which create and perpetuate the problems and hence the policy alternatives that might be advocated to remedy the conditions. On one side is a variety of liberal approaches; on the other a more radical structuralist (sic) view" (ROBSON, 1977; 481-482).

Robson's liberal social geography can be divided into two main streams. One direction attempts to establish an individualistic and group perspective (where a group is little more than a collection of individuals) and defines social geography as "the understanding of the patterns which arise from the use social groups make of space as they see it, and of the processes involved in making and changing such patterns" (JONES and EYLES, 1977:6). From this perspective (spatial) level-of-living problems are largely comprehended as a question of the uneven distribution of individual resources between different groups in the population. In the main it is theories from social psychology that inform this perspective.

The other tendency takes a managerial perspective as its starting point. This conception, which is more problem orientated, defines social geography as "the analysis of the social patterns and processes arising from the distribution of, and access to, scarce resources . . . . ., in other words, it must tackle the socio-spatial outcomes of the scarcity and inequitable distribution of desirable resources (goods, services, facilities) in Western society" (JONES and EYLES, 1977:6). In this managerial perspective level-of-living problems are taken to be questions of system management within given economics and social policies. According to this view for instance, there is a given system of industries, sectors, branches and firms. Some of these are expansive and initiating economic growth, and can thus contribute to growth in their locations – but at the expense of areas lacking these industries. Congestion problems are created at the centre, and problems of regional decline at the periphery, and these are taken to be the chief cause of regional and social inequalities in levels-of-living. The major theoretical sources for this perspective are sociology and welfare-economics.

The 'radical' variant of social geography is no more homogenous theoretically. It consists of different sub-groups ranging from 'critical theory' to anarchist perspectives, including a whole range of marxist positions. To oversimplify severely, however, we can characterise radical social geography as stressing structural relations in the analysis of social problems. A structural perspective takes as its starting point the economic system – or more properly the mode of production where economic relations are also social and political – so as to unveil the built-in contradictions in the development of society. Such a structural perspective does not direct its attention solely towards isolated, and so usually idealised, economic social or political conditions as *the* cause of social conditions and change. Rather analysis would be based on interrelated material reality and the social contradictions this produces; which are seen as the motive force for change, and thus responsible for the development of problems like different level-of-living conditions. From this point of view cultural and social phenomena cannot be meaningfully studied separately from the way people interact and combine to produce and distribute the wherewithal to live and built their societies (ASHEIM, 1978). It is important, therefore, to see people as active agents making history, but making it socially (rather than purely individually). In Marx's words, to repeat a well-known extract from *The Eight-*

eenth Brumaire of Louis Bonaparte:

"Men make their own history, but they do not make it just as they please; they do not make it under circumstances chosen by themselves, but under circumstances directly encountered, given and transmitted from the past" (MARX, 1972:10).

This stress on people as creative and active would distinguish a structural perspective in general from structuralism. Structuralism tends to reduce people to passive "support agents expressing particular combinations of the social structure through their practice" (CASTELLS, 1976:78); that is, history is reduced to a determinism of structures.

In the rest of this essay I aim to examine the different liberal and radical directions existing in today's social geography. The objective is to decide whether these various approaches function as ideology, or as critical analysis, in relation to the rest of society. Perhaps for many it might seem "undoubtedly more comfortable to debate the nature of explanation within an agreed framework of the empirical theory of positive social science" (ROBSON, 1977: 485). To continue the quotation from Robson, however:

"The rules of the debate are now in process of being refashioned and whether the conflicting interpretations will be resolved by compromise and fusion, or by the emergence of any one as a new paradigm for social geography has yet to be determined" (ROBSON, 1977:485-486).

These questions of the relations between different theoretical positions, and of what practice such positions can lead to, have distinct implications for the philosophy of science. Therefore, they cannot be answered until we subject them more clearly to epistemological examination. I shall briefly attempt such an analysis in the next section.

The Philosophy of Science Perspective

The epistemological break in the development of thought in social geography, taking place around 1970, has often been interpreted as a fundamental reassessment of the positivist ideal of social science. In my opinion this has in fact only amounted to a partial reassesment of the positivist method of understanding the world. The demand for 'social relevance' in human geography *can* indeed imply a critique of positivism's ideal of value-free neutral research. But the solutions to this problem that are usually propounded are inadequate. It is not enough, for a critique of positivism, to change the object of geographical research from functions to individuals (or groups of individuals). Nor is it sufficient to start out with a declaration of personal values and viewpoints — only to 'forget' the implications of these in the succeeding work (cf. BLAUT, 1974; BUTTIMER, 1974; SMITH, 1977). None of these attempts at providing a solution come to grips with the central problem with which any fundamental critique of positivism must begin. This is the problem of positivism's view of the relationship between social science as theory with that science's object — society, and how this relationship should be understood. In other words, we are concerned with the problem of the relationship between subject and object, between scientific form and content, and how this relationship is articulated (SAYER, 1979).

Positivism claims this relationship between subject and object to be purely external; that is social sciences as theory, and society as objective reality, can be taken as being independent from one another. This point of view holds important implications for the form taken by social science. Firstly, this underlies the positivist 'dream' of a unity of science based on natural science, and of using theories and models from natural science to study society. The classic example in human geography is, of course, the application of gravity and potential models to the analysis of interaction patterns, and other 'social physics' analogues. Secondly, however, the assumption of externality and independence of subject and object leads to the conclusion that it is possible to establish uniform and universal criteria for a given, true knowledge about society that is independent of that society itself.

These special criteria for 'true knowledge' in positivism are based on the assumption that all scientific knowledge about the world is drawn from perception, that is, knowledge is based on empirical observations. The problem with this empirical definition of meaning is that it, in itself, is not empirically testable. In turn the positivistic scientific ideal cannot fulfill its own primary demand

for a universal and comprehensive criterion on what is, and what is not, true and reliable knowledge about society. This is so because positivistic science is incapable of reflecting on the *internal* relationship between scientific form and content which always exists in social science. Among other things this internal relationship implies that it is not possible to obtain a historical, universal and unconditional knowledge about society. Positivism, which assumes this is possible, is paradoxically led to the position where one starting point is as good as any other. For under these conditions, the questions becomes that of whether knowledge is instrumental, as measured by the ability to predict — but the question as to whether knowledge is reliable or true cannot be answered (GREGORY, 1978).

Within this perspective it is the researcher, as a subjective individual, who in the last resort becomes the judge of what is 'right' and what is 'incorrect'. The choice between theories, models and methods is reduced to a question of values, of who has 'the best belief'. As Chisolm says:

> "In the last resort, the choice between one set of basic assumptions and another is a metaphysical matter, a question of belief that is not amenable to scientific analysis" (CHISOLM, 1975:176).

But this 'solution' does nothing to save positivism's basic assumption of the separation and independence of facts and values; on the contrary, we are left only with values — the 'facts' have gone. There is no longer any basis for claiming that something is 'science' as compared to any other intellectual activity, such as politics, literature or art. The one grades into the other without any meaningful distinction. This does not only mean the destruction of positivism's scientific ideal, but also it removes the claim of social science to be scientific — *science is turned into ideology* (ASHEIM, 1978).

Instead of simply ignoring this problem, or even trying to solve it philosophically in the abstract, a Marxist epistemology takes as its starting point the internal relationship between scientific form and content. The main difference between positivist and Marxist epistemology is that Marxism does not justify the separation between science and ideology on universalised principles, supposedly separated from that society it produces knowledge about. Marxist epistemology is not justified philosophically or transcendentally, but practically. The criterion to establish how far the individual reaches a 'true' knowledge about reality is seen by Marxism to be the individual's practice in the interaction between subject (the individual) and object (the material structure), where the immediate result is change in the object. The individual is at the same time, an active subject who changes society, and also a passive object who is changed by society as objective reality. This contradiction is resolved through the individual's practice, where a unity of thesis and antithesis is achieved.

In a less abstract way this means that the society which social science produces knowledge about is not something given, and unambiguously independent, of that practice which the social scientist (as well as others) undertakes. This is the real problem which every social scientist is confronted with.

"Positivist science is not, therefore, a social science which does not take up a position on those social phenomena it describes; rather it is a social science which *believes* it does not do so. Positivisim is, in other words, an ideology, or false consciousness" (ENERSTVEDT, 1976: 383).

Marxist epistemology is superior to positivism not because it represents a 'better' choice, or, what is sometimes seen as necessary, a logically consistent solution to the positivist problematic on positivism's premises. As I have already shown, this is not possible. Rather Marxist epistemology is superior because it dissolves the positivist problematic.

The Development of Theory

The liberal and Marxist directions in current social geography differ most clearly in three ways. These are the positioning of production *vis-à-vis* distribution, the conception of the relationship between the individual and society, and, last but not least, the understanding of space as a component in the analysis of social problems.

Production and Distribution

The 'division of labour' between economic geography and social geography — which is itself a result of positivism's fragmentation of the social sciences — has reinforced a tendency to separate distribution (consumption) from production. Economic geography often describes production as a purely technical matter, and leaves supposedly 'social' questions of distribution and welfare to social geographers. They, in their turn, presume distributional problems to be simply a question of uneven distribution and inequal access to goods and services which are *already* produced and localised. This presumption is held equally whether distributional problems are expressed as inequality between social classes or between towns and regions.

A good example of this is Smith's book *Human Geography: A Welfare Approach.* Here social geography is defined as the study of *who* gets *what, where* and *how* (SMITH, 1977:7). This definition focuses on the four major tasks which Smith assumes social geography should have. First, social geography has a positive, descriptive task (what something *is* — 'who gets what, where'); secondly, an explanatory task ('how'); next, a normative evaluating task (how something should be); and finally, an innovatory or alteration task (how something can be done after deciding who should get what, where). The crucial point in such a scheme is the explanatory task. And when Smith points to the reasons for existing regional inequalities in levels-of-living his explanation is almost totally based on distributional relations in society. Thus:

"For example, the location of an industry might be regarded as an independent variable (cause) in an explanatory model, with areal variations in human well-being, suitably defined, as the dependent variable (effect). The spatial patterns of private productive capacity, public service facilities, expenditure on social programmes, movement of people to work, can all be viewed in the same way. We need to know far more about the origin of these individual patterns if we are really to understand how they contribute to human well-being as a spatially variable condition (SMITH, 1977:9).

But this is not sufficient. In order to explain the existence of regional and social inequalities in 'human well-being' we have to recognise that these inequalities do not, primarily and independently, arise from conflicts between individuals and groups over the distribution of society's produce. On the contrary, these are founded on the way in which production is organised in society, and a vital feature of this is the separation of the direct producers from control over the means of production. Thus distributional relations are fundamentally connected with the distribution and control of the means of production in society. Without such control, it clearly follows that one has less power to decide *what* is produced, *how* it is to be produced, and *for whom.* Conflicts over distribution find their origin, therefore, in the social relations of production (SANTOS and SAYER, 1979).

Within the production system individuals exist in relation to one another as employer and employee, subordinate and superior and so on. But in the distribution system, in contrast, different members of society relate to one another in a fundamentally different way. We can illustrate this by an example (NAUSTDALSLID, 1974).

Employer and employee stand in a qualitatively different relation to the production system. The latter contributes to production by selling his labour power to the former, while the employer — by virtue of his ownership rights over the means of production — disposes of the worker's labour power as he sees fit. While the employer's income is determined by the profits of production, the worker's income is determined by the price paid for his labour power. The relationship between them, the question of equality and inequality, is thus one of *qualitative* differences which are objectively defined by their position in the social structure.

To turn to the distribution system, we find that much of this difference becomes hidden. Instead, we are confronted with another type of inequality between the two, which consists of a difference in material standard of living. Behind this difference, of course, lies the imbalance of power in the system of production, which leads to income differentials. But as long as we see these two members of society as confined to the distribution system, the differences between them have changed

form. They are no longer qualitative differences, but *quantitative.* Both stand in a qualitatively equal relationship to the distribution system — they are consumers. We are now dealing with a relative position on a continuous scale, no longer is their relation one of qualitative differences in the social structure. The difference between them is a quantitative difference, the ability to consume, determined by the size of their incomes. What is not 'relevant' (apparently) in this connection is *how* the varying size of incomes is determined.

This simple example illustrates how social relationships — despite the built in interconnection between systems of distribution and production — change their form and content according to the context in which they are to be understood. The division between social and human geography thus both reflects and mystifies our social reality. This division is simultaneously correct in its reflection of current practice and understanding of society, and incorrect in mystifying social practice, in that it uncritically reproduces superficial explanations of this practice. In other words, this division functions ideologically.

Society and the Individual

Within liberal social geography the tendency is to one-sidedly focus the analysis of social phenomena onto the individual. This easily leads to an 'explanation' of social inequalities as being essentially accidental where, for instance, inequalities are founded on the uneven distribution of individual resources. These in turn are then said to be conditioned biologically, or at least within the supposedly independent and isolated personal confines of the family. (See COMMUNITY DEVELOPMENT PROJECT, 1977, for a critique of this in British urban policy.) The trouble with this procedure is, among other things, that it is necessary to take an idealistic, unreal viewpoint of the individual's reality as the starting point for analysis. The possibilities for explanation based on an isolated individual level is further limited to those situations where an intentional analysis seems relevant. That is, analysis is limited to situations where there is an accordance between individual intentions and effects, where the actors, through their actions, produce their intended results (intention - consequence). Very often the forcing of social change into this intentional framework ('voluntarism') will produce a mystification of social relationships and social change. Much geographical work on urban change, residential mobility and access to housing resources, which has based explanation on individual intentions and perceptions in isolation, shows this clearly. (See GRAY, 1975; GRAY and BODDY, 1979.)

Social change *can* be a result of individual intentions and actions producing the intended change. But often the consequences are not in accordance with the individual's plans or desires — the consequences are a result of actions, and interactions, not of intentions. Intentional analysis completely neglects such problematic constellations of unwanted, or unexpected, consequences of human action. For example, there can be situations where the actors know that their actions are harmful even to themselves, but where they are forced to act in this way even if they desire to act more rationally. Similarly actors may behave rationally, as they see it, but because their actions are in fact interactions with others — who may have different intentions, and possibly also more power to effect the action — the result of their action, and the action itself, is mitigated or can even be something quite different from what they intended. There can also be actions which are rational on an individual level, but which collectively have a dysfunctional or even destructive effect (structural irrationality). Such effects can be termed sub-optimal in that the outcome is inferior to other possible results. We have, therefore, discordance between the actual result and that which is both better and possible. (See, for instance CROMAR, 1979.)

Another situation where analysis on the individual level does not suffice is that where a set of actors take decisions individually, but the effects interact and produce consequences that nobody had either intended or promoted. These unintended effects arise as a result of external relations in society. The error here lies in generalising a situation which may be valid to each individual in the group as being valid to the group as a whole, and in relation to other groups. What is true for each member does not necessarily apply to all members simultaneously. When the actor acts as if he was acting alone, this error becomes realised, and everyone acts on conditions that combine to defeat these individual intentions. Plans which could have been put into effect under constant conditions (*ceteris paribus*) become unrealisable because everyone tries to realise them and so changes these conditions. It is not sufficient to understand the development of intended or desired effects in analysing social phenomena, it is also necessary to explain unintended results, which are formed as a result of social interactions and social structures (HERNES, 1975; 1976).

For this purpose it is necessary to develop a theory of structural change. Such a theory is best based on dialectical, historical materialism, which takes as a starting point the way in which different social groups react to contradictions in society, and thereby dissolve or strengthen these contradictions. In the analysis of regional and social enequalities, therefore, we need to operate in both 'micro-' and 'macro'-levels. At the micro-level one concentrates on the conditions behind individual decisions. But, if these decisions are not located in broader, structural relationships the research will not amount to an analysis of social change as transformed and transmitted by individuals. Individual action must not only be analysed on the basis of observed, actual behaviour, but it is also necessary to consider the limits and possibilities that macro-level structural relations — for example class relations in society — place on individual actions. Theories of social change must show how structural relations influence the motives and actions of individuals, and how these actions (practice) in turn can dissolve those conditions giving rise to social laws and tendencies. A valid theory of social change demands that both micro- and macro-level relations, and the dialectical relationship between the levels, are incorporated (HERNES, 1976; SANTOS and SAYER, 1979).

Concepts of Space

In human geography, the general question of the relationship between scientific form and content in the social sciences receives a specific expression — the relationship between space and object. This specific problem can be formulated in the following way; is the object subordinated to space in geographical analysis, or is the object dominant and space subordinate? It is here that we return to the two epistemological breaks in the more recent history of geographical thought. The first entailed transition from concepts of absolute space to relative space, from a descriptive to model-making chorology. The second break is, however, more fundamental. This entails a rejection of the notion of human geography as the science of space, as chorology. The object of human geography is rather social processes perceived as space, something which implies a relational concept of space (HARVEY, 1973; ASHEIM, 1979; HANSEN, 1979).

The concept of relative space understands space both as relative location and as relative to the type of social processes being studied. The major task of geography is then to discover 'spatial laws', that is empirical and statistical regularities in the covariation of spatial phenomena ('spatial analysis'). This 'spatial' covariation is understood, in the traditional positivist way, as surface phenomena torn free from the social processes they are part of.

Such a concept of space implies that the object is subordinate to space; the role of geography is to be a some sort of 'interpreted geometry', something which very often results in various forms of 'spatial fetishism'. This refers to the use of space as the explanatory variable, employing notions such as 'spatial process' and defining the object of study as 'the *spatial* organisation of human society'. But, as Folke points out (among others), "This definition tends to obscure the fact that the organisation of human society is a social, not a spatial phenomenon" (FOLKE, 1973: 18). This positivist geography of spatial processes makes the opposite error to other social sciences such as economics and sociology. While these attempt to examine society without space, positivist geography studies space without society.

The book *Geography and Inequality* (COATES *et al.*, 1977) provides a good example of the problems of using the concept of relative space in social geography. For instance, the book states that:

> ". . . the root causes of spatial inequality cannot be tackled by spatial policies alone, therefore. Inequalities are products of social and economic structures, of which capitalism in its many guises is the predominant example . . . Thus it would seem that we are led to a rather pessimistic conclusions. In part this is so the spatial; or geographical, approach does not offer the holy grail" (*Ibid.*, 1977:256).

The authors mean by this that 'spatial policy' can handle symptoms, repair existing damage but not engage the causes of the problems. "Many of the causes, consequences and manifestations of inequality are dominantly structural rather than spatial in nature", and, as a result of this "spatial solutions to inequalities are, in themselves, insufficient" (*Ibid.*, 4-5). They conclude that "the real cause of inequalities lies in the structure of societies, and is in part represented by the way in which these organise space; thus the solution of inequalities must be sought in the restructuring of societies" (*Ibid.*, 256-257). As Anderson maintains, "Social inequality is not replaced by 'spatial inequality' for the latter term is meaningless independent of social content — one cannot choose between 'spatial' and 'social', one must have both" (ANDERSON, 1973:3).

This impasse, the conflicts and contradictions it entails (a result of the limitation of social geography's object in founding analysis on spatial inequalities) can neither be solved by an "appeal to pragmatism — that spatial engineering might meet pressing social needs while permanent solutions are sought — nor by (their) claim that any alternative social structure to capitalism will need to develop spatial policies" (BODDY, 1978: 458-459). To solve these problems, which are "endemic in geography as a whole" (*Ibid.*), it is necessary to achieve nothing less than the removal of a fundamentally inadequate conceptualism of human geography — the chorological. It is not enough to give the subject a more socially relevant content when the starting point and method of analysis remains severely flawed. Rather the need is for an alternative concept of space, where the object dominates and space is subordinate, that is, where space is not separated from and understood independent of the object under study.

Such a concept has to consider space as a *property* of the object (society). In such a way space and object are understood as totally integrated. Harvey calls this concept of space 'relational', where space is an integral part of the object (HARVEY, 1973); the object is not just seen as reflected *in* space, for space does not exist independently of process. This concept of space implies that location and distance must be considered together with those social processes of which they are a part. The land use pattern in a town is not just a function of distance from the town centre, but also of social relationships such as those concerning property ownership, access to capital, technical development in the construction industry, and so on. Distance and location are therefore just one part of a more extensive social structure (HANSEN, 1979). Without this integration, the importance of 'spatial concepts' in explaining socio-spatial inequalities easily becomes over-exaggerated, e.g. NYSTUEN (1968).

If space is seen as a property of the object, then society must be seen as social space, where social processes unfold. Society is thus a spatial structure, and social processes vary from place to place. Different social processes entail given contradictions, leading to different geographical patterns of distribution with varying socio-spatial characteristics.

This approaches Harvey's notion that spatial structures should be conceived as "things which 'contain' social processes in the same manner that social processes are spatial" (HARVEY, 1973:11) and similarly Santos states that "history after all, is not written outside of space, and an a-spatial society does not exist. Space itself is social"(SANTOS, 1977:3). Space, understood as a social phenomenon, is thus shaped by the very same social laws which generate social processes and does not exist by itself. Social processes *produce and represent* social space; process is not just reflected *in* space (ASHEIM, 1979).

One of the consequences of this relational concept of space is that is no longer possible to talk of 'geographical' theories of the causes of inequality; rather we must develop *social science* theories. Similarly, we cannot simply talk about spatial inequalities, but *socio-*

spatial inequalities. Necessarily, therefore, we have to develop explanatory abstraction from phenomena which remain unique in relation to the object of study. The problem is that of abstract social processes which, in different conditions, can result in different, concrete socio-spatial appearances. This produces the need for "a theory which penetrates through social forms to discover the more basic socio-spatial forces which are continually re-creating spatial inequalities" (PEET, 1978:4). Coates *et al.* also admit this in stating that "inequalities are very deeply rooted in the ethic of a capitalist society" where, "to understand the dynamics of spatial patterns in non-socialist countries, therefore, it is necessary to understand the dynamics of capitalism (COATES *et al.*, 1977:253).

Unfortunately, their understanding of 'the dynamics of capitalism' is very poor. They imagine profit to be 'born of shortage' instead of seeing it as the manner in which surplus labour is realised under those specific social relations of production prevailing in capitalism, and they see inequality as caused by the 'ethic' of capitalism, rather than by its structure. Similarly they claim that "space and the pattern of location are manipulated for the benefit of capitalism" (*Ibid.:*255), implying that capitalism is personified, rather than being seen as a specific form of economic and social structure resulting in an uneven distribution of 'goods' and 'bads' between different social groups. And finally the authors claim that "life in a capitalist society is a conflict between individuals and groups, for that society's products". (*Ibid.:* 234). Here they fail to understand, and repeat, what I earlier pointed to as one of the main weaknesses of liberal social geography, the examination of distribution in isolation from production. As Boddy puts it, in reviewing their work:

"Inequality stems from the nature of capitalist production, from separation from and possession of the means of production, rather than from the manner in which a given set of products (mysteriously produced by "society") is shared out among individuals and groups" (BODDY, 1978: 459).

One consequence of such lack of understanding of the capitalist mode of production will be that "the dynamics of the specific mode of production is lost, and where, consequently, the class nature of the structure of society can be completely submerged" (MASSEY, 1974:234).

In order to capture social development as it reflects reality it is crucial to take as a starting point for analysis those groups and classes that have interests in furthering or hindering a given development. Different classes in the regional social structure use social space differently, and social contradictions appear as contradictions between the needs of different social groups in regard to the development of infrastructure, the use of land, the provision of services, and so on. Social processes do not only, therefore, produce a social differentiation (division into classes), but also a geographical differentiation. Only historical materialism, with its theory of class struggle, takes any definite position on this question.

The View of Practice

HARVEY (1973) discriminates between three main types of social science theory: first 'counter-revolutionary theory' and 'status quo thoery' which are liberal and positivist theories in the main, and 'revolutionary theory' which is most often formulated on a dialectical, historical materialist basis. A good example of 'counter-revolutionary theory' would be an individual-based, voluntaristic theory of socio-spatial inequality, without material foundations. Such a theory expresses the need of the late capitalist state to understand welfare problems as matters of distribution at the individual level alone.

Traditionally, information about social conditions have been collected on individuals and at the individual level — only to a much lesser extent has information been gathered on the structure of soceity. This has applied almost as much to social science research as it does to official statistics; thus national censuses are predominately collections of data about individual consumption patterns while in urban geography, for instance, factorial ecology — almost entirely based on an uncritical acceptance of the census as a data source — was used to describe 'urban' social structure and 'urban' problems. Because of this bias to consumption and to the individual

level, the information base for public policy leads to political action formed around an individualistic interpretation of society, rather than a structural perspective. With better information on the individual, compounded by voluntaristic analysis, public policy will aim to increase the individual resources of the population, so as to enhance or compensate for the individuals' ability to compete for goods on the market or in the political arena. Policy is not so likely to aim for a change in *structural conditions* in society, which determine *how* people can use their resources, and what they can achieve with the resources they have. A policy which simply tries to change individual resource levels will only have limited effects, therefore. It may improve conditions which are individual in their character, but it will be irrelevant or just as likely have negative or dysfunctional effects in attempting to solve problems of a structural nature. A 'counter-revolutionary theory' will thus have a clear ideological effect, in defusing awareness and displacing attention from fundamental questions to partial or non-existent problems. Such a theory would also have a legitimising and a conserving effect in society, by not pointing out which social mechanisms are the cause of various social problems, and thereby preventing an understanding of how unwanted social developments can be changed. Instead we are presented with idealistic (and often moralistic) appeals, with little effect other than to hinder people's understanding of reality.

'Status quo' theories are often erected on what I earlier called the 'system' or 'managerial' perspective (see pp.3-4). In this case the problem-solving mechanism is supposed to lie in central government, which should (and can) even out differences and regulate relations between sectors, activities, regions and social groups. This perspective will stress the need for reorganising social mechanisms, and of taking account of the total effects of actions in the system. The method for achieving such solutions is to increasingly remove social problems from the market and into the political arena (reformism). We might also add here as 'staus quo' theories those descriptive accounts of social conditions which, although they often include implicit voluntaristic interpretations, are sufficiently illuminat-

Geoforum/Volume 10/Number 1/1979

ing and sufficiently un-interpreted to fall either way and possibly form the basis for reformist or even revolutionary demands. (A good example might be descriptions of social conditions in contrasting regions or urban areas.)

However, the possibilities for the political system to actually 'govern' the development of society depends on two conditions. Firstly, the organisational structure and the problem structure should coincide; that is the political system should perceive and treat the problems in an adequate way. Given the nature of the capitalist state and the dominance of particular interests, this seems unlikely in general. Secondly, however, it is important that problems actually are 'management problems' which can be solved by changing the control systems which steer their social articulation (for example, a transition from the market as regulating mechanism to the political arena). Alternatively, problems might demand a more fundamental change in the social and economic structures (the 'base') of society. I shall expand on this a little by presenting a brief example.

If we look for a moment beyond the critique of the welfare state which limits itself to saying that too little has been done to redistribute wealth and create greater equality, we can raise the question of whether it is even possible to create social equality through wealth redistribution and within the structural limits of the welfare state. Logically it is possible to create 'equality' between persons A and B with regard to how much of a certain good they possess. But if the relation between A and B is that of employer and employee, for instance, these criteria of equality have little meaning. A and B are not different because one of them *has* more of something than the other, but because one of them *is* something else than the other. They exist as counterparts in an objective social structure, and it is precisely this structure that defines the relationship between them. In this case it is not possible to achieve equality, or a greater degree of equality, between the two through redistribution of wealth or goods, simply because their unequal relationship is not something that can be redistributed. A major presumption of welfare state policies, in the assumption that they are

relevant to solving social problems (i.e. the assumption that these problems are 'managerial' in nature) is that these problems exist in the form of quantitatively unequal distribution of 'goods'. Moreover, it must be assumed that these goods are those where the welfare state (the 'superstructure') can have some influence over distribution (NAUSTDALSLID, 1974). In other words 'status quo' theories represent a geography of the welfare state adapted to the premises and conditions of the social establishment. To work with this system-management or managerial perspective, therefore, is to run a severe risk of remaining limited to the concepetion of 'piece-meal' social changes, where most probably (but remaining undiscovered) it is more basic structural changes that are necessary. The social result of using such theories will be, in this case, a reproduction of inequality (although it may be 'shifted around the system' a little). In other words, such theories will essentially sustain the status quo. (See FOREST *et al.*, 1970; DUNFORD, 1979.)

The welfare state and its 'status quo' theories cannot therefore, solve problems of a more qualitative nature, precisely because it is not a tool for dissolving more basic structural contradictions in the system, such as the mechanism and relations of class society. If the researcher is interested, therefore, in contributing to an improved level-of-living for the weaker social groups, it becomes an important task of social science research to allow these groups the possibility of becoming more conscious of structural contradictions. Thus Hernes claims that:

> "the real task of social science is clearly, therefore, to remove collective illusions and to provide a non-mystifying presentation of concrete reality and its relationships. This demands developing concepts which reflect realities, and theories which can disclose underlying processes" (HERNES, 1976:109).

When the contradictions connected to any given social problem are understood, it will be seen that the solutions are not simple, *technical* questions, but primarily *political* questions. Only by using a structural perspective based on 'revolutionary theory' is it possible to lay bare contradictions in society, so that social science can disperse ideology and have a *critical* function in society. It is here that the major difference lies between adapting to, and changing, the structure of society. The construction of theories about modes of production, surplus product and social classes is a presupposition to the ability to understand social change and relations. In turn this understanding is a *necessary* condition for that practice (the sufficient conditions) to dissolve objectively existing relations of social development. Marxism thereby represents a philosophy of the social sciences which is both relative and absolute. It is absolute in the sense that it can give a 'true' understanding under specific historical and material conditions. But at the same time it is relative in that, by existing as a *preface* to a political practice, it can be an active element in changing society.

The concept of space as the property of the object makes human geography more politically (and practically) relevant, in that the actors in the political (class) struggle become more precisely identified as groups in regional social structures. And, if we do admit people as the dominant influence on the past, present and future, it is to this that our scientific activity should be connected. Social change has always happened when the 'impossible' has been made possible through change in the social relations of power.

Acknowledgements — The author would like to thank S.S. Duncan, F. Hansen, B. Lenntorp and J. Widberg for comments on earlier drafts. Translation from the Norwegian was carried out by S.S. Duncan, T. Klette and H. Valestrand.

References

ANDERSON J. (1973) Ideology in geography: an introduction, *Antipode* **5**, 3.

ASHEIM B. (1978) Regionale ulikheter i levekår (Regional inequalities in level-of-living) NOU (Norwegian Official Inquiry) 1978:3.

ASHEIM B. (1979) Forståelseform, romoppfattelse og planleggning (Epistemology, the conception of space and planning) *Häften för kritiska studier* **2**.

BERRY B. (1973) A paradigm for modern geography In: *Directions in Geography*. R.J. Chorley (Ed.) Methuen, London.

BLAUT J. (1974) Commentaries on Values in Geography, In: *Values in Geography*. A. Buttimer pp.44-45.

BODDY M. (1978) Review of Coates B. *et al.* Geo-

graphy and inequality, *Environment and Planning A* **10**, 4.

BUTTIMER A. (1974) Values in geography, Resource Paper No 24, AAG, Washington D.C.

CASTELLS M. (1976) Theory and ideology in urban sociology (originally 1969) In: *Urban Sociology: Critical Essays,* C.G. Pickvance (Ed.). Tavistock, London.

CHISHOLM M. (1975) *Human Geography: Evolution or Revolution?* Penguin, Harmondsworth.

CROMAR P. (1979) Spatial change and economic organization: the Tyneside coal industry (1751-1770), *Geoforum* **10**, 45-57.

CHORLEY R.J. (1973) Geography as human ecology, In: *Directions in Geography,* R.J. Chorley (Ed.), Methuen, London.

COATES B., JOHNSTON R. & KNOX P. (1977) *Geography and Inequality,* Oxford University Press, Oxford.

COMMUNITY DEVELOPMENT PROJECT (1977) *Gilding the ghetto: the state and the poverty experiments,* CDP.

ENERSTVEDT R. (1976) Något om förhållandet mellan filosofi och vetenskap (Some thoughts on the relationship between philosophy and science) In: *Positivisme, Dialektikk, Materialisme,* R. Slagstad (Ed.), Universitetsforlaget, Oslo.

FOLKE S. (1973) First thoughts on the geography of imperialism *Antipode* **5**, 1.

FORREST R. *et al.* (1979) The inner city: in search of the problem *Geoforum* **10**, 109-116.

GRAY F. (1975) Non-explanation in urban geography *Area* **7**, 4.

GRAY F. and BODDY M. (1979) The origins and use of theory in urban geography: household mobility and filtering theory, *Geoforum* **10**, 117-127.

GREGORY D. (1978) *Ideology, Science and Human Geography,* Hutchinson, London.

HANSEN F. (1979) Kulturgeografiens objekt: samfundsmessige processer opfattet som rum (The object of human geography: social processes perceived as space) *Haften för kritiska studier* **2**.

HARVEY D. (1973) *Social Justice and the City,* Edward Arnold, London.

HERNES G. (1975) *Makt og avmakt (Power and Powerlessness),* Universitetsforlaget, Bergen.

HERNES G. (1976) Struktur og dialektikk (Structure and dialectics), stencil, Bergen.

JONES E. (Ed.) (1975) Introduction In: *Readings in Social Geography,* Oxford University Press, Oxford.

JONES E. & EYLES J. (1977) *An Introduction to Social Geography,* Oxford University Press, Oxford.

MASSEY D. (1974) Social justice and the city: a review, *Environment and Planning* **6**.

MARX K. (1972) *The Eighteenth Brumaire of Louis Bonaparte* (originally 1869), Moscow.

NAUSTDALSLID J. (1974) Interessedimensjioner i norsk distriktsutbyggning (Conflicts of interest in Norwegian regional policy), stencil, Oslo.

NYSTUEN J.D. (1968) Identification of some fundamental spatial concepts, In: *Spatial Analysis: A Reader in Statistical Geography,* B. Berry, D. Marble, (Eds.), Prentice-Hall, New Jersey.

PEET R. (1978) Introduction, In: *Radical Geography,* R. Peet (Ed.), Methuen, London.

ROBSON B. (1977) Social geography, *Progress in Human Geography* **1**, 3.

SANTOS E. and SAYER A. (1979) The political economy of agrarian reform and spatial organisation in Chile, *Geoforum* **10**, 59-80.

SANTOS M. (1977) Society and space: social formations as theory and method, *Antipode* **9**, 1.

SAYER A. (1979) Epistemology and conceptions of people and nature in geography, *Geoforum,* **10**, 19-43.

SMITH D.M. (1977) *Human Geography: A Welfare Approach,* Edward Arnold, London.

Geoforum, Vol. 10, pp.19-43, 1979.
Pergamon Press Ltd. Printed in Great Britain.

Epistemology and Conceptions of People and Nature in Geography

ANDREW SAYER, *Brighton, U.K.

Abstract: The paper attempts to integrate two major issues of debate in geography which are conventionally discussed separately: epistemology and conceptions of the relationship between people and Nature. Whichever issue we start with, two concepts are essential: intersubjectivity and labour. Knowledge of natural objects is tied to labour, which both subjects ideas to a kind of test and changes our position within Nature. All knowledge depends upon intersubjective understanding between people, but this implies that in social science, and hence in human geography, the traditional subject-object relationship should be recast as a form of communication between 'knowing-subjects'. These relationships are not limited to some separate sphere of epistemology but are constitutive of society in Nature itself. Labour, though traditionally overlooked in geography, is the most active and transformative process in changing Nature and society, and intersubjectivity is an essential element of the irreducibly *social* character of human life. In this attempt, the paper outlines and justifies a historical materialist perspective through critical engagement with positivist and humanist approaches. It is then argued that false conceptions of people and Nature in geography are grounded in the structure and self-understanding of our own society such that a critique of these ideas becomes a critique of our society.

1. Introduction

This paper attempts a critical discussion of epistemology and conceptions of people and Nature in geography. In doing so, it tries to integrate several spheres of discussion which are normally separated. Geographers have usually seen fit to discuss epistemology and methodology in isolation from the philosophy and object of the discipline (e.g. HARVEY, 1969; AMEDEO and GOLLEDGE, 1975; and even to a certain extent GREGORY, 1978). In geography's 'philistine' period (cf. OLSSON, 1975: vii) — that is, at the peak of the so-called 'quantitative revolution' — geographers happily turned their backs on traditional geography's amateurish reflections on the philosophy of the subject and the relations between 'man' and Nature (e.g. SAUER, 1952) and contented themselves with a zealous but narrow concern with scientific methodology. In this paper I want to reinstate the interests in philosophy and conceptions of people and Nature in geography, but, by drawing more extensively on philosophical literature, avoid the embarrassing parochialism of traditional geography's ventures into this area.

It is implicit in what follows that answers to questions about the way we know and the reliability of our knowledge must be provided jointly with answers to questions about the nature of our object of knowledge, and about the social situation under which both our knowledge and much of the object of study is produced. As we shall see, we can posit neither a simple relationship between knowing-subject and object of study in epistemology nor any simple bi-polar relationship between people and Nature. Rather, there is a partial interpenetration of subject and object, such that society's material structure and its self-understanding interact in

* School of Social Sciences, University of Sussex.

19

complex ways that must be delimited if either a satisfactory epistemology or an adequate conception of people and Nature is to be worked out.

The approach will be as follows; after providing a fuller justification for a concern with conceptions of people and Nature in geography (section 2) a historical materialist conception of people and Nature is outlined stage by stage. At each stage, epistemological implications will be raised and contrasts drawn between elements of corresponding epistemological positions and conceptions of people and Nature in what are termed positivist and interpretive social science. The former position would include most of spatial analysis, regional science and behavioural geography, the latter the humanist and phenomenological geography popularised by writers such as Tuan, Relph, Buttimer and Lowenthal. Most of the points raised in this critical engagement revolve around the questions of *intersubjectivity* and the nature of 'the *social*' and the role and implications of *labour*. In the fourth section, following up our attempt to delimit the interpenetration of subject and object, we look at how orthodox conceptions of people and Nature originate in the form of bourgeois society, and in turn how these conceptions *react back upon* that social reality. Finally in the conclusion, having discussed concrete examples of this interpenetration both in society at large and in the work of certain geographers, we attempt to summarise the implications at a more abstract level.

2. Conceptions of People and Nature — Are They Needed?

In most discussions of the nature of geography and its object of study, two themes have been dominant; a concern with *space* (whether it is a matter of spatial patterns, relations of structures) and a concern with the interaction between people and nature, 'environment' or 'land'. Discussion of the latter is now rare, for with the rise of positivist geography in the 1960's, a preoccupation with scientific *method* developed, and insofar as discussion of the *object* of study was felt to be worthwhile, the first theme grew at the expense of the second. So, if we are to resurrect a concern with conceptions of

people and Nature some brief justification is in order. This we can provide by discussing why positivist geographers have had so little to say on the subject. This disregard derived from the positivist philosophy of science which dominated the 'new geography' in which debates about such vague subjects as the essential character of people ('man') and Nature were considered to be 'metaphysical' and/or meaningless, or at least irrelevant. Since any claims about the subject could not be solved in a straightforward fashion by reference to unambiguously observable 'facts' there was no point in discussing them. Moreover, since positivism assumes a unity of method for all science, whether social or natural, epistemology and methodology were considered to be indifferent to the nature of the object of study and so the results of discussions of conceptions of people and Nature could not have any significance for 'science'.

This is not to say that the 'new' geographers were always or even occasionally aware of these aspects of positivist epistemology or knew what the abhorred 'metaphysics' was. Rather, these attitudes were absorbed informally in an atmosphere in which obsession with techniques and the mimicking of what were supposed to be the methods of natural science formed the dominant ethos and in which metaphysical discussion on people and Nature seemed to epitomise all the problems of the discredited, traditional, unscientific geography.

However, positivist geographers could not escape from metaphysics so easily, for since nothing that they studied could be said to exist outside Nature and Society, they could not possibly avoid taking some stance on the subject. Believing in the possibility of an observation language uncontaminated by theoretical presupposition, positivists might have argued that the content of this stance would be founded upon the firm bedrock of 'facts' instead of metaphysical speculation, and therefore that it is was purely an *a posteriori* matter. The problem with this argument is that a fact which is uninterpreted is simply meaningless. To try to strip away 'interpretations' of facts in order to reach a kernel of incontrovertible knowledge is to strip away any understanding. The interpretation of particular facts is always influenced by our interpretation of the most basic categories of experience, such as 'things', 'matter', 'mind', 'time', 'space' and 'Nature' and it is examination of these that constitutes metaphysics (HARRÉ, 1972). Those writers − whether positivist or non-positivist − who, following the logical postivists, tend to use the term metaphysics in a purely pejorative way are usually quite uncertain as to what it means. Since conscious or unconscious metaphysical commitments influence our more specific interpretations of the world, we can scarcely avoid examining them and so we admit without apology that much of what follows about concepts of people and Nature is quite metaphysical.

This positivist belief in the possibility of an atheoretical, neutral observation language and hence in the avoidability of theoretical and metaphysical presuppositions led, by default, to an unaware absorption of commonsense notions as the basic anchor point of knowledge. This is hardly a safe foundation, for the most important characteristic of commonsense is its taken-for-granted character as a body of eternal truths. Some of its ideas may be correct, others incorrect, but since it is by definition *unexamined,* and *uncorrected* (NOWELL-SMITH, 1974), it is inevitably internally inconsistent, Unless we 'problematize' basic categories like 'social', 'Nature', and 'individuals', we are bound to absorb these inconsistencies into our analysis. Therefore, the issue of how we conceptualize people and Nature *must* be placed back on the agenda of geographical inquiry.

3. Historical Materialist Perspectives on People and Nature and their Epistemological Implications

This section outlines an alternative conception of people and Nature which is considered to be consistent with a historical materialist perspective and uses this to criticise certain liberal conceptions of people, Nature and epistemology that are current in geography. However, although the proposals put forward here owe much to Marx[4] and marxists such as SCHMIDT (1971), TIMP-ANARO (1975), GOLDMANN (1969), OLLMAN (1971), SARTRE (1968), COL-LETTI (1972), MESZAROS (1970; 1972),

WALTON and GAMBLE (1972) and BUR-GESS (1976), the manner of presentation and some of the emphases will be rather unconventional, as I intend to draw out some epistemological issues which normally get submerged in such discussions. To do this I have drawn upon the work of critical theorists such as APEL (1967, 1972), HORKHEIMER (1972) and HABERMAS (1971;1976), who have probed the relations between epistemology, social theory and human interests much more deeply (albeit more abstractly) than have these more conventional marxists. Also, in comparing various epistemological positions in social science, I owe much to several excellent texts on the philosophy of social science, such as KEAT and URRY (1975), GIDDENS (1976), SMART (1976), BENTON (1977), FAY (1975) and BERN-STEIN (1976).

I shall pay special attention to some of the issues raised in debates between phenomenology and historical materialist, critical, social science since flirtations with the former have become quite popular in recent years in geography (WALMSLEY, 1974; TUAN, 1971; BUTTIMER, 1976; RELPH, 1970, 1976; GALE, 1972; LOWENTHAL, 1961). As will become clear I think these geographers have failed to grasp some of the more important insights of the intepretive philosophical tradition in which phenomenology is situated and instead have adopted its most dubious elements (cf. ENTRIKEN, 1976; GREGORY, 1978: ch.4).

As the argument that follows is quite complex, it may be helpful first to anticipate some of the main conclusions in order to deal with some possible sources of misunderstanding. The general thrust of the argument in this section will be that most of the questionable elements of liberal conceptions of people and Nature and epistemology stem from two main sources: −

A. An inadequate recognition of the nature and role of *intersubjectivity* in social life − a failure shared by both positivists and, ironically, by those humanist geographers who have championed the study of subjectivity in geography.

B. A distortion or wholesale omission of the nature and implications of *labour* as the most active and fundamental interaction between people and nature.

The discussions of A are especially complex and lengthy and no doubt to some the concern with these issues will be taken to belie an idealist or at least non-marxist standpoint. Certainly, as HABERMAS (1972: 52-53) has argued Marx himself, in his later theoretical writings, tended to reduce all human action and the self-generative process of life wholly to labour and production, but in his material investigations of concrete social forms he took full account of interaction outside labour in terms of intersubjective norms and values and in terms of ideological forms. Where we do make limited concessions to elements of these philosophies outside the marxist tradition, it is argued that when all the caveats about their validity are taken into account, plus the points related to B, the overall argument does not involve any retraction of the basic elements of historical materialism on the contrary, it reinforces them. Too often, I feel, marxists have given unnecessarily crude expositions of historical materialism: and its epistemology, cavalierly patched-up with unilluminating and unexplained assertions that certain relationships are 'dialectical' (always italicised, of course) and this failure owes much to the widespread disregard of recent developments in the philosophy of the social sciences which have yet to be processed by any of the 'heavyweight' marxist theoreticians.

Having completed the preparatory forewarnings, we can now begin the stage-by-stage outline of our historical materialist conception of people and Nature. For the sake of brevity the argument will be presented in form of numbered 'theses'.

(i) The Unity of People and Nature

We must begin by recognising that people and Nature are not separate: we are part of Nature and to start in the conventional manner with such a separation followed by a listing of interactions would be to prejudice every other aspect of the exposition. Nature is *internally differentiated* and properly speaking we should refer not to interactions between people and Nature but to 'inner-actions' within Nature.[5]

This leads us immediately to the question of the form of this internal differentiation, in particular to a discussion of those characteristics and 'inner-actions' which humans share with other parts of Nature and those which are particular to humans. Failure to resolve these issues, as will be shown later, into conceptions which oscillate between a naturalisation of humanity and a humanisation of Nature (BURGESS, 1976).

Some of these distinctions and 'inner-actions' are uncontroversial: for example the division between inanimate and animate Nature and 'inner-actions' in the shape of humans' physical metabolism with outer Nature through such processes as respiration, sexual reproduction, death, ageing, eating. However, as we will see, the form of this metabolism is distinct from that of other animals and the nature of the difference *is* controversial. In fact it is argued here that it is these unique characteristics of human life which are most frequently misunderstood and misrepresented in geography.*

(ii) Intersubjective Meanings and the Nature of 'The Social'

Firstly, *unlike* other forms of life, human life is *social*. By this we mean far more than that individual people interact with one another in groups. A society is more than the sum of its parts: 'the social' is not reducible without residue to the characteristics of the present individual members of a society.[6] Nor does population equal society. In particular, what distinguishes a society from a mere group or aggregate is that the interaction is *meaningful;* that is, the 'social' is grounded in the production, negotiation and use of 'intersubjective meanings'. We do not merely interact with one another purely in the manner of mechanical causation of physical stimulus and response as postulated in behaviourist social science,[7] for we also act on the basis of *understanding.*

Now at this point, it is essential to distinguish between *behaviour* and *action.*[8] By 'behav-

---

*For example, the ecosystem approach to human geography tends to blur these distinctions and reduce human beings to the status of top carnivore (STODDART, 1967).

iour' we mean nothing more than a purely physical movement or change, such as falling asleep, breathing, that is, doing things which lack 'intrinsic meaning structure'. In contrast, doings which we call 'actions' are not wholly reducible to physical behaviour even though they may be coupled with it. Actions are constituted by *intersubjective meanings:* putting a cross on a ballot paper, conducting a seminar, getting married, arguing, doing arithmetic, going on a demonstration are all examples of doings whose nature *depends* on the existence of certain intersubjective meanings. We differentiate between a carnival , a fascist demonstration and an anti-fascist demonstration not simply by the physical movements of a crowd of people marching down a street, for this 'behaviour' might differ very little in each case, but by reference to the meanings that the actions have for participants. In the sphere of 'action' as distinct from behaviour, meaning is not merely *descriptive* of the world, it is also *constitutive.* A community of geologists uses shared concepts to describe and explain the nature of granite, but the granite itself is impervious to the content of the *concept* of granite. However, while geographers might use concepts like *'lebensraum'* amd 'fascism' in describing Hitler's Germany, the *object* of study would have been different had these concepts or something similar to them not existed as intersubjective meanings in that society.

In case the word 'constitutive' is misinterpreted, it should be noted that we do not wish to imply that constitutive meanings and rules necessarily 'produce' or 'generate' social practices, but merely that the practices would not be what they are if it were not for these meanings. For example, the use of money in exchanging commodities requires an intersubjective understanding of the function of money − what it 'stands for' − but it takes more than the 'concept' of money to 'produce' money.

Failure to recognise the constitutive role of meaning in society is characteristic of positivism and indeed of some positivistic variants of marxism. For both these groups the consequences of this failure are disastrous because it renders the nature of their own scientific activity unintelligible (APEL, 1972).

To maintain this position they would have to argue that they could do science without understanding any concepts. Since science is a part of society, then the meaningful character of social action has to be conceded.

Althusserian marxists are right in distinguishing between the 'real object' and the 'thought object' and in insisting that the concept dog (thought object) does not bark, but there is an exception to the latter stricture when the real objects involve human action − most obviously in the cases of political conflicts, mass media and ideologies − because here concepts very definitely do 'bark'.[9] In the case of positivistic marxism, a refusal to acknowledge this would render the concept of 'false consciousness' redundant, and more generally lead to a profoundly conservative view of people as nothing more than objects in history rather than the (potential) subjects of history. Ironically, the attempt to purge marxism of anything which might sniff of idealism, itself leads to a form of idealism in which ideas and ideologies have no material force but hang mysteriously above and out of contact with society.

Having introduced the concept of constitutive intersubjective meanings and established the behaviour-action distinction, we must now make several important qualifications which distinguish our view from that of 'interpretive' social science (which includes phenomenological approaches, and is used most widely in sociology and anthropology) which usually champions these concepts.

(iii) Qualifications about 'Constitutive Intersubjective Meanings'

Interpretive social scientists such as WINCH (1958) seem to associate the existence of intersubjective meanings and rules in society with the existence of a social consensus in which these meanings and rules are fully understood. However, we would argue that misunderstandings can also be constitutive of action (LICHTMAN, 1970) (e.g. misunderstanding of other societies by colonialists) and that even where rules and meanings of actions are understood, people may still disagree and dispute them (TAYLOR, 1971). I may fully understand the intersubjective meanings associated with voting, to do with political parties, elections, governments etc., such that I am able to participate in voting, but I may simultaneously dispute the legitimacy of every one of these concepts. Intersubjective meanings, like the common sense of which they are the content, need not be coherent, consistent or correct. In fact, as GELLNER (1962) argues, the material force of many concepts in societies (e.g. 'the national interest') derives from their ambiguity, hypocrisy and inconsistency. This reinforces our earlier warning about the dangers of a failure to scrutinise commonsense notions.

Meanings and rules are not always expressed in language, nor are they reducible to linguistic expressions. Rather they are bound up with action and institutions so that practices such as casting a vote or signing a cheque presuppose the existence of particular intersubjective meanings, social rules and other practices (TAYLOR, 1971). Therefore the disputes over intersubjective meanings in society mentioned above, are by no means academic or semantic in character, for since they are bound up with practices and the material form of society they involve disputes over *material interests*. For example, we may enter a dispute about the similarity or dissimilarity of tax evasion and welfare-scrounging — but to do so would not be simply a matter of conflict of ideas, but one of conflicting material interests and practices.

> "The meanings and norms, implicit in these practices are not just in the minds of the actors *but are out there in the practices themselves,* practices which are essentially modes of social relation, of mutual action".[10] TAYLOR, 1971: 177 (our emphasis).

Not all concepts known in society are constitutive of social practices to the same degree. Some such as religious beliefs have lost their force as the material effectivity of the practices in which they are grounded in the wider society has declined. Some refer to practices which have a constitutive role in other societies, but not in our own (e.g. witchcraft, caste). Obviously, 20th century westerners do not have major systems of intersubjective meanings concerning witchcraft and taboo because their understanding is not necessary for engagement in social relations in the west.

In other cases, intersubjective meanings which at first sight do not appear to be part of common sense and everyday social practices, are on closer scrutiny, found to be embedded in them. For example, the concept of 'competitive individualism' is not an *explicit* part of common sense yet once it has been pointed out, it is possible to see that it is embedded in a wide variety of social practices. Likewise, in the case of our own subject of people and Nature it can be argued that the ideas embodied in the 'suburban ideal' of Nature as an arena of recreation "from which the facts of production had been banished" [Raymond Williams quoted in HARVEY (1978)][11] are firmly grounded in the evolving structure of capitalist society. We are not generally aware of these 'deeper layers of meaning' and yet they are both supportive of practices and institutions and are in turn reproduced by the latter. And it is often the case that once these deeper layers enter our consciousness, efforts are made to change them: the fact that they remain hidden for the most part is an important factor in their continued existence.

(iv) Intersubjectivity — 'The Individual' and 'The Social'

Although constitutive meanings are negotiated by the individuals and expressed in their writings, they are not wholly reducible to opinions of those individuals: they are not free emanations of the thought of isolated individuals, nor are they simple responses of isolated individuals to Nature. If they were so, there would be purely subjective understanding, involving no intersubjective communication. But this is an impossibility for we cannot acquire the human qualities of understanding without entering into social relations.[12] In the extremely rare cases of individuals who have been brought up outside society ('wolf children') the most important and distinctive human characteristics have been found lacking, they cannot speak or perform simple logical operations, they have atrophied sensory perception and some could only walk on all fours! Our understanding is fashioned out of concepts which are *available* in our society, and which *denote* a much wider range of objects than individuals, and those concepts are usually to some extent productions of societies.

We would therefore take issue with the emphasis and characterisation of 'individuals' in humanistic approaches in geography such as the writings of Yi-fu Tuan (e.g. YI-FU TUAN, 1976), which situate asocial individuals in nature and in some nebulous 'culture' without specifying the structure of social relations and their material basis. At first sight it may appear that it is *individuals* who, *do* things in life, whereas 'classes', 'institutions' and even 'societies' appear to be mere aggregations of individuals or even abstractions. Howver, as LUKES (1968) shows, as soon as we ask the question — *Which aspects* of individuals are being granted a privileged status in such accounts? — it becomes clear that no matter whether the answer is individual 'characters', 'ideas', 'beliefs' or 'actions'[13] none of these aspects can be defined asocially. To attempt to *reduce* society to individuals or individuals to mere expressions of society is misleading and quite unnecessary: both of these opposed positions involve a dual misrepresentation of each of its terms. Therefore, the common objection of phenomenologists and the like, that marxists fail to consider the individual in society can often be turned back against them.[14] Indeed in positivist and behavioural geography the consequences of this asocial characterisation of individuals can be seen in the tendency to attempt to explain macro-phenomena by reference to some autonomous realm of individual preferences — which inevitably gives an entirely voluntaristic view of the world (cf. GRAY, 1975). Ironically, despite their avowed hostility to naturalistic approaches which objectify human experience, phenomenological approaches which interpret the subjectivity of this experience in abstraction from intersubjective meanings and social norms invite similar regresses towards either psychologistic explanations of this experience which situate its origin in our 'inner Nature', or behaviourist explanations which characterise it as a purely physical response to stimuli in 'outer Nature'.

The point that intersubjective meanings are not reducible to individuals' opinions or preferences has important epistemological and methodological implications, for it means that the positivist practice of doing opinion surveys in order to produce what purport to be 'brute data' on the subject is misconceived.

Such data cannot tell us *why* people have *these* opinions. They have to be interpreted and this can only be done by establishing relationships between opinions, intersubjective meanings, material interests and practices (TAYLOR, 1971). In other words we cannot fully understand the social world without interpreting its intrinsic meaning structure, though this is exactly what positivists try to do when they treat social science as involving no more than the construction of syntactical relations (through models) among 'brute' data.

(v) Against Idealism

In contrast to the idealist tendencies of many interpretive social scientists (e.g. WINCH, 1958) we have no intention of *reducing* all social pehnomena to this 'basis' in intersubjective meanings or social rules.[15] Many of the most important social relations exist in virtue of force and necessity, although they may be rationalised in such a way as to set up some general consent for their existence. In the case of the all-important social relations *of production,* the relations are maintained through the control of people's physical reproduction by means of *social* restrictions on access to the means of production, the disposal of labour-power (our capacity to work), and of the control over labour and its products. In a capitalist society, if you lack means of production and subsistence, to survive you have to sell your labour-power to those who own and control the means of production. You need to understand a little about certain social rules to do this (which is not to say that you have to follow them uncritically), but it would be a disastrous idealist fallacy to suppose that the social structure of capitalism was instituted on the basis of agreed-upon rules. These rules are supportive of the material practices and are *imposed* and enforced through sanctions involving material and social deprivation.

This type of fallacy is characteristic of those phenomenological approaches which attribute to peoples' desires and perceptions that which is done to them and which they are compelled to do or to accept. In particular, *'power'* relationships between people are characterised by the *lack* of or *disregard* for democratically-negotiated intersubjective meanings (LUKES,

1974; VON WRIGHT, 1971, ch.IV). Again, although the starting point is very different, the effect of this neglect of power and material social structure is much the same as that of the common positivist practice of explaining social phenomena in terms of preferences of individuals (GRAY, 1975; SAYER, 1976).

(vi) Criticism in Social Science and the Relationship between Theoretical and Actor's Accounts

Unlike some advocates of interpretive social science such as WINCH (1958) or SCHUTZ (1965), we do *not* wish to argue that social scientists should not criticise concepts in society. One may grant that sometimes criticism may be based on misunderstanding, but there seems to be no reason why we cannot understand intersubjective meanings in the actors' own terms *and* then go beyond the latters' self-understanding to provide an analysis which is implicitly or explicitly critical of that common sense view. Marx's analysis of false-consciousness is an excellent example of this in that it simultaneously determines the *origin* of certain ideas, their material effects *and* shows them to be false. So ideas and practices may be false or mistaken, but it may be true that they exist and have material force. The material practices of capitalism and much of the content of political economy are mutually reinforcing in that the ideas of the latter are based *on* and are implicit *in* the former. We can criticise liberal social geography and political economy not just because they are in one sense 'false' or 'incorrect' but also because in the other sense it is 'true' or 'correct' that these (false) practices exist.[16] We would therefore argue for a distinction between *theoretical* accounts and *actors'* accounts. Although there should be some relation of the former to the latter (at least they should not ignore constitutive meanings and actors' accounts), they should not be reducible to the latter, (as SCHUTZ, 1965, seems to advocate) for such reduction would merely reproduce common sense. And if we cannot go beyond common sense. there is no need for any kind of science.[17]

A theoretical category such as 'surplus value' is related to the everyday categories of 'profit',

'rent' and 'interest' in capitalist society in that it theorises their origin: *both* sets of categories are used by Marx, and the latter, being grounded in practices which have intrinsic-meaning structure, are *part of* concrete social reality. If on the other hand, we take concepts from social physics, and locational analysis such as 'population potential' or 'spatial autocorrelation' there is no such intimate tie between the theoretical concepts and the constitutive meanings and practices in the object of study. Whereas, 'surplus value' and the other concepts to which it is linked — such as profit maximisation, and competition between firms — contain implicit assumptions that people are conscious subjects, the concepts of locational analysis treat them as mere objects, as 'data' and consequently misunderstood the nature of their object of study by creating a thought object which negates the essential qualities of the real object.

The relationship between theoretical and actors' accounts is a fluid one. Elements of the former may become incorporated into the latter and become constitutive of social practices in the way that the concepts associated with I.Q. tests became constitutive of certain practices in British education, and urban systems analysis has become constitutive of certain practices of British structure planning. This raises the important issues of the relation of subject (analyst) to object (society) and the role of criticism in social science. In social science there is a partial identity of subject and object of knowledge (GOLDMANN, 1969), and since the objects (other people) are also knowing subjects, the relation between subject and object should not merely be a platonic one of passive reflection, or description, explanation and prediction, that is, a one-way process emanating from the subject as in natural science.[18] Instead, the production of knowledge should involve both subject and object in *interaction*, negotiation of meanings and criticism. All science requires criticism of ideas and practices within the scientific community, but where ideas and 'actions' are part of the object of study, *social* scientists can be critical of their object. And if we accept that science is redundant unless it goes beyond common sense, then criticism of society becomes not just an option, but a necessity: to fail to criticise is to fail to improve upon common sense.

This argument is ignored or rejected by both positivists and phenomenologists. In the former, science is limited to description, explanation and prediction of *objects;* and our proposals would be seen as an illegitimate introduction of 'values' into science. The problem with this response is that science — positivist or whatever — must attempt to sort out good and significant arguments from bad amd pointless arguments to *evaluate* its own understanding. But if science aims to go beyond common sense understanding and if we recognise the constitutive role of the both science and common sense in society and yet deny that evaluations of social practices should be part of science, we produce an atrophied and inconsistent concept of reason and rationality, and one which is cut off from and alien to our lives rather than intrinsic to them. Such a science makes a virtue of the denial of the nature of its object of study as knowing subjects and, in its normative role of providing prescriptions for society, can only operate within a *technically*-circumscribed rationality which avoides evaluation of human needs. When it has to make recourse to moral judgements, the values invoked are disconnected from the lives of people in society (ADORNO *et al.,* 1976; MESZAROS, 1972: 62). To put this crucial but difficult point in another way: the fact-value distinction itself is very much a product of this type of thinking, for as TAYLOR (1967) shows, it treats values as simple statements for which no rational support can be given. For example, a value statement is understood to be of the type '*X'* is good or bad, *full stop,* rather than '*X* is good or bad because it relates in a particular way to certain human needs *Y'.* In making this reduction, positivism removes such statements from the domain of rational discussion, and yet, as is the case with its rejection of constitutive meanings and unintentional action [see (vii), this has the effect of rendering unintelligible its own practice as science, for the values on which it is based — such as the search for 'truth' and logical consistency — cannot be given any defence under this conception of values. As Popper has admitted, these values have simply to be taken as 'pure decisions' [cf. ADORNO *et al.,*

(1976), especially the papers by Popper, Habermas and Albert].

In the case of phenomenology, the narrow concern with 'restoration of meaning' as the comprehensive description of the facts of consciousness tends to produce an unquestioning faith in the rationality of this consciousness (RICOUER, 1965; GOLDMANN, 1969). As is clear in Yi-fu Tuan's bland outpourings (e.g. YI-FU TUAN, 1971b) the crucial elements of *scepticism* and *criticism* are absent. Phenomenology makes much of the notion that people are subjects, but in fact does not treat them as such because it fails to engage critically with their self-understanding.

(vii) Intentional Actions and Teleological Explanation

The study of society must also come to terms with *intentional actions.* Although not all actions are intended, failure to take account of those that are produces a picture of a society whose intersubjective meanings are inert and merely descriptive or regulative, and in which there is no concept of *agency:* Understanding these alone may clarify the form and significance of actions but would not explain why actions *occur* (FAY and MOON, 1977). Our actions are not limited to instinctive, reflex and habitual modes, but can be directed towards the realisation of certain goals. In such cases 'teleological explanation' in which we say '*X* was done in order to produce *Y*', is appropriate. In an attempt to standardize methodology across all the sciences, positivists, such as Hempel, have often tried to reformulate teleological explanations in the casual form — '*X* causes (or is followed by) *Y*' (HEMPEL, 1965). These attempts have failed on two counts. Firstly, the reformulation misses the point that the fact that *X* is necessary for *Y* is itself part of the explanation of the occurrence of *X* (RYAN, 1970: Ch.8). Secondly, whereas failure of *Y* to follow *X* constitutes a failed casual explanation, failure of action *X* successfully to produce *Y* does not vitiate a teleological statement: the truth of the statement that I am writing this paper in order to improve upon existing conceptions of people and Nature and epistemology is not affected by whether I succeed or not (VON WRIGHT, 1971: Ch.IV). We may grant that teleology has been rightfully purged from the non-human sciences where it took the form of vitalism, but as with inter-subjective meanings, intentional action in society can only be denied by rendering our own practice unintelligible. In science (whether positivist or not) and in engineering, knowledge that, say, water turns to steam (event Y) when heated to $100°C$ (event X) enables us to produce Y by producing X. Whereas the spontaneous production of steam in outer nature is to be explained causally, the *act* of producing steam in society is to be explained both causally and teleologically – both by reference to causes and reasons (cf. VON WRIGHT, 1971: Ch. VI). Whereas causes are either causes or they are not, reasons are open to *evaluative* assessment, as good or bad reasons. In trying to reduce all kinds of explanation to causal form, positivism is unable yet again to make sense of its own activity.

In introducing the behaviour/action distinction, and the concepts of constitutive meanings and intentional action and then making numerous caveats about their implications we have tried to distance ourselves from both the positivists on the one hand and the idealist tendencies of interpretive social scientists, in particular phenomenologists, on the other. Given the complexity of the arguments and the interactions within society and Nature that they describe, it is impossible to encapsulate what we consider to be a correct view of society and Nature in every statement. Taken on their own, out of context, some statements may seem idealist, some vulgar materialist. It is only in synthesis that they can be fully understood, and we have yet to introduce the most important element in this synthesis, the one which transcends the idealism-materialism and mind and matter dualisms – labour.

(viii) Labour – its Social Character and its Transformation of Nature

The active transformation of nature for the purposes of survival might generally be called labour, and in the case of human beings it has certain distinctive characteristics which are absolutely central to the understanding of society. I shall argue that labour is the most important and the most neglected interaction between people and Nature.

Human labour is a form of intentional action (see above, section 5) which *transforms, organizes and/or moves parts of nature to serve as 'use-values' for our consumption*. Unlike the merely instinctive and habitual labour of animals, the labour of humans is predicated upon our power to 'monitor our own monitorings' and consciously and intentionally to *produce* transformations of nature. The end-product of labour is envisaged in the mind of the worker before the work begins and then is made real or 'objectified' through labour. The structure of this process is the same as that of intentional action: knowledge that seeds (X) under conditions, p, q and r becomes vegetables (Y) spontaneously in nature is used *to produce Y under the worker's direction* by first producing X – sowing seeds, and conditions p, q and r – preparing and watering ground. This is sometimes called the 'teleology of labour' (WALTON and GAMBLE, 1972).

In so far as labour involves a transformation of Nature from within, we can only work as Nature does, by working with its given materials: we can only change Nature by obeying Nature's laws.[19]

Since human transformations of nature are based on understanding and intentions, human labour is not 'behaviour' but *action*. Human labour is also in several senses distinctively *social*, involving not only an interaction between each individual and outer Nature, but also an interaction between people. In the more obvious sense, this is so because human individuals always produce with and for others besides themselves. However, taken in isolation this statement appears to be only contingently rather than necessarily true, and invites the response – surely it is at least *possible*, though admittedly extremely rare in practice, for individuals to produce purely for their own consumption? The problem with this reply is firstly that the species would fail to *re*produce itself if it failed to produce for its young (which is the case for non-human as well as human labour) and secondly (and this is the most frequently overlooked point) that even the labour of Robinson Crusoe was based on socially acquired skills learned before his isolation. The labour of an asocial 'pure' individual would, like the behaviour of wolf children [see above, section [4] (iv)], be unrecognisable as *human* labour.[20] Human labour, as distinct from animal labour requires understanding of Nature's mechanisms, and this knowledge is not innate but socially acquired.[21] Knowledge of Nature is never produced through an unmediated reflexion of the subject upon Nature, but always uses 'means of production' in the form of the existing social knowledge.

The needs towards which labour is directed, the form of the labour and the product of labour all have a social aspect. In particular, labour does not take place under *any* social relations, but under determinate interlocking *social relations of production*. In these the control of labour and its product, are determined by differential social control over the means of production, labour-power (our capacity to work), the labour process itself and the product of labour. The manner of appropriation of Nature, i.e. the form of our metabolism with Nature, is determined by the social relations, chiefly to do with ownership and control, and these forms of appropriation have the effect of reproducing those social relations. The separation of workers from the means of production means that their appropriation of Nature is governed by the interests of capitalists, and in turn this serves to reproduce the workers as wage-labourers because it does not give them the control of the means of production to enable them to become anything else, and it reproduces the capitalists as the owners and controllers of production. Therefore there is a *necessary* relation between the form of appropriation of Nature and the social relations of production.

Liberal theory only recognises a *contingent* relation between production and social relations, such that the former is seen as a purely technical process which is affected in an external fashion by 'social factors': Witness the frequent remarks in geographical studies of the Third World that certain social (or 'cultural') 'factors' inhibit development — such as lack of education, different cultural values. This separation is also present in the conventional treatment of income distribution and inequality in social geography as unequal access of different groups of consumers (i.e. existing *outside* production) to a bundle of goods which has already been produced (e.g. COATES *et al.*, 1977).

(ix) Labour and Self-change

Labour is the most *active* and *effective* relation between people and Nature, for it is through our labour that we transform our environment. The manner of this transformation depends upon social relations but can also react back upon those social relations. In changing our social and 'natural' context, we change ourselves, for as we have already argued our character as people does not simply emanate from within us, but is developed through our interactions with others: 'the human essence is the ensemble of social relations' (6th Thesis on Feuerbach, MARX, 1974a). As we develop new forms of control over Nature and our social relations (e.g. through the development of telecommunications), we develop new needs for new use-values and information (e.g. information on world current affairs) and new means for satisfying them (television broadcasts) and as a result we become a different kind of people (more/less socially aware, apathetic/callous/ concerned). It follows that we must take account of the ability of people to change themselves. This does *not* mean that we must adopt a voluntarist account of society and history in which all that happens is a simple function of the human will, for:—

> "Men make their own history, but they do not make it just as they please, they do not make it under circumstances chosen by themselves, but under circumstances directly encountered, given and transmitted from the past" (MARX, 1972, 18th Brumaire of Louis Bonaparte:10).

Although human labour gives rise to the potential for self-change, not all self-change is intended, and where it is, it is not always realised.

(x) Appropriated Nature and the Object of Labour

The objective results in 'outer Nature' of our labour constitute *'appropriated Nature'* and consists of objects of consumption and means of production. Appropriated Nature includes objects such as houses, machines, factories, reservoirs, computers, livestock, ploughed fields – all those objects for which bourgeois thought, having *separated* people and society from Nature can find no place in either and has to label 'artifical and unnatural' objects. Once again this separation and omission stems from capitalist ideology and the real, concrete social forms of capitalism in which it is grounded.

Although the *object of labour* (the thing being worked upon) and the conditions under which work is done are usually within appropriated Nature, the *original* conditions of production themselves have not been socially produced. Obviously we cannot fabricate new use-values out of nothing, and since we must always work upon pre-existing substances we have to acknowledge the fact that so-called 'environmental' constraints do have a significant effect upon societies. It is precisely the nature and extent of this effect that has been at the centre of most geographical discussions on people and Nature, but it is only when this relationship is taken in isolation that it presents any difficulty. That is, it is only a problem if we don't take into account the central role of labour in transforming both Nature and Society. When this happens. the effects of appropriated Nature and the forms of social organisation are hopelessly confused with the effects of this 'virgin Nature'.

(xi) Labour: Its Philosophical Implications

The philosophical implications of the 'sensuous human activity' of labour are enormous, for it is only by reference to labour and its teleological character that we can *transcend the dichotomy of the material and thought, and the dualism of materialism and idealism* Labour is *simultaneously* a material, practical process *and* meaningful, intentional action. In constructing a building we both transform parts of Nature (sand, wood, stone), objectify human knowledge and reproduce or modify certain social relations.

It is also the human faculty of self-changing through the teleology of labour that makes social development profoundly historical, in contrast to the merely evolutionary development of other forms of life. This means that

whereas laws in nature are universal and eternal, laws of social action are *historically-specific* and can be changed through human practice. Whereas we can control Nature only by obeying its laws, we can change the very terms of social laws, by *disobeying* them. And yet, as cause and effect of its failure to come to terms with the fact of human self-change, positivist science, such as locational analysis, expects to find invariant, universal empirical regularities of human behaviour. Any regularities discovered at a particular point in time are hopefully expected to hold true for the future while repeated failures to corroborate such regularities are treated as failures of the individual scientist or model, rather than as evidence of qualitative self-change of history. As a result, such an approach *reifies* every social fact it encounters; the social facts of the development of cities, the conventions of political activity, even the evaluation of the built environment, are treated as in principle no different from the facts of mineral composition, topography and meteorology. But laws and facts of society can only continue to operate so long as human practice, knowledge and social relations remain unchanged; the law of value can only work as long as we have unplanned competitive production for profit. Marxism, recognising the partial identity of subject and object, attempts to take account of its own effect in changing the object. As a result, marxist theory is the only theory which can survive and indeed theorise a break-down in or surpassing of its categories and laws. Marxist theory of capitalism tries to understand the conditions of its own dissolution in changed human practice. It is only if we understand firstly that *social* laws are historically-specific and can be disobeyed and changed and secondly that practices and material forms may be 'false' that it is possible to make sense of Marx's famous statement that 'The philosophers have only interpreted the world in various ways; the point is to change it' (Theses on Feuerbach, MARX, 1974b).

We have reached this conclusion that categories used in the study of society should be historically-specific by working upon some very general abstract categories such as 'Society', 'intersubjective meanings', and 'labour'. These abstract categories cannot be applied in an unmodified form in concrete studies, for they always take on particular forms according to the historical situation. Each of these categories cannot stand for an isolated real object; labour cannot exist apart from the subject of labour (a person) and an object of labour (raw material); intersubjective meanings presuppose people who articulate them and objects denoted by them; 'Society' is not a thing but a set of relationships. To serve as *concrete* concepts these categories must be relationally defined:[22] What *kind* of labour? What *kind* of labourer? Under what *kind* of technical conditions and social relations? Unless we make these concepts concrete their use can only lead to a concealment of historical change. Certainly, General Motors needs labour, but *wage*-labour and not serf-labour or slave-labour. Likewise feudal lords depend on the labour of others for their existence, but not just any labour. If workers have either completely free access to land or no ties whatsoever, there is no need for them to produce a surplus on which the lord can live. There is therefore no 'natural' reason why peoples' interaction with Nature should take the form of serf-labour, slave-labour, or working for capital as wage-labour. But in any given historical period the interaction with Nature is locked into a determinate structure of social relations and the eternal necessity of labour (in *abstract* terms) misleadingly gives the appearance of an eternal necessity of those social relations. Bourgeois thought characteristically confuses abstract necessity with concrete historical forms of that necessity so that 'earning a living'/'getting a job'/'surviving' are often treated interchangeably.

As Harvey's discussion of Malthus shows, this confusion is characteristic of theories of overpopulation (HARVEY, 1974). Malthus' work on overpopulation might initially appear to be concerned with a value which is essential for the whole population – the survival of society. In fact it was based on assumptions that the existing class structure was the only (natural) one possible, and, therefore, it followed that a landed class was necessary to consume surplus product without pushing up its numbers, for if the labouring classes were to consume it they would inevitably reproduce at an excessive rate. In openly embracing neo-Malthusian

analyses of underdevelopment and overpopulation, modern geographers have made the same error. As Timpanaro remarks,

"For too long the ruling classes have attributed to 'Nature' . . . . the iniquities and sufferings for which the organisation of society is responsible" (TIMPANARO, 1975:17).

The naive positivist assumptions that social science involves a simple bipolar relationship between subject and object and that it should seek out regularities among matters of fact, ignoring the contingent status of social facts, refusing to see that their production is open to negotiation according to peoples' interests, social norms and power structures, means that even when it is used normatively it can only change its object in accordance with what are mistakenly supposed to be its universal eternal laws and entities. Given that historical conjunctures reflect class-dominance, this 'piecemeal social engineering' can only work according to the interests of the dominant class. In this way, regional policy, supported by regional science, takes capitalist social relations as given and the regional problem as an engineering or managerial problem, as a malfunctioning of control, to be dealt with by policies which do not interfere with those social relations but assist in their reproduction in backward areas.

By now, it should be clear that whether we are talking about normative or descriptive uses of positivist and humanist approaches in human geography and social science, these problems cannot be dealt with in the sphere of 'methodology' as traditionally conceived, or, in the case of normative applications, by the adoption of more radical intentions by the investigator. In the first place, all of these problems relate to issues which are unknowingly presupposed in methodological discussions: that is, they relate not to secondary questions of testing hypotheses, problems of induction and deduction, and so on, but to primary problems of the relationship of subject and object, about the nature of the knowing subject and the object of knowledge and what their implications are for the possibility of understanding. In the second place, even if the intentions of the researcher are quite radical, adoption of positivist and humanist approaches inevitably involves a foundation in what we have tried to show are inadequate and incoherent answers to these primary problems ·and hence results in an inability to solve more concrete and practical problems. Whether social science is seen in terms of explaining and controlling reified social relations or, in the humanist case, in terms of developing an understanding of subjectivity, neither will take us far beyond the uncorrected ideas of common sense and both will produce what Harvey has termed 'status-quo' or 'counter-revolutionary' theory (HARVEY, 1973: Ch.4).

In this section we have attempted to develop an immanent critique of positivist and humanist positions regarding epistemology and conceptions of people and Nature. We have started by taking a combination of contested and uncontested premises and then tried to discover their limits by counterposing them, by drawing out their presuppositions, and by checking whether they can be consistently applied reflexively to the actual activity of these forms of science (cf. CRAIB, 1977 for a discussion of this method). The conclusions drawn from this process have been used to derive an alternative conception, some of whose elements, such as the idea of science as critical activity, might appear outrageous when considered in isolation or as premises (as they are so often presented in marxist discussions), but which can be arrived at logically from much less controversial starting points. No mystical conversion experiences or gestalt switches between incommensurable paradigms should be required.

4. From Criticism of Thought to Criticism of Society

Although the implications of the interpenetration of subject and object might already seem complex, we have still not gone very far; we have yet to show how this interpenetration applies to our own subject-matter. That is, *informal* versions of conceptions of people and Nature are, like any other system of constitutive meanings, out there in society itself, and likewise the way in which epistemological positions inform the practice of science *in* society can often be discerned. And since there are serious problems with these conceptions *about* society and knowledge, and insofar as they have a constitutive

role, they must also be problems *in* and *of* society. As with other constitutive meanings, although one can argue that, in varying degrees they 'generate' certain practices in society, the direction of influence is usually much stronger in the reverse direction. Accordingly, it is not so much that false ideas produce 'false' [in the sense introduced in 3 (vi)] practices but that 'false' practices maintain the reproduction of their constitutive meanings simply because of the difficulty of resisting the conclusion that 'what *is* in society, is what *must* be.

Disentangling these interpenetrations of thought and practice and attacking them *in thought* will usually only 'leave the world as it was', as Wittgenstein said of philosophy. We cannot merely 'think' these ideas and practices away because they are not reducible to pure 'errors of thought'. Their persistence derives from the way in which they are embodied in practice and therefore they can only be changed through practice. However, if this change is to be produced consciously, it must be based on a critical theory of society.

In this section, then, examples will be given of the way in which problems of conceptions of people and Nature in geographical thought unknowingly reflect *real* problems *in* society. As such we will be attacking not just false ideas but ideology for as Mepham has argued:—

"Ideology is not a collection of discrete falsehoods but a matrix of thought *firmly grounded in the forms of our social* life and organized within a set of interdependent categories" (MEPHAM, 1972, our emphasis).

(i) People as the Subjects or Agents of History

I have argued against deterministic conceptions of people and Nature which do not acknowledge the nature of people as subjects or agents in history. Now in our own lives, we are rarely able to recognise ourselves as the conscious intentional producers of our own social relations and material conditions of existence in anything more than very limited ways. In the main, we have to submit to what already exists, despite the fact that on reflection we may realise that these conditions are socially produced. In capitalist society it is particularly true that the results of our actions — our own products — take on 'naturelike' qualities in the sense that they react back on us as *blind forces* to which we must submit. This is most obvious in the economic sphere, where we hear of the market 'rising' and 'falling', of 'downturns', 'booms', redundancies, and inner-city decline. Although all of these are outcomes of the actions of human agents we have to respond to them, and we are told that we must 'face up to' these harsh economic 'facts', just as we must face up to bad weather, floods and earthquakes. In this way the naturalisation of social relations is a problem *in* and *of* society.

Despite the fact that these economic phenomena are associated with an ever-increasing technological control over outer Nature, the constantly enlarging sphere of 'appropriated Nature' comes to dominate us. Paradoxically, although this technology is commonly seen as the replacement of the 'natural' by the artificial, the latter assumes the former's quality of blind force or fate. As the forces of production — appropriated Nature — come to dominate us, so the sphere of life in which it seems meaningful to talk of effective human agency and subjectivity becomes ever more restricted, ever more reliant on the pre-packaged form of consumer goods and ever more privatized, while *subjectively felt* social relations become increasingly intransitive and reduced to interpersonal relations connected with shared consumption.

It is hardly surprising therefore, that humanist geographers who aim to restore and do justice to the essential subjectivity of life, can only discover it in the realm of the passive reflection of individuals, in the form of their *private* life style and in their selection and use of commodities, while seeing economic forces as of a piece with natural constraints. Yi-fu Tuan illustrates the point for us beautifully: —

"Consider the house as man's environment and his world. The walls have to be of a certain strength in order to rise to a certain height and bear the roof of a certain weight. *Economic constraints place limits on some aspects of the house:* for example its size, the kinds of material used, its site and location. *Within these physical and economic constraints* the owner of the house has the freedom to establish his world, his scale of values and meaning. He may want to do this by

painting the walls an unusual colour, by arranging furniture geometrically and leaving the front door always unlocked" (YI-FU TUAN, 1971a: 181, added emphasis).

and in a more recent article he describes his approach in the following terms:

"Humanistic geography builds, critically, on scientific knowledge. The rules and laws formulated in science are perceived to function as fate in the human drama. People obey physical and economic laws whether they recognise them as such or not; people are also the playthings of chance. The humanist geographer must be keenly aware of the constraints on human freedom . . . . Unless he knows the impersonal forces of an economy he cannot estimate to what degree human beliefs and ventures are founded on illusion" YI-FU TUAN, 1976:273).

Tuan's humanist intentions are subverted by his happy, even eager acceptance of the nature-like quality of capitalist forces and by his omission of our most active relationship with outer Nature and the one through which we can most clearly objectify and recognise our own character as human subjects — labour. As a result he can only celebrate the circumscribed and privatized subjectivity of bourgeois existence without understanding its origins.

As to its claims to be *critical,* nothing could be more false, for this so-called humanist geography can only accept the contingent facts of social organization as inevitable. We might reformulate Tuan's final sentence of his 1976 quotation thus:

"Because he believes in the inevitability and nature-like quality of the forces of the economy, Tuan cannot estimate to what degree human beliefs and ventures are founded on illusion".

As regards the question of *who* are the agents of subjects of history we generally find that the answer is 'individuals' in conventional views and 'classes' in marxist views. I would agree that if we are talking about *effective* subjects of history the former views are incorrect and yet understandable given the nature of capitalist society. Capitalism is characterised by a formal freedom of individual workers to dispose of their labour-power as they wish: heavy constraints on mobility of labour only impede the volatile dynamic of capitalist development. An individual worker who cannot tolerate being a wage-labourer can always give up his or her job and struggle to survive without adequate means of subsistence. But this freedom of individuals leaves the structure of social relations which regulates our metabolism with Nature intact: the employer can always take on another worker. The fact is that this individual freedom to 'take the job or leave it' (assuming there is a job of course!) supports rather than challenges the stability of capitalism. The only way this smooth reproduction of the social relations of production by replacement of individuals can be changed is where wage-labourers act as a class to prevent this substitution. An individual does not constitute a social relation and so is not an effective historical agent in changing social relations. It is even difficult for, say, large masses of British car-workers to change their social relations of production when this substitution can always take place on the other side of the globe. So it can be shown both that the view that individuals have an apparent freedom to act is quite understandable, and that the marxist ascription of the role of historical agents to classes is not an arbitrary and tendentious premise [as it sometimes appears – as in Marx's 1857 Introduction (MARX, 1973)] but a rationally defensible description of our society.

(ii) The Ideology of 'No Labour'

We have noted the silence of geographers' conceptions of people and Nature on the subject of *labour* and its social character, but in what social forms could the ideology be said to be grounded?

Firstly, there are the general characteristics of the vast majority of academics who articulate these conceptions; they tend to come from social backgrounds in which the experience of labour other than the purely mental variety is limited. As academics their subsistence depends upon the surplus labour of others so that they can limit their *own* interaction with Nature to one of reflexion. As WILLIAMS (1973) shows in his fascinating historical analysis of the content and origins of changing attitudes towards the country and the city, the fact that the vast majority of writers lived off the labour of others and had

no personal experience of agricultural labour had an enormous impact on what they saw as 'Nature'. For example, there are recurrent themes of Nature as countryside, as a place of rest and natural abundance, the fruits of which are gifts for the taking. This is the view of a *dormitory* population of temporary escapees from the city who consistently managed to overlook (or at least evade any unpalatable implications of) the generations of labour which had arduously tilled, husbanded, fenced and drained the land, which has *produced* both the countryside and its 'natural gifts' and the surplus which supported the landed classes and their extravagant properties. Nowhere is this view more apparent than in the landscaped parks in which it was consciously objectified – a countryside 'from which the facts of production had been banished' and which was intended purely as an object of *reflexion,* and yet which could not possibly have been created except as the result of the exploitation of others (WILLIAMS, 1973:105,124). Secondly, there is the deepening tendency in capitalist production to develop a separation of the moment of conception, of design and planning from the moment of execution, or a separation of mental and manual labour, so that what we termed the essential characteristics of *human* labor are often scarcely evident in the labour of many individuals. Thirdly, while labour is an 'abstract necessity' for the survival of any society, in capitalism this takes the concrete form of production of commodities in which the production, consumption of use-values and reproduction is subjugated to the requirements of production in the pursuit of profit. It is therefore not surprising that 6 days a week spent banging windscreens into car bodies is not seen as sensuous human activity (though even in this, human capacities of intentional, consciously-monitored action are still required in some small degree) (BRAVERMAN, 1974), or as a fundamental active relationship with outer Nature (though this still involves the transformation of objects in Nature by means of Natures' forces).

If the general form of labour is one in which the worker is expected to follow orders which are means to the ends of appropriation of profit rather than use-values as defined by the worker; if neither the means of labour nor its end-product are the producer's own property, it is not surprising that labour, production and economics appear as neither natural nor social. Yet with deeper analysis which does not take these facts for granted but asks how they are socially produced, we can show that the problem is not merely one of illusion but of social reality itself. Consider the following pair of relationships between people and Nature; firstly the situation where following a bumper harvest crops are destroyed, despite the fact that millions of undernourished people need those crops; secondly, the situation in pre-revolutionary Cuba where capitalist sugar plantations included vast acreages of unused land so that the peasants were pushed out onto the worst land and forced to become wage-labourers at the time of the sugar harvest in order to survive (HUB-ERMAN and SWEEZY, 1961) In both cases we can see how our essential relationships with Nature can be jeopardised by social relations which support the irrational logic of profit. In capitalist society we continually negate our position within Nature: in attempting to obey the mutable social laws of capitalism, we are forced to attempt to disobey the immutable laws of Nature — in the case of the Cuban peasants, to be forced to attempt to live without being able to labour.

Given the complex, divided and contradictory form of our society, it is hardly surprising that the bulk of literature in geography and social science, which self-righteously abstains from evaluating its objects of study, can only reproduce partial aspects of the appearance of capitalism and project them onto everything it encounters. The class nature of our society is such that neither the social character of labour nor its absolute necessity for social reproduction is immediately obvious, despite the fact that the existence of these classes depends on these social relations of production. Some, but not all individuals can live entirely off the labour of others, but since this situation is experienced through the consumption of *things* — commodities, the social dependence is hidden. Some may even appear to live by making money out of money, without any intervention of labour. But of course bits of paper and coins do not *create* use-vaues and hence wealth. Certainly, investors may get a positive return on their investments, but they can only buy something

with that 'return' if others, elsewhere, have produced more than they consume such that this 'return' can be realised by those who consume without producing. It is *these* real social forms which conceal the social relations of capitalist production and which lead economic geographers and development theorists to believe that underdeveloped regions' problems stem from a lack of 'finance' or 'capital' or 'entrepreneurs' and that regional development is fundamentally determined by the 'evolution of society's consumer demands' (MANNERS, 1972:1).

(iii) Nature and Alienation

In popular and geographical literature, 'Nature' has often come to mean 'wilderness' — that part of the world which appears to be virtually unaffected by human development and as such, as babbling brooks, moors, forests and wild parks, it has become particularly sought after as an object of leisure-time consumption. It is always very apparent that what we have termed 'appropriated Nature' is often seen as the antithesis of Nature. In fact, it is often not seen as part of society either. Since the technology which dominates social life in capitalist society is so clearly a human product, we tend not to think of it as 'natural', and although, potentially, technology promises to liberate us from toil, when in the service of production for profit it also deskills and hence dehumanises that toil (BRAVERMAN, 1974). So, in as much as capitalist technology limits and suppresses our individuality, it seems scarcely 'social' or 'human' either. As this alienated appropriated Nature expands so Nature-as-wilderness shrinks. By definition, the experience of the latter does not take place through labour. Nevertheless, even moors, babbling brooks, mountains and deserts eventually become commodities — packaged experiences for sale — and those who can afford to seek out unsullied Nature are pushed into ever more remote regions.

These are not eternal facts of human existence but contingent facts of recent history in which life has become even more divided into working and socialising, and even — with the separation of the means of production from the worker and the consequent spatial separation of home and workplaces —

into working and living. It is in such real divisions that the conceptual fragmentation of geographers' views of society and Nature originates.

(iv) The Roots of the Fragmentation of Human Geography

The division of human geography into 'social', 'economic', 'political' and 'cultural' geography is no exception. Let us consider what is meant by some of these commonsense categories. The 'economic' is conventionally taken to include markets, trading relationships, production units and their location, whereas the 'social' refers to relationships *outside* production, in particular outside the private sector to classes consisting of people of similar characteristics, to interpersonal relationships and possibly to their attitudes. Neoclassical economics and the location theory which derives from it see production as capital does, as a technical combination of qualitatively equivalent 'factors of production'. They cannot pose let alone answer questions about the social relations of production. Industrial psychology examines the social relations of production, but as SHAW (1972) notes, it forgets that they are anything to do with capitalist production. In these conceptions there is no way of looking at social relations in the workplace in terms of the requirements of capitalist production which force firms to increase output per worker, come what may. Similarly, those commonsense and academic conceptions of the domain of 'the political' which limit it to a sphere of negotiation and conflict over social organisation and resource allocation *outside* the sphere of private industry are, in a sense, accurate because bourgeois democracy *institutionalizes* such conceptions and uses them to defend its legitimacy. Likewise, although the division between the economic and the social seems quite arbitrary and irrational when closely examined, it is nevertheless clearly grounded in bourgeois social forms. After all, 'the social services' do deal with certain human relations *outside* private production and carefully support without interfering with the latters' interests, and councils and committees for economic development largely exclude those relationships which do not involve private and state capital, or exchange relations. Geographers and other social scientists, taking

these categories as 'givens' not surprisingly produce a fragmented picture of our society, even though, in their interdisciplinary leanings, they may pay lip service to the belief that the social individual is not separable from the economic or political individual. Consequently, economic geographers, seeing production as a purely technical matter, leave the question of the distribution of wealth to social geographers who assume that distributional problems, whether they take on a class, urban, or regional expression, are simply a matter of an unevenly distributed bundle of already-produced goods.[2]

In all these formulations, we see a confused and unexamined reproduction of the problems which are embodied in capitalist society itself. Whereas in feudal society the 'inner-relations' of the mode of production are immediately visible in a nakedly political form in which the landed classes live off the labour of others, the inner relations of capitalism are hidden behind relations of free exchange of commodities. Like democracy, the geographers view stopped at the factory gate, at employment statistics and the external data of production. And of course there are real forces in society which attempt to suppress the inherently political and social character of production and turn it into a smoothly functioning, purely technical machine. Social relations of control and authority of suppression of attempts of workers to decide on the content, speed and object of work are necessary to ensure the survival of firms against competitors who have greater social control over their workforce and hence higher labour productivity and profits.[23]

The attempted restriction of the categories 'social' and 'political' and the practices they denote to spheres which do not threaten capital accumulation is a type of 'socially-necessary illusion' in capitalism. It is only by breaking down such illusion that capitalism becomes intelligible. For example, the *origin* of income inequalities, class differences and 'spatial' inequalities is unintelligible unless we break with the view that distribution is a separate matter from production. Harvey's discussion of redistribution of income through urban 'spatial' processes can only offer explanations of transfers of income between classes whose existence is taken as given (HARVEY, 1973:Ch.2).[24] We cannot see why there are classes in the first place unless we recognise that distribution is fundamentally a distribution of the means of production. If you don't control the means of production then you inevitably have less power to determine what is produced and for whom: the conflict over distribution is ultimately a conflict over production. The demarcations between social, economic and political geography mirror and mystify our social reality. They are both largely correct and mystifying in so far as they uncritically reproduce the false basis of those practices and ideas.

(v) Positivism in Society

As a matter of expositional convenience, we separated the discussion of those aspects of social life involving communication and understanding through intersubjective meanings from those involving labour. In all societies these two aspects must be to some extent interdependent. On the one hand the content of social knowledge could not have acquired its complexity and predominant reliability without the teleological objectifying and verifying qualities of labour as a species of activity which subjects knowledge to test.[25]   On the other hand, the complexity and power of human labour could not have developed without communication and assessment of this activity among communities of knowing-subjects.

However, in many ways — in particular through the separation of 'living' and 'working' — a certain degree of separation of these interdependent aspects has evolved in capitalism but with a dominance of the technical or instrumental rationality (based on the control of objective processes of Nature) over the essentially moral and evaluative character of communication as mutual understanding. But this separation is paradoxical, for the less we can negotiate, participate and initiate in the sphere of labour and technical rationality, the more we take it for granted. The other side of the coin is that as interaction, communication and culture become pre-packaged and technically controlled, the more they lose their essential multi-lateral and

transitive quality and the less important and effective become our own views on their content (WILLIAMS, 1973:295-296).   This *real* separation is both mirrored in and reinforced by the positivist insistence upon a separation of cognition and evaluation and fact and value in science. The imbalance of the dominance of technical rationality is reflected in the privileged position positivism gives to technical knowledge as science and its treatment of questions of values as non-science or even non-knowledge. In its extreme form of behaviorism, it legitimises the management of grievances by the use of physical force or 'behaviour control'. Positivism's misunderstanding of the nature of its object study in social science has become a constitutive element of our society and has therefore almost been successful in creating its object in its own image as a society in which social relations have become 'naturalized'. Geographers have participated in this process in blissful ignorance of its implications.

Having presented some examples of the origin of the problems, raised in section 3, in the structure of our society, we will end this section by pointing out a paradox which runs through all these examples. Insofar as it is true that 'false' practices exist, social theories underpinned by naive epistemologies which merely accept their facticity without question will superficially appear to be 'true' or correct, while the historical materialist theory will seem to *conflict* with what is actually the case. Yet a defining characteristic of any materialism is its respect for what actually exists, regardless of what we may think. The theory we have presented does not deny the existence of these social facts, but it does deny that they represent the only possible social world or that this a rational world. Its project is not just to record the contingent facts of history, whether objective or subjective, but to show how they were produced so that social relations may be de-reified, and so that the potential for our becoming conscious, rational, humane and effective subjects of history can be realised. Again, although the notions that sometimes the world may be at fault and not our theories, and that science can and should deal with the potential as well as the actual may seem outrageous when posed in isolation against the background of commonsense and conventional understanding of science, as we have tried to show, their logical derivation from relatively uncontroversial premises is perfectly possible.

5. Conclusions

(i) A lack of awareness of the influence of theoretical, metaphysical and epistemological presuppositions in our studies of what we believe to be matters of fact means that our geographical knowledge is grounded not in the firm bedrock of such 'facts' but in the uncorrected, unexamined and frequntly incoherent presuppositions of vulgar common sense.

(ii) No amount of preoccupation with *methodology* — with procedures of empirical study, induction, deduction, models of explanation, theories of hypothesis testing and so on, can make up for this lack. In order to produce even minimal guarantees of the reliability and sense of knowledge we have to deal with the broader questions of the nature of our objects of study — as in the case of conceptions of people and Nature, the nature of knowing-subjects and the conditions of our existence as such — chiefly by reference to 'intersubjectivity' and labour, and above all the complex relationship between subject and object. The claims of historical materialism and critical theory to provide a sounder and more meaningful kind of knowledge relate to these latter issues rather than the narrow concerns of methodology.

(iii) Although positivism conventionally disregards such issues, not even its own practice can be given a coherent account without recourse to values, concepts of intersubjectivity and so on.

(iv) Different positions regarding the relationship can be summarised as in Figure1. In (a), subject is part of the object of study. In the as discrete, and the production of knowledge is viewed as a one-way process emanating from S. In cruder versions this may take the form of a 'bucket theory of knowledge', (POPPER, 1972: 341-361) in which facts are 'collected' till they simply 'add up' to 'knowledge'. But even in more sophisticated epistemologies in which the social production of theory and knowledge and the theory-laden nature of facts are recognised, the relationship

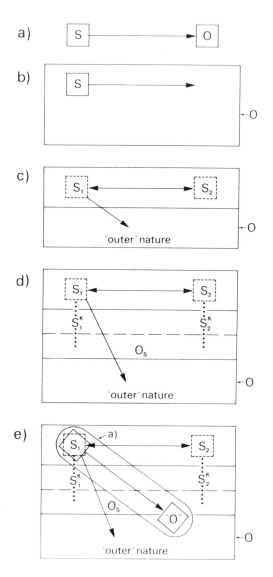

Figure 1. The relationship between subject and object in social science.

between subject and object may still be as in (a).

In (b) it is acknowledged that we are part of nature and society and so the knowing subject is part of he object of study. In the case of *social* science — (c) other people are also knowing subjects and yet still part of the object. S_1, represents the investigator, S_2 these 'other people' who are investigated. Since S_1 and S_2 usually live in a common culture and economy and hence participate in similar or at least related meaningful actions, understanding S_2 involves interaction between S_1 and S_2. Even in anthropology, where there is little or no initial conceptual and practical connexion between S_1 and S_2, some such connexion must be established in order to understand S_2 and their society (cf. WILSON, 1970).

In (d) it is recognised that the realm of 'the social' has an internal differentiation of decisive epistemological importance. Both $S1$ and S_2 act on the basis of some understanding of O as a whole. As this understanding is conditioned by and constitutive of social practices, and as it informs our transformations of Nature through labour, both the knowledge of S_1 and S_2 (S^k_1 and S^k_2) and the objectifications of that knowledge in social relations, activities, technologies and appropriated Nature (O_s) themselves become part of this object of knowledge. In this sense, epistemology, social theory and society itself interpenetrate. Moreover, since false as well as correct ideas may have a constitutive role in society, problems are not reducible to errors of thought. Insofar as the domination of objective social forms over our conceptions of them is generally much stronger than the effect of ideas which are not yet constitutive in changing social practices, these problems can only be solved or changed through *practice*.

As we have argued in section 4, false conceptions of the relationship between subject and object, and people and Nature can be both constitutive of and reflective of a society in which social relations are reified. Therefore we must try to understand the implication of a false, naive conception of these relationships – such as (a) – being part of the object. It is this complex situation that we have tried to represent in (e). Theory produced under the terms of (a) cannot completely resist the implications of its situation within the structure of relationships represented in (e), although it is commonly unaware of them. One of the main reasons why it appears to be successful is that in producing a 'short-circuit' across these complex relationships it may seem to produce 'correct' knowledge in the manner described at the end of section 4. The most common form of this 'short-circuiting' is where theory is unknowingly grounded in common sense, and does not appreciate the constitutive role of that

common sense in the society being studied, so that the theorist is well satisfied by the unsurprising discovery that the world is just as the theory says it is! It is in terms of an awareness of the situation described in (e) that critical theory can justifiably claim to understand ideologies such as (a) better than they understand themselves.[26]

(v) The inseparability of epistemology, social theory and conceptions of people and Nature is such that an almost identical series of diagrams could drawn up to correspond to the stages of our outline of the latter in section 3 As Alan Wilson has often said, "This will be left as an exercise for the reader!"

Notes

1. The term positivist geography is used to refer to the modern, quantitative geography that developed in the 60's and early 70's. While this included a very eclectic array of tendencies, there is little doubt that a positivist conception of the subject was dominant insofar as the following characteristics obtained; a belief in the possibility and desirability of value-free science; a belief that what were thought to be the methods of natural science should be emulated in social science; a belief that the only basis of reliable knowledge about the world was experience, observations, data; the related belief in a theory-free observation language; a belief that theoretical explanations should take the form of deductive systems; a belief that the relation between subject and object in science is merely one of reflection, and so on. For introduction to critiques of positivism in geography, see GREGORY (1978), and in social science see KEAT and URRY (1975), FAY (1976), GIDDENS (1976), SMART (1976), and for critiques of a positivist interpretation of natural science, see BHASKAR (1975), HARRÉ (1970; 1972).

2. With the rise of General Systems Theory, indifference of method (and even theory) to the nature of the object of study came to be considered a *virtue*. This dubious view was generally defended by entirely *separate* arguments advocating the development of interdisciplinary science. It is perfectly possible to support the latter without accepting the former.

3. Anticipating a later argument, this grounding in unexamined common sense has a major ideological implication: Lukacs writes:

   "Thus when 'science' maintains that the manner in which data immediately present themselves is an adequate foundation for the scientific conceptualisation and that the actual form of these data is the appropriate starting-point for the formation of scientific concepts, it thereby takes its stand simply and dogmatically on the basis of capitalist society. It uncritically accepts the nature of the object as it is given and the laws of that society as the unalterable foundation of 'science'." LUKACS (1971) *History and Class Consciousness,* p.7. quoted in BURGESS (1976).

4. It is perhaps unwise to single out the more polemical works such as the *Preface to A Contribution to the Critique of Political Economy* as references for Marx's conception of people and nature, for although they contain some of Marx's most explicit statements on the matter, these tend to be somewhat one-sided, simplistic aphorisms which give little indication of the richness and sublety of the conception which *informs* his more scholarly works – in particular, of course – *Capital.* Many of the faults of vulgar materialist perspective derive from a facile adoption of such aphorisms without an understanding of the maturer conceptions. Schmidt's work is perhaps the most successful synthesis of the latter (SCHMIDT, 1971).

5. cf. OLLMAN, 1971, part 1 on the 'Theory of Internal Relations'.

6. This relates to the debate between methodological individualism and methodological holism. See O'NEILL (1972), LUKES (1968), ISRAEL, (1970) and BHASKAR (1978).

7. Behaviourism takes the view that scientific explanation should take into account only observable behaviour. To find an explanation of one type of overt behaviour, we must refer not to unobservable motivations, intentions or expectations, whose existence cannot be an implicit 'stimulus-response' form of explanation of behaviour, which by-passes mental processes, or at least makes them appear unproblematic and/or mechanical. In its stronger versions, behaviourism may constitute a substantive theory about individuals and society, regarding all behaviour as purely physical in its nature. In its weaker forms, as a methodological principle, it could be said that it merely asserts and follows in extreme form the empiricists requirements of empirical evidence as the sole basis of knowledge. See SKINNER (1972), NAGEL (1961), WATSON (1931) (–pro-behaviourist); CHOMSKY (1959), HARRÉ and SECORD (1972), FILMER *et al.* (1972) (anti-behaviourist) and also the collection edited by BRAYBROOKE (1965) for debates between both sides; and STEA and DOWNS

(1973) for an extreme example of behaviourism in geography.

8. In epistemological debates a parallel distinction is often drawn between *explanation* (of behaviour) and *understanding* (of action). There is a vast literature in sociology and the philosophy of social science concerning the nature of these and whether the latter is (as positivists believe) dispensable and reducible to the former. See – GIDDENS (1976) as a useful introduction to the debates; ABEL (1948) for the positivists view; and APEL (1967;1972) and VON WRIGHT (1971) for antipositivist arguments.

9. This does not imply that there must be an identity of theoretical concepts and concepts used in the wider society [See below, 3 (vi)].

10. "The situation we have here is one in which the vocabulary of a given social dimension is grounded in the shape of social practice in this dimension; that is, the vocabulary wouldn't make sense, couldn't be applied sensibly, where this range of practices didn't prevail. And yet this range of practices couldn't exist without the prevalence of this or some related vocabulary. There is no simple one-way dependence here. We can speak of mutual dependence if we like, but really what this points up is the artificiality of the distinction between social reality and the language of description of that social reality. The language is consitutive of the reality, is essential to its being the kind of reality it is. To separate the two and distinguish them as we quite rightly distinguish the heavens from our theories about them is forever to miss the point" TAYLOR (1971, pp. 174-175. [Page numbers refer to CONNERTON (1976)].

11. See also the interesting comments of WALKER (1978) on the same subject.

12. "What the ontology of mainstream social science lacks is the notion of meaning as not simply for an individual subject; of a subject who can be a 'we' as well as an 'I'. [TAYLOR (1971) p. 182 in CONNERTON (1976)]. The ontological basis of history is the relation of men without other men, the fact that the individual 'I' exists only against the background of the community" (GOLDMANN, 1969, p.28).

13. Marx comments ". . . the self-interest already is a socially-determined interest, the goals of which can be achieved only within the conditions determined by society, which also provides the means" (quoted in ISRAEL, 1970, p.147). See also, the 6th Thesis on Feuerbach in MARX (1974).

14. However, as Sartre argues, there are grounds for complaint when some Marxists reduce the characteristics of an individual to nothing more than the bearer of a simple social relation of production so that an individual is simply classified as bourgeois, peasant, proletarian or whatever. "Valéry is a petit bourgeois intellectual, no doubt about it. But not every petit bourgeois intellectual is Valéry . . . The héuristic inadequacy of contemporary Marxism is contained in these two sentences" (SARTRE, 1968:p.56). To claim to understand individuals in this way, is, as Sartre argues, not materialist but idealist, for it reduces something concrete to a pre-given *category* and fails to discover the *actual* constellation of relations entered into by the individual which makes her different from other individuals.

15. An example is WINCH'S statement that "Social relations are expressions of ideas about reality" (1958, p.23). It is clear from the rest of his book that he doesn't think social relations are anything *more* than this. See also Gellner's critique of Winch's idealism (GELLNER, 1968).

16. It is in *both* these senses that Marx's 'Capital' is 'A *Critique* of Political Economy'.

17. In fact it is scarcely possible to *study* common sense *without* becoming critical of it because the moment of study penetrates the taken-for-granted character of its ideas. We cannot help but discover deeper 'layers of meaning' of which the actor is unaware. In its desire to study consciousness, *just as it is,* in presuppositionless manner, phenomenologists inevitably set up a tension between the opposed goals of 'restoration of meaning' and 'de-mystification' or 'reduction of illusion' [RICOUER (1965) in CONNERTON (1976)].

18. In practice, positivism can only recognise this partial identity in a few restricted spheres — in particular in the case of self-fulfilling prophecies in forecasting applications: it cannot recognise its own contribution to the development of a society in which the interests of technical control have come to dominate all other interests in life. In its philosophizing it can only reduce this interpenetration of subject and object to an equivalent of the (entirely different) problem of the influence of measuring instruments that continually plagues physics (HORKHEIMER, 1972, p.214).

19. "It is absolutely impossible to transcend the laws of nature. What can change in historically different circumstances is only the *form* in which these laws can express themselves." Society's "existing structure determines the form in which men are subjected to these laws, their mode of production, their field of application, and the degree to which they can be understood and made socially useful . . . . . Nature can only be ruled in accordance with its own laws" [MARX, quoted in SCHMIDT (1971), p.98]. By 'laws of nature' I mean those transfactually active mechanisms which constitute ways of acting of, and which derive from the properties of objects i.e. the realist view, and not the mere empirical regularities which are denoted laws in positivism i.e. the Humean concept of laws (see BHASKAR, 1975). We cannot rule out the possibility that these mechanisms and properties may change (the 'big' problem of induction) (see HARRÉ and MADDEN, 1975). As far as we know they have not changed yet, but if they were to in the future, it is unlikely that we would be unable to perceive the change and start to reconstruct scientific knowledge (HARRÉ and MADDEN, 1975, Ch.4). While our knowledge of nature's laws is always in principle revisable (the 'little' problem of induction) this does not of course mean that nature itself changes when scientific theory is revised.

20. "The human being is in the most literal sense a (. . . . political* animal . . . .), not merely a gregarious animal, but an animal which can individuate itself only in the midst of society. Production by an isolated individual outside society — a rare exception which may well occur when a civilized person in whom social forces are already dynamically present is cast by accident into the wilderness — is as much an absurdity as is the development of language without individuals living *together* and talking to each other" MARX, 1973 p.84).
*sometimes translated as 'social' animal.

21. Note that the truth of this statement is not purely analytic and circular for it is still an empirical question whether and where and when such objects exist. i.e. yes, it is true that we have made the qualities of intentionality and social determination part of our *definition* of human labour, but it is still an empirical question whether anything complies with this definition. What lies at the root of this anticipated misunderstanding is the belief — widely held in all sciences influenced by positivism — that logical necessity is the *only* form of the necessity and that there is no such thing as natural necessity (see HARRÉ, 1970, 1972; HARRÉ and MADDEN, 1975; BHASKAR, 1975 and KEAT and URRY, 1975).

22. "The concrete concept is concrete because it is a synthesis of many definitions, thus representing the unity of diverse aspects. It appears therefore in reasoning as a summing up, a result, and not as

the starting point, although it is the real point of origin, and thus also the point of origin and imagination. The first procedure attenuates meaningful images to abstract definitions, the second leads from abstract definitions by way of reasoning to the reproduction of the concrete situation" (MARX, 1974, p.141).
(Note the contrast between 'concrete' concepts as theoretical constructions in marxism and the *a*-theoretical 'empirical data' of positivism.)

23. 68.4% of hours lost in industrial disputes in British Ford factories involved grievances over work content, 10.4% over discipline, and only 4.8% over pay (COUNTER INFORMATION SERVICES, 1977).

24. Harvey obviously no longer holds this position.

25. Such tests are, of course, fallibile.

26. No doubt some will say that this is 'dialectical'. Maybe it is, but I don't see that anything is added by saying so.

References

ABEL T. (1948) The operation called Verstehen, *American Journal of Sociology,* **54,** pp. 211-218, and in: *Readings in the Philosophy of Science,* H. Feigl & M. Brodbeck, (Ed.).

ADORNO T.W. *et al.* (1976) *The Positivist Dispute in German Sociology,* Heinemann, London.

AMEDEO D. and GOLLEDGE R. (1975) *An Introduction to Scientific Reasoning in Geography,* John Wiley, New York.

APEL K.O. (1967) *Linguistic Philosophy and the Geisteswissenschaft,* Dordrecht.

APEL K.O. (1972) Communication and the Foundations of the Humanities, *Acta Sociologica* **15,** 7-27.

BENTON T. (1977) *The Three Sociologies,* Routledge & Kegan Paul, London.

BERNSTEIN R.J. (1976) *The Restructuring of Social and Political Theory,* Blackwell, Oxford.

BHASKAR R. (1978) *A Realist Theory of Science,* Leeds Books.

BHASKAR R. (1978) On the possibility of social scientific knowledge and the limits of naturalism, *Journal for the Theory of Social Behaviour* **8,**1.

BRAVERMAN H. (1974) *Labour and Monopoly Capitalism,* Monthly Review Press.

BRAYBROOKE D. (1965) *Philosophical Problems of the Social Sciences,* Macmillan, N.Y.

BURGESS R. (1976) Marxism and geography, *Occasional Papers No. 30* Dept. of Geography, University College London.

BUTTIMER A. (1976) Grasping the dynamism of life-world, *Ann. Ass. Am. Geogr.* **66,** 277-292.

CHOMSKY N. (1959) Review of verbal behaviour by B.F. Skinner, *Language* **35,** 26-58.

COATES B.E.. JOHNSTON R.J. & KNOX P.L. (1977) *Geography and Inequality,* Oxford U.P., London.

COLLETTI L. (1972) *From Rousseau to Lenin,* NLB, London.

CONNERTON P. (1976) *Critical Sociology,* Penguin.

COUNTER INFORMATION SERVICES (1977) *Anti-Report on the Ford Motor Company.*

CRAIB I. (1977) Lukacs and the Marxist criticism of Sociology, *Rad. Philos.* **17,** 26-37.

ENTRIKEN J.N. (1976) Contemporary humanism in geography, *Ann. Ass. Am. Geogr.* **66,** (4).

FAY B. (1975) *Social Theory and Political Practice,* George Allen & Unwin, London.

FAY B. & MOON J.D. (1977) What would an adequate philosophy of social science look like? *Philosophy Soc. Sci.* **7,** 209-227.

FILMER P., PHILLIPSON M., SILVERMAN D. & WALSH D. (1972) *New Directions in Sociological Theory,* Collier, Macmillan, London.

FRISBY (1974) The Frankfurt School: critical theory and positivism In: *Approaches to Sociology,* (Ed.) J. Rex, Routledge & Kegan Paul, London.

GALE S. (1972) On the heterodoxy of explanation: a review of David Harvey's Explanation in Geography, *Geographical Analysis* **4,** 285-322. Also Harvey's reply, On obfuscation in geography: a comment on Gale's heterodoxy.

GELLNER E. (1962) Concepts and Society, *The Transactions of the Fifth World Congress of Sociology* and reprinted In: *Rationality,* B.R. Wilson (Ed.) (1970) Blackwell, Oxford.

GELLNER E. (1968) The new idealism — cause and meaning in the social sciences, In: *Problems in the Philosophy of Science* I. Lakatos and A. Musgrave (ed.). Amsterdam, North-Holland and reprinted in E. Gellner (1973) *Cause and Meaning in the Social Sciences.*

GIDDENS A. (1976) *New Rules of Sociological Method,* Hutchinson.

GOLDMANN L. (1969) *The Human Sciences and Philosophy,* Cape, London.

GRAY F. (1975) Non Explanation in human geography, *Area* **7,** 228-235.

GREGORY D. (1978) *Ideology, Science and Human Geography,* Hutchinson, London.

HABERMAS J. (1972) *Knowledge and Human Interests,* Heinemann, London.

HABERMAS J. (1976) The analytical theory of science and dialectics, In: *The Positivist Dispute in German Sociology,* T.W. Adorno *et al.* (Ed.), Heinemann, London.

HARRE R. (1970) *The Principle of Scientific Thinking,* Macmillan, London.

HARRÉ R. (1972) *The Philosophies of Science: An Introductory Survey,* Oxford U.P., London.

HARRÉ R. & MADDEN E.H. (1975) *Causal Powers,* Blackwell, Oxford.

HARRÉ R. & SECORD P.F. (1972) *The Explanation of Social Behaviour,* Blackwell, Oxford.

HARVEY D. (1969) *Explanation in Geography*, Arnold, London.

HARVEY D. (1973) *Social Justice and the City*, Arnold, London.

HARVEY D. (1974) Population, resources and the ideology of science, *Econ. Geogr.* **50**, 256-277.

HARVEY D. (1978) Labour, capital and class struggle around the built environment in advanced capitalist societies, In: *Urbanisation and Conflict in Market Societies*, K.E. Cox (Ed.). Methuen, London.

HEMPEL C.G (1965) *Aspects of Scientific Explanation*, The Free Press, New York.

HORKHEIMER M. (1972) Traditional and Critical Theory In: P. Connerton (Ed.). *Critical Sociology*, Penguin.

HUBERMAN L. & SWEEZY P. (1961) *Cuba: Anatomy of a Revolution*, 2nd ed. Monthly Review Press, N.Y.

ISRAEL J. (1970) The principle of methodological individualism and Marxian epistemology, *Acta Sociol.* **14**, 145-149.

KEAT R. & URRY J. (1975) *Social Theory as Science*, Routledge & Kegan Paul, London.

KIRK W. (1963) Problems of geography, *Geography* **48**, 357-371.

LICHTMAN R. (1970) Symbolic interactionism and social reality: some Marxist queries, *Berkeley J. Sociol.* **15**.

LOWENTHAL D. (1961) Geography, experience and imagination: towards a geographical epistemology, *Ann. Am. Geogr.* **51**, 241-260.

LUKACS G. (1971) *History and Class Consciousness*, Merlin Press, London.

LUKES S. (1974) *Power: A Radical View*, Macmillan, London.

LUKES S. (1968) Methodological individualism reconsidered, *Br. J. Sociol.* **19**, 119-129, reprinted in his *Essays in Social Theory*, Macmillan, London.

MCLOUGHLIN J.B. (1969) *Urban and Regional Planning: A Systems Approach.*

MANNERS G. *et al.* (1972) *Regional Development in Britain*, John Wiley, London.

MARX K. (1972) *The Eighteenth Brumaire of Louis Bonaparte*, Progress, Moscow.

MARX K. (1973) *Grunrisse*, Penguin.

MARX K. (1974a) *The German Ideology*, C.J. Arthur (Ed.). Lawrence & Wishart.

MARX K. (1974b) *Theses on Feuerbach* in collection, *The German Ideology*, C.J. Arthur (Ed.). Lawrence & Wishart.

MEPHAM J. (1972) The theory of ideology in 'Capital', *Rad. Philos.* **2**.

MERCER D.C. & POWELL, J.M. (1972) Phenomenology and related non-positivistic viewpoints in the social sciences, *Monash Publications in Geography*, **No. 1** Melbourne.

MESZAROS I. (1970) *Marx's Theory of Alienation*, Merlin Press, London.

MESZAROS I. (1972) Ideology and Social Science,

Socialist Register (1972) R. Miliband, J. Saville (Ed.). Merlin.

NAGEL E. (1961) *The Structure of Science*, London, Routledge & Kegan Paul.

OLSSON G. (1975) Birds in Egg, *Michigan Geographical Publication, Dept of Geography, University of Michigan*, **1**.

O'NEILL J. (Ed.). (1972) *Modes of Individualism and Collectivism*, Penguin.

NOWELL-SMITH G. (1974) Commonsense, *Rad. Philos*, **7**.

OLLMAN B. (1971) *Alienation: Marx's Conception of Man in Capitalist Society*, Cambridge.

POPPER K.R. (1945) *The Open Society and its Enemies*. Vols. I & II, Routledge & Kegan Paul, London.

POPPER K.R. (1972) *Objective Knowledge*, Oxford U.P., London.

RELPH E.C. (1970) An inquiry into the relations between phenomenology and geography, *Can. Geogr.* **14**, 193-201.

RELPH E.C. (1976) *Place and Placelessness*, Pion, London.

RICOUER P. (1965) In: *Critical Sociology*, P. Connerton, Penguin.

RYAN A.R. (1970) *The Philosophy of the Social Sciences*, Macmillan, London.

SARTRE J.P. (1968) *Search for a Method*, Vintage Books, N.Y.

SAUER C. (1952) *Agricultural Origins and Dispersals*, American Geographical Association, N.Y.

SAYER R.A. (1976) A critique of urban modelling, *Prog. Plann.* **6**, Pt. 3, 187-254.

SCHMIDT A. (1971) *The Concept of Nature in Marx*, NLB, London.

SCHUTZ A. (1965) The Social World and the Theory of Social Action, In: *Philosophical Problems of the Social Sciences*, D. Braybrooke (Ed.). Macmillan, London.

SHAW M. (1972) The coming of radical sociology, In: *Ideology in Social Science*, R. Blackburn (Ed.). Fontana.

SKINNER B.F. (1972) *Beyond Freedom and Dignity*, Cape, London.

SMART B. (1976) *Sociology, Phenomenology and Marxian Analysis*, Routledge & Kegan Paul, London.

STEA D. & DOWNS R.M. (1973) *Image and Environment: Cognitive Mapping and Spatial Behaviour*, Arnold, London.

STODDART D.R. (1967) Organism and ecosystem as geographical models in: *Models in Geography* R.J. Chorley, P. Haggett (Ed.). Methuen, London.

TAYLOR C. (1967) Neutrality in Political Science In: *Philosophy, Politics and Society* III, P. Laslett and W.G. Runciman (Ed.). and reprinted in *The Philosophy of Social Explanation*, A. Ryan (Ed.).

TAYLOR C. (1971) Interpretation and the science of man, *Review of Metaphysics*, **25**, pp. 3-51 and reprinted in *Critical Sociology*, P. Connerton

(Ed.). (1976) and in *The Philosophy of Society*, R. Beehlec, A.R. Drengson (Ed.). (1978).

TIMPANARO S. (1975) *On Materialism*, NLB, London.

TUAN YI-FU (1971a) Geography, phenomenology and the study of human nature, *Can. Geogr.* **16**, 181-192.

TUAN YI-FU (1971b) Man and nature, *Commission on College Geography Resource Paper* No. **10**, Association of American Geographers, Washington D.C.

TUAN YI-FU (1976) Humanistic geography, *Ann. Ass. Am. Geogr.* **66**, 266-276.

VON WRIGHT G.H. (1971) *Explanation and Understanding*, Routledge & Kegan Paul.

WALKER R.A. (1978) The transformation of urban structure in the 19th century and the beginning of surburbanisation, In: *Urbanisation and Conflict in Market Societies*, K.R. Cox (Ed.). Methuen, London.

WALMSLEY D.J. (1974) Positivism and Phenomenology in human geography, *Can. Geogr.* 8, 95-107.

WALTON A. & GAMBLE P. (1972) *From Alienation to Surplus Value*, Sheed & Ward.

WATSON J.B. (1931) *Behaviourism*, Routledge & Kegan Paul, London.

WILLIAMS R. (1973) *The Country and the City*, Paladin.

WILSON B.R. (1970) *Rationality*, Blackwell, Oxford.

WINCH P. *The Idea of Social Science*, Routledge & Kegan Paul, London.

Geoforum, Vol. 10, pp.45-57, 1979.
Pergamon Press Ltd. Printed in Great Britain.

Spatial Change and Economic Organisation: The Tyneside Coal Industry (1751-1770)

PETER CROMAR, * Sheffield, U.K.

Abstract: Concepts of economic power and organisation are rarely considered by historical geographers in their attempts to explain change in space economies. In this paper an attempt is made to use these concepts to explain and understand the changing geography of the Tyneside coal industry from 1751 to 1770, a time when the industry was dominant nationally. At the beginning of the period the Tyneside industry was itself dominated by a monopolistic group, the Grand Allies, a dominance partly maintained through control over the use of land. Their dominance was broken by a combination of technological and economic developments as exploited by a competing group of capitalists based on the emerging banking system. The monopoly of the Grand Allies was broken but replaced, in a more developed form, by the Limitation of the Vend, and by 1770 the geographical and economic structure of the industry had changed dramatically. Underpinning this changing geography was the interaction of social and political structures, including the interdependence of enterprises with a developing political economy. It is in this interaction that the understanding of change in space economies must be sought.

Historical geographers have hitherto been loathed to consider questions of economic power and organization in their attempts at explaining changes in space economies. In the few cases where a theoretical framework has been used[1] it has been one based on the neoclassical theory of the firm, incorporating some elements of locational analysis. Many criticisms have been made recently of this sort of approach[2] and it is not proposed to reiterate them here but rather to provide an empirical example of a different form of analysis based on some concepts derived from Marxist economics. In essence traditional analysis has viewed the firm in isolation from the rest of the social, political and economic environment within which the firm exists. By contrast this alternative approach focuses attention on structure and organization, on the pattern of dependency between enterprises, on how the economy

keeps going, what is supposed to happen, and hence what makes the economy break down and what makes it develop into an economy of a different kind. In this paper this alternative approach is used to provide an analysis of the development of the Tyneside coal industry from 1751 to 1770.[3] The Northumberland and Durham coalfield was of immense importance at this time and Mitchell and Deane[4] point out that this coalfield, at least until the end of the eighteenth century, dominated the national industry and that shipments of coal from the north east may be regarded as indicators of total British output. The period 1751-1770 saw the end of the dominance of the Grand Allies and saw moves towards the setting up of the 'Limitation of the Vend', a more formally organized cartel, in 1771.[5] It is especially important to realize that these two dominant industrial structures were markedly different and represent the response of the coal owning capitalists to different economic and technological environments.

*13 Grange Crescent, Sheffield.

Historical Background

Before 1700 capital and control in the Tyne-side coal industry was effectively concentrated in the ranks of the Company of Hostmen, a merchant gild who alone possessed the right to trade in coal. By the time of their incorporation in 1600 they had a virtual monopoly of the Tyneside coal industry. As the demand for coal continued to increase throughout the seventeenth century, especially from London and the Thames Valley, the hostmen increased and expanded their power sufficiently to dominate effectively not only the coal industry of Tyneside but also the municipal government of Newcastle upon Tyne. By 1700 however, the large capitalists who controlled the Company were coming to realize that in many ways their interests were identical with those of the non-hostmen coal owners and so the barriers to the entry of new competition,[6] based on the institutional necessity of membership of the Company of Hostmen, were effectively lowered.

At the same time as this source of a barrier to entry was being eroded the shallow and more easily worked coal seams near the River Tyne were becoming exhausted. Technological constraints at the time, in the form of the inefficiency of early steam engines, meant that the coal owners had to expand laterally, by means of waggonways,[7] rather than sinking deeper pits. In the period up to 1726, when the Grand Allies[8] were formally constituted, the future Grand Allies engaged in a massive investment of capital with the aim of gaining control of many of the 'factors of production', the control of which is vital to the erection of significant barriers to entry. The monopolistic property of space became very important in this period as the Grand Allies either blocked off the collieries of their rivals by their use of wayleave power[9] or they paid rent for coal lands and collieries which they did not intend to work (negative wayleaves and dead rents respectively).

1726-1750 saw the continued spatial spread of the coal industry into the area between the rivers Derwent and Team (Figure 1) and a further increase in the power and control of the Grand Allies. Throughout this period the Allies made constant initiatives to bring about a 'regulation' (a price and output fixing arrangement) in the coal trade and so enable the realization of monopoly profits. Conflict within the capitalist class was manifest however as the major group (the Grand Allies) attempted to subjugate their rivals (especially Ridley). Because of the primitive nature of the banking system at the time, however, and the massive circulating capital requirements, the Grand Allies could not afford to pursue a price-cutting war for long periods, and so they sought other ways to dominate their rivals. The most successful of these was the policy of differentially increasing their rivals' costs, by the use of negative wayleaves[10] and dead rents, and a 'regulation' was reimposed in 1747 (after previous attempts in 1727 and 1733) when their main rival, Ridley, was almost bankrupt. By 1750 the coal industry on Tyneside was effectively dominated by the Grand Allies.

After the period of a stationary market for coal from 1727 to 1750, demand for coal in London, where the Northumberland and Durham coalfield had a virtual monopoly until about 1850 when the national railway network was completed, began to expand again, imports into London increasing from 458,376 London chaldrons in 1750 to 613,842 London chaldrons in 1770 (Figure 2).[11] Sweezy suggests that this increase in demand encouraged a rapid expansion in the Tyneside coal industry such that "it seems reasonable to assume that by the end of the 1760s the expansion in productive capacity had rather overshot the mark for complaints of excessive competition had begun to be heard from various quarters and the coal owners seemed ready for a somewhat more comfortable arrangement."[12] As will be demonstrated in this paper there were very significant changes taking place in the Tyneside coal industry at this time but they were not associated with a massive increase in the number of working seasale collieries (which had only increased from 27 to 31) nor with a significant increase in the size of collieries.[13] What had expanded was the number of collieries producing best quality coal and these collieries were mainly located north of the Tyne and outside the control of the Grand Allies. The way in which the *de facto* monopoly possessed by the Grand Allies in 1750 came to be broken up is explained not only by the technological changes (especially the

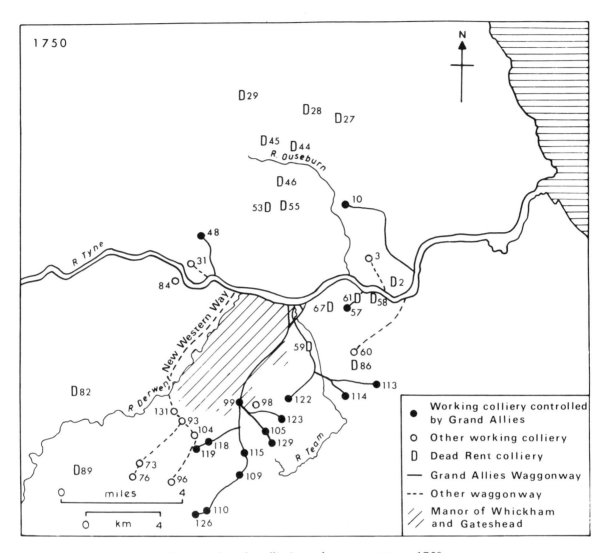

Figure 1. Seasale collieries and waggonways *ca.* 1750.

improvement of the steam engine) but also by the changes in the financial institutions of the time, especially the formation of local private banks. These banks performed the function of acting as middlemen between those who were looking for capital and those who were looking for opportunities of transforming into capital their reserves of ready money.

Theoretical Expectations of Change in the Tyneside Coal Industry 1751-1770

In the period from 1751 to 1760 the demand for coal from London fluctuated wildly while the increased price (Figure 2) was due in no

small part to the effects of the Seven Years War (1756-1763). Since fluctuations in the level of demand will tend to reduce the level of investment[14] it is theoretically feasible that this period from 1751 to 1760 saw an essential marking of time by entrepreneurs as they tried to consolidate their previous capital investments. Furthermore in a situation of excess capacity it is probable that variations in demand would be met by a change in the level of utilization of existing plant rather than by investment in new plant. This failure to invest would be compounded in an industry with a monopolistic structure, especially with regard to technical progress, for the monopolists could take a smaller

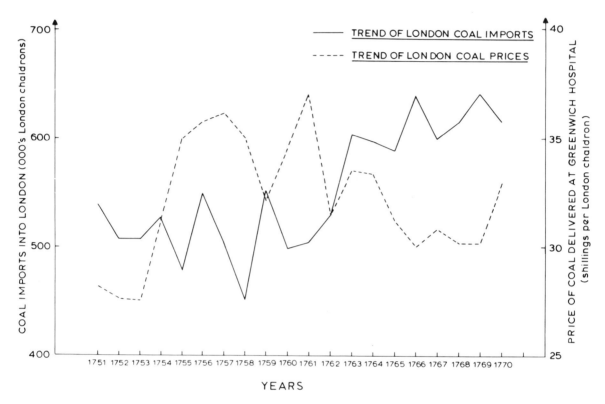

Figure 2. Coal imports and prices at London 1751-1770.

amount of super-profits rather than risk capital in new techniques which would reduce costs. So in the period before 1760 there would theoretically have been a minimum of new investment until entrepreneurs reformulated their expectations as a result of the increasing trend in prices. Even after 1760 it would be likely, theoretically, that capital investment would be made mainly by new entrepreneurs if they could gain access to capital resources, rather than by the old established entrepreneurs who may well have had large amounts of capital already tied up in existing collieries and technology. In order to see how far these theoretical expectations conform with the reality of change in the Tyneside coal industry it is first proposed to describe the spatial expansion of the coalfield in this period and then to present a more complete analysis which takes into account the social political and economic context within which this spatial change took place.

Spatial Expansion of the Coalfield 1751-1770

In 1750 (Figure 1) the coal industry on Tyneside was massively concentrated in the area between the Derwent and the Team, with only four working seasale collieries (out of 27) located north of the Tyne. By 1770 (Figure 3) the distribution had changed considerably, there now being 12 working collieries north of the Tyne out of a total of 31, accompanied by an expansion of the waggonway network north of the Tyne.

In the area north of the Tyne and east of the Ouseburn four new collieries had been opened, that at Walker (5)[15] being the first attempt to exploit the deeper part of the Tyne coal basin below a depth of 400 ft. Walker colliery was open by 1761. Chirton colliery (26) was leased to Burdon and Harrison in 1754 for a term of 31 yr at a certain rent of £320 per annum (16/- tentale) with the proviso that, if necessary, £2000

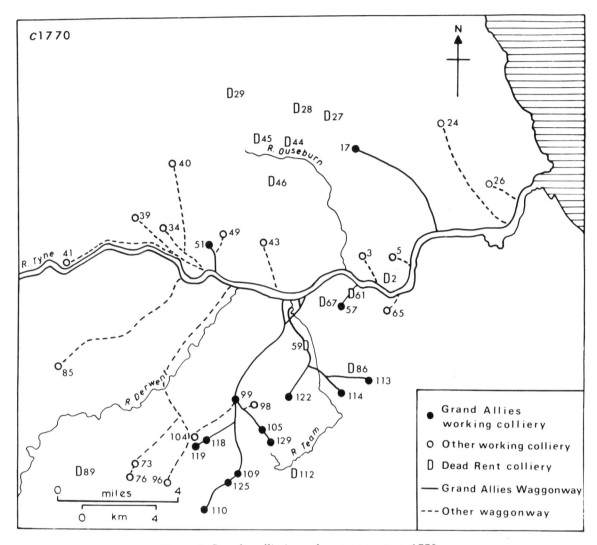

Figure 3. Seasale collieries and waggonways *ca.* 1770.

was to be spent on winning the colliery.[16] It was certainly open by 1756 for it was already having drainage problems[17] and by 1767 the geology was creating more problems for the owners.[18] Shiremoor colliery (24) was opened by Gibson, Bell and Brown between 1755 and 1760 and had 4495 yd of main waggonway in 1760 when the materials in the colliery were valued at £6000 and the expected profit on an annual vend of 1200 tens was *ca.* £6000 per annum.[19] The other new colliery in this area was a new winning of Longbenton (17) by the Grand Allies whose previous winning at Longbenton (10) had been exhausted by 1763. The old waggonway to Walker Staith was pulled up and

relaid from the new colliery to Winchomblee Staith by November 1764. Prior to this winning the Grand Allies had been treating with Ralph Millbank for a wayleave through Willington for Grand Allies' coals from Longbenton, Killingworth and Willington.[20]

The area north of the Tyne and west of the Ouseburn had been dominated by landsale collieries for about 30 yr before 1730 but by 1770 it was very much involved in the seasale trade with new collieries being opened at Fenham (43), East Denton (49), Denton (51), Greenwich Moor (40), Walbottle (34), Throckley (39) and Wylam (41). All these collieries used steam engines. Fenham was leased in

1765 for 31 yr at a certain rent of £400 per annum (23/6 tentale) with a proviso that £2000 be spent in the first 2 yr.[21] The estimated winning cost was much larger than this, however, being £6000 initial capital investment including the provision of a steam engine, the upkeep of which was estimated at £600 per annum.[22] The colliery was working by 1767 under the name of Beaumonts. East Denton was won just before 1770. The colliery at Denton was a new winning by the Grand Allies who had been advised to take this course in 1753 when West Denton (48) was nearly exhausted.[23] By 1770 the rent for Denton colliery was 32/- tentale (probably the highest on the coalfield) but the expected profit (after allowing for interest on capital advanced) was still £1.10s.0d. per ten on a cost price of £5.10s.0d. per ten.[24] Greenwich Moor colliery was probably won before 1770 by Bell and Brown, while sinking began at Walbottle colliery, for the Duke of Northumberland, in 1768. By 1770 coal was actually being worked and the colliery was offered for lease at a certain rent of £500 per annum (20/- tentale). The cost of winning, including the building of a waggonway, had been £12,000 while the upkeep of the engine was estimated at £500 per annum. Since the estimated profit for the lessee was only 10/11 per ten or £660 per annum[25] (after interest on the capital advanced had been allowed for) and the risks were high it is not surprising that the lessees worked the colliery to the limit without the usual regard for safety or indeed fairness to the lessor. Throckley colliery, which had long been a landsale colliery sublet to Brown, became a seasale colliery before 1761 after the control of the lease reverted from the Grand Allies.[26] The colliery, which used part of Blackett's Wylam waggonway, was worked by Bell and Brown and paid £500 per annum in wayleave rents.[27] Wylam colliery, the family colliery of the Blacketts, had been a landsale colliery in 1728 but it was working for seasale by 1764 when 917 tens, 12 waggons of coal from Mr. Blackett's Wylam colliery were led over part of the Earl of Carlisle's land from 1 May 1764 to 30 April 1765.[28] The total wayleave rent paid by Wylam colliery was £800 per annum but since no rent was paid for the colliery itself as it was worked by its owner, Blackett could still make an expected annual profit of £1500 on a vend of 1200 tens in 1767.[29]

South of the Tyne there had been nothing like this dramatic change but the number of working collieries had dropped from 23 to 19 as the effects of competition from the new collieries north of the Tyne (producing the highest quality coals) began to make themselves felt. One of the results of this new competition was the adoption of 'screening' by the old established collieries in the Derwent-Team area. "The superiority of the new collieries in quality and adjacency to the river was naturally and by the aid of steam engines so great, that the inferior collieries were obliged, in order to keep up competition, to resort to a practice so blameable that nothing can justify it except the plea of self-preservation. It was this, to pass their coals through a screen or sieve, and so separate the round and the large from the small, that they might meet in the market. This practice was a sacrifice of labour and of materials, so that the smallest coals passing through the screen were made worse than useless."[30] A very early example of the way capitalism exploits natural resources solely in the interests of private profit rather than for the good of society as a whole? There is no evidence here that the operation of the market exchange economy produced an optimum use of resources as neoclassical theory would have us believe.

In the area between the Derwent and Team the collieries at Burdon Moor (123), Beamish (115), Bryansleap (131), Burnopfield (93) and Lanchester Moor (126) had all been closed, probably by 1760 and certainly before 1767[31] while the only new colliery was opened at Stanley (125) by the Grand Allies. The lease of Stanley was obtained by the Grand Allies in 1754 for a term of 63 yr at a certain rent of £300 per annum (14/- tentale) and the colliery was certainly in production by 1757 when "the second pit in Stanley colliery was beginning to sink".[32] West of the Derwent George Silvertop's colliery at Stella (84) had been closed and he had transferred operations to his Whitefield colliery (85) using the old Clavering Stella waggonway. East of the Team Gateshead Fell (60) had been closed and Heworth (65) reopened, certainly by 1767 when it was selling 8000 chaldrons with an estimated profit of £6000 annually.[33] Sometime after 1750 Friar's Goose colliery (58) was opened but it was drowned out by 1763 when Alderman Ridley refused to allow the lessee of Friar's Goose the use of his steam engine at Heaton, which Ridley used to drain his Byker colliery (3). "When the Mr. Ridley's colliery at Heaton left off working the lessee of Friar's Goose colliery offered him £200 a year for the use of his engines at Heaton for to preserve Heaton water from falling down to their colliery, but Mr. Ridley would not take less of them than £500 a year. The two engines together if sold would not have been worth more than five or six hundred pounds, he might have had this £200 a year for perhaps twenty years — for the want of these fire engines of Mr. Ridley's Friar's Goose was lost and given up."[34] In the pursuit of his own profits Ridley was prepared to forgo this potential gain of perhaps £3400[35] because to have taken it would have meant an increase in the capacity on the coalfield with the attendant possibilities of increased supply, reduced prices and hence diminished profits.

It is apparent, however, that the above outline of the spatial changes in the location of the Tyneside coal industry from 1751 to 1770 does not, and cannot, in itself provide an explanation of the processes responsible for the changes. It is naive to equate changes in spatial form with process, not only because of the problems posed by equifinality and multifinality[36] but also because these changes must reflect the more fundamental social, political and economic reality within which these changes occur and only within which they have meaning. It is this more concrete analysis of social, political and economic conjunctive to which I now turn.

Capitalist Policy and the Changing Economic Situation

Activity in the coal industry from 1751 to 1760 largely conformed with the theoretical ideas proposed earlier. The older established capitalists, notably the Grand Allies and the group comprising Lord Windsor, Mr. Simpson and Mr. Ridley, consolidated their investments in the collieries in the area between the rivers Derwent and Team. In 1752 Henry Witham

leased one sixth of Collierly colliery (73) to Lord Windsor for 21 yr at a certain rent of £115 per annum (22/6 tentale) and in the next 2 yr Windsor and Simpson renewed wayleaves from Mrs. Emmerson and Richard Hodshon, both for £60 per annum certain.[37] In 1754 Windsor and Simpson leased Lanchester Common colliery (75, 77) from Harrison for 21 yr at £900 per annum certain (15/- tentale) but the colliery does not appear to have been worked until 1775 when the Grand Allies were in control of the lease. The Grand Allies leased Stanley colliery (125) in 1754 for £300 per annum certain (14/- tentale). In 1755 Ridley sunk two new pits at Bushblades (96) at a cost of £932.5s.0d.[38] while further wayleaves for Collierly were bought in the next year from Mr. Scarfe for £12.12s.0d. per annum certain and from Mr. Grieve for £15.15s.0d. per annum certain.[39] In the same period the Grand Allies were working Longbenton (10) to what must have been near capacity for in 1751 the vend was 42,904 Chaldrons (over 90,000 tons) and in 1752 was 35,618 chaldrons which brought in receipts of £24,072.5s.0d. while the total production and transport cost was £13,299.11s.3d.[40]

After 1760 the demand for coal from London increased markedly with much less fluctuation than previously (Figure 2). The result of this increasing trend of demand with low fluctuation would tend to be an increase in the expectations of entrepreneurs. These expectations would be further enhanced by the successful application of the improved steam engine at Walker colliery (5) and the resulting possibility of the extension of the worked area of the coalfield into previously unconsidered areas. These increased expectations could not be realized, however, without capital and it was probably the emergence of a banking system giving wider access to capital which provided the basis of much of the growth which took place in the Tyneside coal industry between 1760 and 1770.

Before the setting up of the Newcastle Bank in 1756[41] capital for investment in coal mining had to be internally accumulated, by and large, and this meant that the large coal owners had massive advantages over potential newcomers into the industry since the established coal owners alone had access to the capital resources necessary for investment in seasale collieries. Because of this differential access to capital resources it is hardly surprising that there was very little change in colliery ownership from 1700 to 1750. After the setting up of the banking system this situation began to change: money capital flowed into the banks from people holding liquid capital, principally the large landowners, together with traders who accumulated more money than they could profitably invest in their own business. On Tyneside this capital became available to new entrepreneurs willing to speculate in coal mining. Speculate may not be the correct term, however, when it is remembered that William Brown, the major new coal owning capitalist (in partnership will Bell, one of the proprietors of the Newcastle Bank), was the foremost colliery engineer of the day and so undoubtedly possessed a certain monopoly of skill.

The Newcastle Bank was jointly owned by Ralph Carr (whose grandfather was William Cotesworth, one of the original Grand Allies), Matthew Bell (probably connected with the Bell family who were prominent members of the Company of Hostmen in the seventeenth century), John Cookson (who controlled a salt and chemical monopoly at South Shields), and Joseph Airey. It was mainly Bell who invested directly in coalmining, becoming a joint owner with Brown of the collieries at Shiremoor (24), Greenwich Moor (40), Throckley (39) and probably also Walbottle (34) but the Newcastle Bank itself was also expending its business rapidly. Unfortunately no direct evidence remains of any definite link between the growth of bank business and investment in coal mining, apart from the involvement of Bell, but it seems probable that the link was a strong one, especially given the overriding importance of the coal industry in the economy of the North East in the last half of the eighteenth century.

At the same time as the emergence of a banking system was allowing expansion to proceed apace north of the Tyne the old established coal owners south of the river found themselves in a difficult position as their coals were now of an inferior quality. Moreover, their collieries were becoming more expensive to work as drainage problems had increased while the greater distance they

were from the river as compared with the new collieries meant these older collieries were further disadvantaged by their higher transport costs. The problems of all coal owners were further compounded by the increasing shortage of labour as colliery expansion took place and to counteract the increasing wage rates the 'bond' system was tightened up. The 'bond' system had been common in the north-east for many years before the 1760's as Ashton and Sykes point out[43] but it may well have been of little significance until the 1760s. Certainly the Armstrong MS which has details of the fortnightly meetings of the Grand Allies from about 1730 to 1770, with few breaks in continuity, does not contain the word 'bond' until an entry for 13 August 1764 reads "The partners pitmen to be immediately bound at all places."[44] This would tend to suggest that the 'bond' was increasing in importance. By 1765 the labour shortage had become more intense and as a result of the policy adopted by the coal owners there was a massive strike. The policy of the coal owners in this conjuncture, to join together and present a common front of capital against labour was the first instance in the coalfield of the concerted power of capital working together against the owners of labour power to protect its own interest. Such policies became much more common later.[45]

Although the bond had been in existence in the north east coalfield from as early as 1703 its nature and complexity increased through time. By 1763 it was indeed a complicated document as is clear from the bond made between Lady Windsor and John Simpson, owners of Collierly (73) and other collieries, and their labour force:

"The parties shall continue at work, without striking, combining, or absenting themselves; shall deliver one corf of coals gratis every pay, or fourteen days; shall be fined one shilling for every corf sent to the bank less than wood full, and shall be immediately drawn to the bank if the banksman call him, and shall deliver one corf of coals gratis for every corf of coals set out (that is, condemned on account of containing stones among the coals); and for the performance of all and singular these conditions, the hewers, drivers of gin horses, onsetters, and banksmen, bind themselves severally and respectively, their and each of their several and respective heirs and assigns in the penal sum of £18."[46]

The customary binding fee which the employer paid the pitman in return for the guarantee for his labour power for 1 yr had for a long time been a purely nominal sum of sixpence or a shilling. However, the period of high prices and increased trade after the end of the Seven Years War coincided with a shortage of pitmen and one or two of the coal owners began to offer higher binding fees, sometimes as much as three or four guineas, as a means of ensuring their labour supply. Late in 1764 meetings of coal owners were held to decide upon ways and means of abating this competition and reducing what was considered to be the 'extravagant' binding money. The outcome of these meetings was that the coal owners decided upon two measures: to force the miners to continue working under their existing bonds for three months after they expired in August 1765; not to hire any man who could not produce a certificate of release from his last employer.

The response of the miners when they got to know of these proposals was dramatic — in August 1765 practically all of the miners in the north east coalfield — some 4000 in all, ceased work in protest and the trade of the ports was paralyzed. After a fortnight the coal owners gave way on the main issue, offering certificates of discharge on the expiration of existing contracts. By this time, however, the miners had raised their demands to include wage increases and the immediate cancellation of existing contracts. Riots and violence followed as the coal owners refused to accede to these demands and so troops were dispatched from York, at the request of the coal owners, after a meeting on 11 September, to quell the strike. Little is known of the further stages of the dispute but it is apparent that repression was harsh for there was a general resumption of working by 2 October and the miners did not have another large-scale strike until 1810.[47] The long-term effects of the strike seem to have been negligible as far as the miners were concerned for the terms of the bond remained much the same for many years. For the coal owners, however, it was much more significant for it was their first attempt to present a

united front against labour and probably did much to convince them of the benefits of co-operation against common adversaries, be they the miners or the consumers of coal.

It must not be imagined, however, that it was only the lessons learned by the coal owners during this struggle with labour that encouraged them to set up the 'Limitation of the Vend', a far more organized form of cartel, in 1771. Conflict within the capitalist class itself had also become more intense and this also encouraged the formation of the cartel. In particular, by 1764 the expansionist policies pursued by the Grand Allies between 1727 and 1750 were beginning to rebound upon them for they had so much circulating capital tied up in dead rent collieries on long leases that they were finding it difficult to respond to the changing technical and economic situation. In 1764 the Allies were paying more than £2300 per annum in dead rents for collieries at Urpeth (112), Derwentcrook (86), Gateshead Park (61), Bensham (67), Medomsley (89), St. Anthony's (2), Brunton (44, 45), Fawdon (46), Dinnington (29), Wideopen (28) and Westlade (27).[48] Such heavy fixed expenditure meant that it was often inconvenient for the Allies to take new collieries but they still used their wayleave power, where possible, to limit the output of rival collieries. The inferior quality of their coal, as compared to that from the new collieries north of the Tyne, was also causing the Allies problems and they were not averse to using subterfuge and price-cutting policies in the attempt to retain their share of the market: 9 June 1966 "Agreed that the refuse coals at Benton be sold for oversea at 10/- per chaldron but the name of Benton not to be inserted on the certificate." 29 Jan. 1969 "The great demand for Longbenton coals and the small demand for South Moor makes it necessary to consider what can be done to promote the vend of the latter, whether by falling the price thereof or by advancing the former." 28 Oct. 1769 "When it was agreed to make a trial to vend Tanfield coals from this day (until further notice), making an allowance of 4/- per chaldron for such as are sent to London and 5/- per chaldron for such as they send coastways."[49]
These price-cutting policies soon had the desired effect for it was not long before the subject of 'regulation' was again being aired.[50]

Competition was proving no more advantageous to the owners of new collieries than it was to the older established coal owners and the pressure for a 'regulation' increased until the formation of the 'Limitation of the Vend' in 1771 — a cartel organization that was to continue in existence, with a few short breaks, until about 1845.[51]

Summary and Conclusions

In 1750 the main concentration of activity in the Tyneside coal industry was in the exposed part of the coalfield south of the Tyne in the area between the Derwent and Team with 16 of the 27 working seasale collieries being controlled by the Grand Allies. The entry of new capitals into the Tyneside coal industry was made extremely difficult since the Grand Allies owned most of the good coal lands and strategic wayleaves. The power and control they derived from the ownership of dead rent collieries and negative wayleaves effectively allowed the Allies to control the whole of the Tyneside coal industry and by so doing they were able to extract some degree of monopoly profits. By 1770 this situation had changed considerably for while the Allies were still the most powerful single group of coal owners they now controlled only 14 of the 31 working seasale collieries. Furthermore of the 14 new collieries opened on the Tyne since 1750 only three were controlled by the Grand Allies. These new collieries were concentrated north of the Tyne in the concealed part of the coalfield and in the main produced higher quality coal than that from the older established collieries in the Derwent-Team area. How did this change in industrial and spatial structure come about?

After the stationary market for coal in the 1730s and 1740s had begun to expand again, at first with massive fluctuations, and then, after 1760, with a steady upward trend with low fluctuations, the expectations of entrepreneurs increased. These expectations were further enhanced by the technological development of the steam engine (improved by the use of iron instead of wood for the pumps and joints) which allowed the exploitation of the concealed coalfield in the areas outside the direct control of the Grand Allies.

A further factor here was that the geomorphology of the area north of the Tyne and east of the Ouseburn was nowhere near as deeply incised as that south of the river Tyne and so the area which could be used for a waggonway was greatly increased,[52] thereby limiting the viability of negative wayleaves. The realization of these expectations was encouraged by the emergence of a banking system which probably allowed the penetration of outside capital into the coal industry. The main figures in this new development were Bell (a director of the Newcastle Bank) and Brown (a prominent colliery engineer) who jointly opened three, and possibly four, new collieries from 1760 to 1770. The Grand Allies found it difficult to participate in these new developments for they had not foreseen the possibility of technical progress and so had invested heavily in coal lands which could be worked with the pre-1750 technology but which were too far away from the Tyne to be able to be worked profitably in competition with the new collieries producing better quality coal. As a result of these changes in the technical and economic environment the Grand Allies found that they were burdened with heavy liabilities in the form of certain rents for collieries they could not profitably work. At the same time the profits of the Grand Allies were falling because their collieries in the Derwent-Team area were no longer producing best quality coal. Technical progress and the development of the banking system had effectively destroyed their monopoly.

This destruction of the *de facto* monopoly of the Grand Allies was soon replaced, however, by a more developed form of capitalist organization — 'The Limitation of the Vend' — an early form of cartel. This change in the economic structure of the Tyneside coal industry resulted from two factors: (1) as technological development had increased the size of fixed capital investment also increased, especially with the beginning of the exploitation of the concealed coalfield, and with this there was an increase in the risks associated with investment. In order to minimize these risks, to ensure regular and rapid depreciation of an ever growing amount of fixed capital, the capitalists began to look for possibilities of restricting competition among themselves in order to prevent any fall in prices, and with that a marked fall in their rate of profit; (2) the increasing shortage of labour after 1763 had led to an increase in the binding fees paid to labour. In order to abate this competition for labour the coal owners got together and presented a united front of capital against labour. The results of this action precipitated a massive strike with possibly a short-term victory for the pitmen but in the long run it was the coal owners who gained for it convinced them of the benefits of co-operation and cohesive action against common adversaries, be they consumers or the owners of labour power. It was the interaction of these economic and political forces which best explains the changes in the economic structure and hence the spatial structure of the Tyneside coal industry between 1751 and 1770.

Notes

1. See, for example, HARVEY (1963); LEWIS (1969); SMITH (1963).

2. For example, ROBINSON and EATWELL (1973); KREGEL (1973); HUNT and SCHWARTZ (1973).

3. ASHTON T.S. and SYKES J. (1929), *The coal industry of the eighteenth century*, provide the standard reference, albeit of an inexhaustive nature. SWEEZY P.M. (1938), *Monopoly and competition in the English coal trade 1550-1850*, while much better, did not have the advantage of recently available manuscript material which the present author draws upon.

4. MITCHELL and DEANE (1962).

5. For which see CROMAR (1977).

6. For a fuller discussion of the differing conditions of entry see BAIN (1971).

7. The waggonway was a wooden railway along which coal was transported in waggons pulled by horses. It was a direct precursor of the modern railway.

8. The Grand Allies: Liddell, Bowes, Wortley and Cotesworthy were the largest group of coal owning capitalists in the Tyneside coal industry for most of the eighteenth century. They were especially dominant from 1715 to 1750, see CROMAR (1978).

9. Wayleaves, which represented the legal right to lay a waggonway over someone else's land, were of immense importance in determining the actual spatial pattern of development of the Tyneside coal industry.

10. In 1738 the Grand Allies used their wayleave power to close down the Old Western Way, the main waggonway of their rivals, and this necessitated their rivals building a new waggonway, the New Western Way, at a Fixed capital cost of *ca.* £10,000. This was a massive investment to undertake when the demand for coal was stagnant and over capacity was rife.

11. These figures for imports and prices are derived from MITCHELL and DEANE (1962). A London chaldron was about 28½ cwt, while a Newcastle chaldron was 53 cwt. Throughout the text chaldrons are Newcastle measure unless stated otherwise.

12. *op. cit.*, 35.

13. The mean colliery size *ca.* 1730 was 12,050 chaldrons output (standard deviation 7956 chaldrons) and in 1767 was 11,481 chaldrons (standard deviation 5034 chaldrons). A '*t*' test shows that there is no significant difference between these values. The figures for 1730 are mainly compiled from the Grand Allies Minute Book, North of England Institute of Mining and Mechanical Engineers, Newcastle upon Tyne (hereafter NEIMME) while those for 1767 are mainly compiled from Watson Ms. 10, NEIMME.

14. DUESENBERRY (1958).

15. Figures in parentheses refer to the location of the colliery on the appropriate figure.

16. Johnson Ms. 4.3, NEIMME. Tentale was a form of rent paid by the lessee to the lessor according to how much coal he worked. In general the certain rent was for a specified number of tens of coal and any workings over that amount were paid for by the ten (the tentale rent). A ten was ten chaldrons of coal (approximately 25 tons).

17. Watson Ms. 9, NEIMME.

18. Watson Ms. 5, NEIMME.

19. Barnes Ms. 49.4, NEIMME.

20. Armstrong Ms., Northumberland County Record Office (hereafter NRO), NRO 725 F 53.

21. Watson Ms. 11, NEIMME.

22. Watson Ms. 8, NEIMME.

23. Barnes Ms. 49.4, NEIMME.

24. Watson Ms. 10, NEIMME.

25. Watson Ms. 10, NEIMME.

26. Armstrong Ms. NRO 725 F 51.

27. Watson Ms. 10, NEIMME.

28. Easton Ms. 17.10, NEIMME.

29. Watson Ms. 10, NEIMME.

30. Taken from EDINGTON (1823), p. 57.

31. Watson Ms. 10, NEIMME.

32. Watson Ms. 10, NEIMME.

33. *ibid.*

34. Montagu Ms., Blackgate Museum, Newcastle upon Tyne.

35. £200 per annum for 20 yr: £4000-£600 (the value of the engines) = £3400.

36. This problem is raised by Harvey (1969) *Explanation in Geography*, **166-167**.

37. Johnson Ms. 4.1, NEIMME.

38. Barnes Ms. 49.4, NEIMME.

39. Johnson Ms. 4.1, NEIMME.

40. Watson Ms. 10.54, NEIMME.

41. Carr-Ellison Ms., NRO ZCE 11 (3).

42. The amount of money out on loan from the Newcastle Bank increased from £28, 953.6s.3d. in 1756 to £125,316.11s.9d. in 1770. Carr-Ellison Ms., NRO ZCE 11 (3).

43. *op. cit.*, p. 88.

44. Armstrong Ms., NRO 725 F 53.

45. See for instance CROMAR (1977); SWEEZY (1938); FYNES (1873).

46. From GALLOWAY (1898) *Annals of coal mining and the coal trade*, Vol. i, p. 269.

47. According to FYNES (1873).

48. Armstrong Ms., NRO 725.

49. Armstrong Ms., NRO 725.

50. EDINGTON (1823), p. 57: "... But of this contention, after lasting some years, both parties became weary; they found it prudentially wise to unite in interest, to equalize the price, to regulate the transmission from each colliery and to feed the public at their own prices and according to their own convenience; hence their union became a direct monopoly; it was agreed that the market must be fed and not glutted."

51. SWEEZY (1938), p. 33.

52. The magnitude of engineering problems associated with waggonway building in the Derwent-Team area meant that waggonways had to follow river valleys and so wayleave control of these river valleys became crucial to the coal owners.

References

ASHTON T. S. and SYKES J. (1929) *The Coal Industry of the Eighteenth Century*, Manchester.

BAIN J. S. (1971) *Barriers to New Competition*, Cambridge, Mass.

CROMAR P. (1977) Oligopoly and spatial change: the Tyneside coal industry 1771-1800, *Economic Geography* **53**, 79-94.

CROMAR P. (1978) The Tyneside coal industry 1715-1750, *Northern History* **14**, 193-207.

DUESENBERRY J. S. (1958) *Business Cycles and Economic Growth*, London.

EDINGTON R. (1823) *A Treatise on the Coal Trade*, London.

FYNES R. (1873) *The Miners of Northumberland and Durham* Blyth.

GALLOWAY R. L. (1898) *Annals of Coal Mining and the Coal Trade*, London.

HARVEY D. W. (1963) Locational change in the Kentish hop industry and the analysis of land use patterns, *Transactions of the Institute of British Geographers*, **33**, 123-144.

HARVEY D. W. (1969) *Explanation in Geography*, London.

HUNT E. K. and SCHWARTZ J. G. (1973) (Ed.). *A Critique of Economic Theory*, Harmondsworth.

KREGEL J. A. (1973) *The Reconstruction of Political Economy: An Introduction to Post-Keynesian Economics*, London.

LEWIS P. (1969) A numerical approach to the location of the paper making industry in England and Wales from 1860 to 1965, University of Hull Occasional Papers in Geography, No. 13.

MITCHELL B. R. and DEANE P. (1962) *Abstracts of British Historical Statistics*, London.

ROBINSON J. and EATWELL J. (1973) *Introduction to Modern Economics,* London.

SMITH D. M. (1963) The British hosiery industry in the middle of the nineteenth century: an historical study in economic geography, *Transactions of the Institute of British Geographers* **32,** 125-142.

SWEEZY P. M. (1938) *Monopoly and Competition in the English Coal Trade* 1550-1850, Cambridge, Mass.

Geoforum, Vol. 10, pp.59-80, 1979.
Pergamon Press Ltd. Printed in Great Britain.

The Political Economy of Agrarian Reform and Spatial Organisation in Chile

EDUARDO SANTOS and ANDREW SAYER,* Brighton, U.K.

Abstract: This paper examines the geographical changes associated with the agrarian reforms implemented in Chile between 1965 and 1973. The intentions and results of the Christian Democrat and Popular Unity agrarian reforms were very different; while the former was a limited programme of modernisation and liberalisation, the latter formed part of a revolutionary programme. Nonetheless, a study of the Maria Pinto commune in central Chile shows that, in both cases, the changes in spatial and social organization produced by the reforms had resulted from a complex interplay between a changing class structure and consequent shifts in material interests and political alignments.

I. Introduction

In the relationship between people and their environment, and in the spatial organisation of society, the central place of the social relations of production and the importance of the (particularly political) consciousness of those social relations in society are often not immediately apparent. Especially in the case of our own society, precisely because both are so pervasive, we generally do not notice the historically-specific and socially-produced nature of these social relations, while our consciousness of them does not seem particularly political. But when efforts are made to change both the social relations and that social consciousness, their specific nature and role are thrown into relief. Agrarian reform, particularly where it is a part of a wider programme of attempted socialist transformation, is a case in point. In the example discussed in this paper — the agrarian reform in Chile between 1965 and 1973, and in particular in a part of the Central Zone — the geographical changes can be seen as expressions of the successes and failures of

an attempt to transform social relations between people and the relation of people to the land.

The relationship between social process and spatial structure is in this case, as always, one in which spatial structure both constrains and enables particular forms of spatial interaction, and is itself continuously reproduced and modified by human action.[1] As we shall see, forms of political consciousness have a crucial role in mediating the actions and social relationships which reproduce this structure. This consciousness is not the same as the 'perception' of which behavioural and phenomenological geographers are wont to speak; it is not a subjective, voluntaristic and psychological relationship between individuals and their environment, but an intersubjectively-established understanding which is inseparable from the context of particular social actions and power relationships. The close tie between political understanding and actual experience and practice is particularly clear in the case of attempted revolutionary change. In these cases people attempt to forge new forms of social relations and consciousness, and new ties between them, and efforts to change one without the other are inevitably unsuccessful.

*Division of Urban and Regional Studies, University of Sussex.

Lest it is not already abundantly clear, it should perhaps be said that in stressing these relationships, we are rejecting several characteristic features of geographical approaches to development. We are avoiding the spatial separatist tendency of examining spatial relations in abstraction from the things and processes which they involve and isolated from their social context,[2] and also the treatment of development as a purely technical diffusion or modernisation process in a way that projects a superficial understanding of western sequences and criteria of development onto underdeveloped countries, as if there were no differences in the modes of production involved. We shall not pursue criticism of these approaches any further but simply refer the reader to the critiques of SLATER (1974), BARAN and HOBSBAWM (1961) and FRANK (1969).

II. Agrarian Reform in Chile 1965-1973 Background

The material summarised in the paper is the product of a research project on the agrarian reform process in the central zone of Chile and was carried out by the first author during Allende's Unidad Popular administration (November 1970-September 1973).[3]

Before looking at a case study of agrarian reform it will be useful to provide a general description of the political and economic context of the period of the Christian Democrat and Unidad Popular administrations in Chile and to outline the condition of agriculture and the different approaches to agrarian reform.

It is important to understand the circumstances in which the Christian Democrats came to power in 1964. The elections of September 1964 were dominated by the very real possibility of a victory by Allende's F.R.A.P. parties, and Christian Democrat policies were designed to avert this threat — as was clear from their slogan 'Revolution in Liberty'. Their policies included populist measures such as the 'Chileanisation' of mines (with the objective of 51% ownership of copper mines), agrarian reform and the programme of 'Promocion Popular'. The latter was intended to give the poorest sections of the

urban working class (the 'marginados') a greater influence in the economy and political system.

Three major influences shaped programmes such as the agrarian reform. The first was a combination of populist feeling and the policies influenced by the social doctrines of the Catholic church which favoured underprivileged groups such as youth and women, redistribution of income, 'dignifying' the peasantry, etc. In no way could this be seen as revolutionary — for example, private property was to be respected, and in general a 'middle way' was sought between capitalism and socialism. The second influence was American pressure, through the 'Alliance for Progress' and directly from the U.S. government, for democratic policies which would 'defuse' the possibility of revolutionary change (cf. PETRAS and LA PORTE, 1970). (In fact these populist concessions later served to help light the fuse of revolutionary change.) Thirdly, economic policy reflected the influence of the 'desarrollista' approach of ECLA (Economic Commission for Latin America of the United Nations), namely import substitution and industrialisation.

These influences can be seen in the Agrarian Reform Programme with its aims of closing the gap between urban and rural levels of development, and encouraging the political support of the peasantry. For this 'middle way', expropriations of the larger landed estates (fundos) were designed to turn underutilised land over to peasant cooperatives called 'asentamientos'. There was no intention of interfering with the most efficient capitalist fundos. In other words, the programme involved changing the social structure — in particular by encouraging the development of a rural middle class — but not in a socialist direction. (cf. HERNANDEZ, 1972).

The economic objectives of the Agrarian Reform were important because the contribution of agriculture to the Chilean economy since the war had been small in comparison with other Latin American countries. However, the Christian Democrats were not altogether successful in this aim, and the rate of growth of agriculture (3%) during the 1965-1970 period still lagged behind that of industry (3.6%). By 1967 agricultural products formed only 9.0% of G.D.P. and by 1969 only 3% of exports. Indeed, agricultural production was not even able to keep up with rising domestic demand and consequently agricultural imports grew by almost 400% between the late 50's and mid-60's, until by 1969 they formed 19% of total imports into Chile. (ARANDA and MARTINEZ, 1970, p.116; U.N.- E.C.L.A., 1974, p.90; JOUVIN, 1966, p.490). By the end of the 50's, 24% of the gainfully employed people of the country were involved in agriculture and unemployment in the rural areas reached about 30% (ARANDA and MARTINEZ, 1970, pp.116-120). Given the low levels of productivity and the inequalities of the land tenure pattern (see Table 1), agricultural incomes were both very low in comparison with non-agricultural income (YUDELMAN, 1967, pp.84-85) and unequally distributed within the sector. At the beginning of the 60's, 9.5% (32,600) of the families in the sector received over 50% of total earnings, while 70% (244,000 families) of the 'peasantry' (tenant-farmers, share-croppers, and wage-earners) received only 33.4% of the agricultural income. (ARANDA and MARTINEZ, 1970, p.142).

The mixture of successful progressive reforms and failures of the Christian Democrat administration inadvertently encouraged support for the left, and also produced a political polarisation amongst the middle classes which split their vote and let in Allende's Unidad Popular (U.P.) coalition in the 1970 elections. The parties forming the coalition drew their support from both the urban and rural working class and a number of left-wing middle-class voters. The Communist and Socialist Parties formed the major part of the coalition but the U.P. as a whole gained less than 40% of the vote, and this was not enough to give them enough control and support to carry out their policies.

In evaluating the achievements of the U.P.'s agrarian reform it is essential to keep in mind the severe constraints upon the possible actions of the Allende government.[4] In particular, it was forced to work within the framework of the 'Agrarian Reform Act' (Law No. 16,640) passed during the Christian Democrat period because the support of the Christian Democrat opposition could not be gained to modify the Act. Law 16,640 established a limit of 80 ha 'basicas' — that is an amount *equivalent* to 80 ha of the best irrigated agricultural land — as the minimum size of production units which could be expropriated. It also gave the expropriated owners ('latifundistas') the freedom to select and retain a portion of their land, called the 'reserva', and to keep their machinery and facilities after expropriation. Inevitably, the reservas were always on prime land, while the owners also benefitted from large sums paid to them in compensation and were often able to delay the expropriation by protracted legal battles. Although Law 16,640 effectively prevented the overthrow of capitalist relations of production in Chilean agriculture, significant advances were made which benefitted the peasantry. Approximately 4405 latifundia (6.3 million ha) were expropriated, benefitting 38,000 families

Table 1. Land tenure structure in the agricultural sector (Chile early 60's)

Size of the production unit (ha)	Number of production units	Area (ha)	Area (%)
Less than 5 ha	123,636	207,000	2.4
5 - 50	92,408	1,556,000	5.0
51 - 200	23,959	2,284,000	7.5
201 - 1000	10,158	4,310,900	12.5
1001 - 5000	2601	5,495,400	17.8
More than 5000 ha	730	16,795,400	54.8
	253,492	30,648,700	100.0%

Source: ARANDA and MARTINEZ (1970, p.121).

(U.N. - F.A.O. - I.L.O. 1976, p.99). This was almost three times the number of expropriations carried out in the 6 yr of the Christian Democrat administration.

The Agrarian Programme was given a central place in the U.P. economic strategy and was granted an importance equivalent to that of the nationalisation of copper and key industries. The aims of the Programme were to modify the land tenure structure; to develop an area of social property; to take over the material base and hence the economic and political power of the agrarian bourgeoisie; to reverse the downward trend in the agricultural sector's contribution to the economy, and, by reversing the outflow of capital from agriculture to other sectors, achieve a 5% p.a. increase in output; and generally to develop political support for the government by involving the peasantry more fully in the transformation of Chilean society. However, as we shall see, some of the effects of the U.P. agrarian reform were similar to those of the Christian Democrat reform (see ALALUF *et al.* 1971).

III. Spatial Organisation, Social Classes and Economic Base: The Case of the Maria Pinto Commune in Central Chile

Having provided some background information, we can now turn to the elements of change in a particular rural administrative unit — Maria Pinto — by examining the stages of its historical development in terms of its changing social and spatial structure.

Maria Pinto is a small 'comuna' of 42,000 ha (103,740 acres) situated between the metropolitan areas of Santiago and Valparaiso, the country's two major cities (see Figure 1). In the early 70's, 63% of its population of 6212 inhabitants was distributed among its agricultural production units, 25% in the 'minifundia' — small holdings or rural settlements, and 12% in the town of Maria Pinto (see Figure 2). Agriculture is the main economic activity, and livestock, wheat and barley the main products.

Since the Spanish conquest, the development of the area has been intimately connected

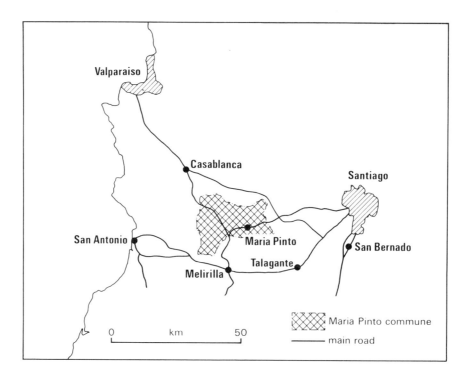

Figure 1. Location of Maria Pinto commune.

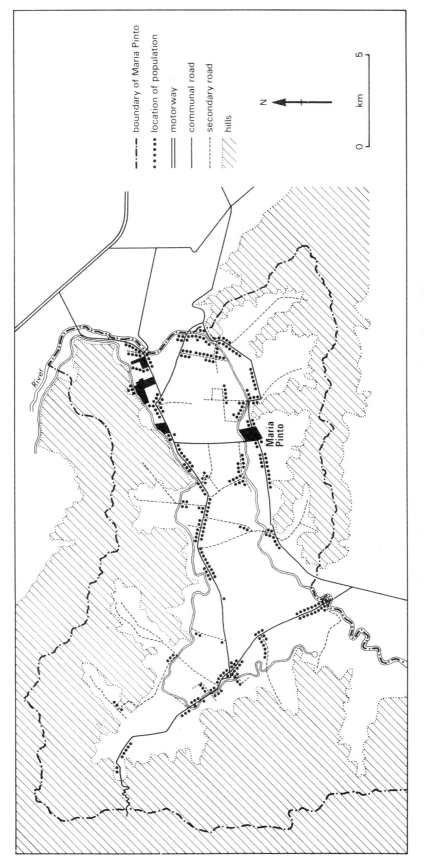

Figure 2. Location of the population in Maria Pinto 1972.

with that of Valparaiso and Santiago (BORDE and GONGORA, undated). In the next section we will trace its origins from the sixteenth century in stages defined according to the form of organisation of production.

(i) *The Spanish Conquest (16th and 17th Centuries)*

In this period, agricultural production was dominated by the 'merced' — extensive livestock farming serving the nearby urban markets. At first these were developed only in the flat valley floors using Indian labour. The ways in which the labour power of the Indians was reproduced were diverse — some were paid in different combinations of money and goods, others were allowed to rent land for their own cultivation. There are records of a small number of black African slaves being used as domestic servants at the end of the century. The land was granted freely to the conqurors by the King of Spain.

As demand increased as a result of further urban growth, production was extended onto the hills. This expansion plus the concomitant need for further control over production and labour led to the development of the 'estancia' in which individual property was defined for each production unit. As the organisation of the estancia required little more than fencing and a small workforce, mainly for control of cattle, the spatial form of the area was extremely simple; a few roads connected the centres of the estancias where the residences of the Spanish landlords and their servants were situated. Huts were also scattered across the hills to serve as shelter for the Indians in charge of the cattle (see Figure 3). By the end of the 17th century nine mercedes and estancias existed in the Maria Pinto area.

(ii) *18th and 19th Centuries*

This period was characterised by major changes in the spatial structure of the area resulting from further extensions of livestock farming and the introduction of cereal production, which, in turn, were in response to rising urban demand and the development of export markets. This involved a new kind of production unit — the hacienda — in which livestock and cereal production could be kept separate. This more intensive kind of agricul-

ture increased labour requirements and marked the introduction of the 'inquilinos' — share-croppers or tenant farmers. These were permanent workers who were remunerated chiefly in kind, rather than in cash, and partly with rights to a small plot and limited pasture rights. The inquilinos were initially Indian but later mixed Indian-Spanish. Later also, the size of the private plot tended to decrease as it was generally found more profitable to increase payments (in cash and kind), and so use the extra land for the landlords' own production. Housing for the inquilinos was generally provided by hacienda owners, who also usually provided rough shelters for temporary workers. The associated increase in population was concentrated in small settlements by the existing roads (Figure 4). Further expansion of the urban markets led to intensification in cereal production and the sub-division of many of the haciendas into small 'fundos' (up to 5000 acres). This intensification was accompanied by investments in water-supply, irrigation, storage facilities and communications with Santiago and Valparaiso and the growth of new settlements as population grew (see Figure 5).

By the end of the nineteenth century there were 5 haciendas, 10 fundos and 3 areas of small property in the 'comuna' (see Figure 6). The spatial and social structures established with these major transformations persisted until the mid 20th century.

(iii) *The 20th Century*

In the 20th century, the typical combination of large holdings (latifundia) and small property (minifundia) was consolidated in the Maria Pinto region. The minifundia were produced by subdividing the old medium-sized holdings of the late 18th century and early 19th century. They are usually defined as those properties below 5 ha, but the average size is 1-2 ha. The owners would subsist partly by working on the latifundia at harvest time and generally when and where the labour of the inquilinos was insufficient, and partly by selling their own agricultural produce or by running small shops or workshops. The minifundia areas also functioned as small service centres supporting the agricultural sector. Apart from the consolidation of these

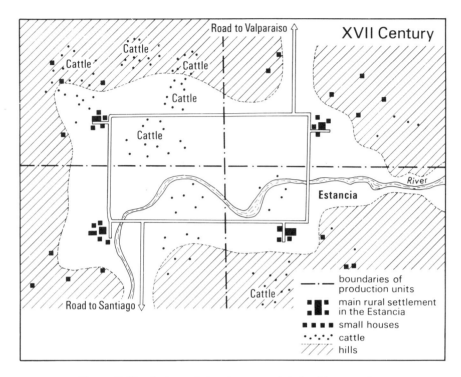

Figure 3. Typical rural structure associated with estancias.

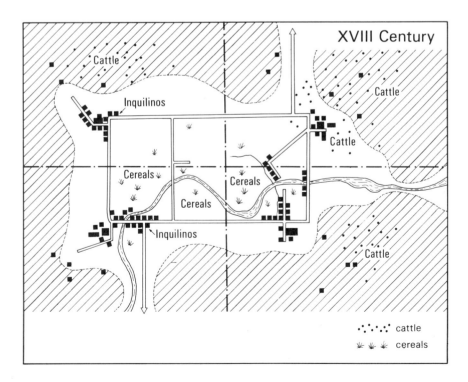

Figure 4. Typical rural structure associated with estancias and haciendas.

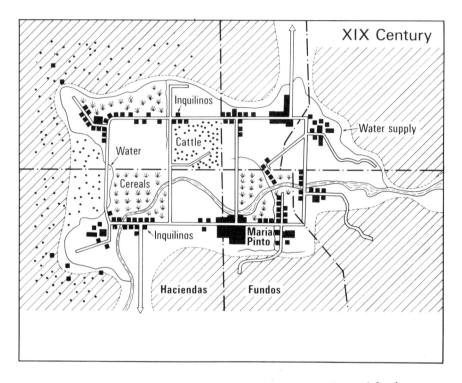

Figure 5. Typical rural structure associated with haciendas and fundos.

landholdings, no major changes in the land tenure pattern occurred prior to 1965, as can be seen from Figures 7 and 8.

According to the information that was available from the 'property file' of the Internal Revenue Service, a highly polarized land-ownership distribution existed in 1965. A small number of landowners controlled 95% of the land in the commune in the form of 18 productive units, all of them over 500 ha (see Table 2). Following the election of the Christian Democrats, pressure from the peasantry to implement the agrarian reform policies built up and led to the passing of the Agrarian Reform Act (Law No. 16,640) in July 1967. By that date a process of subdivision of latifundia had already begun which affected 76% of the land in the Maria Pinto area. These subdivisions were purely nominal transfers of land, usually among members of the same family and were clearly intended to minimise the impact of later expropriations. In real terms, the control and organisation remained the same and the attempted subversion of the Agrarian Reform policy was quite successful; only 11 production units

(2651 ha) representing 6.3% of the total area of Maria Pinto Comuna were expropriated in the period up to September 1970 (election of Salvador Allende). Moreover, delays were created by legal battles over the technicalities of defining the 'hectareas basicas'. Although the quantitative impact of the Christian Democrat government's agrarian reform was therefore quite limited in Maria Pinto, the form of organisation of production – the 'asentamientos' (peasant cooperatives) – that was introduced in the reformed areas had important effects on the attitudes and organisation of the peasantry.

The 'asentamientos' were organised on the basis of each expropriated production unit and those peasants who were both working and living on that unit at the time of the expropriation. They were therefore designated in a piecemeal way without regard for the position of other production units or workers in the area. Consequently, they did not provide a very useful basis for the subsequent socialist transformation of the agricultural sector, although, as we have noted, this was not the intention of the Christian Democrat

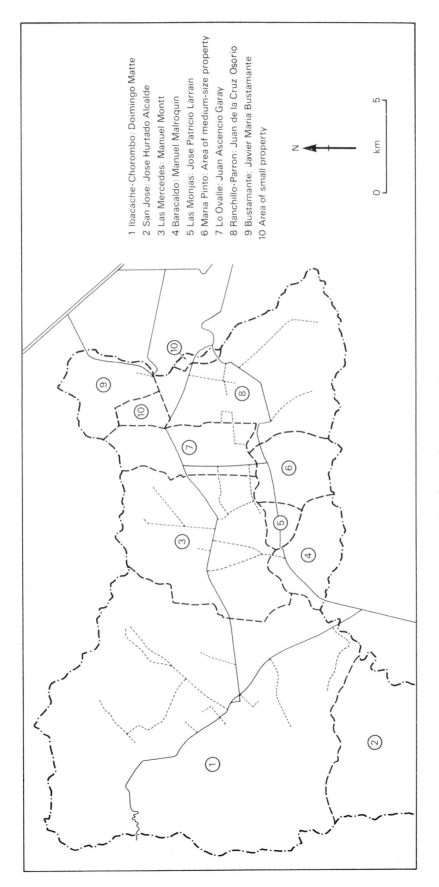

1 Ibacache-Chorombo: Doimingo Matte
2 San Jose: Jose Hurtado Alcalde
3 Las Mercedes: Manuel Montt
4 Baracaldo: Manuel Malroquin
5 Las Monjas: Jose Patricio Larrain
6 Maria Pinto: Area of medium-size property
7 Lo Ovalle: Juan Ascencio Garay
8 Ranchillo-Parron: Juan de la Cruz Osorio
9 Bustamante: Javier Maria Bustamante
10 Area of small property

Figure 6. Landownership in Maria Pinto 1880.

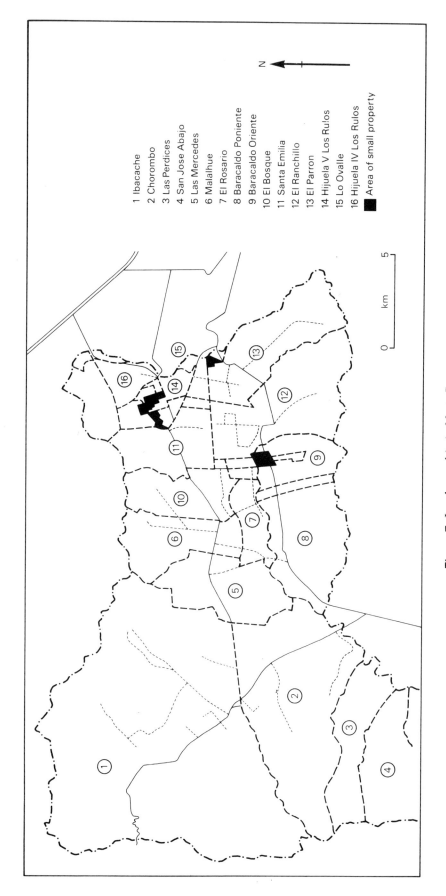

1 Ibacache
2 Chorombo
3 Las Perdices
4 San Jose Abajo
5 Las Mercedes
6 Malalhue
7 El Rosario
8 Baracaldo Poniente
9 Baracaldo Oriente
10 El Bosque
11 Santa Emilia
12 El Ranchillo
13 El Parron
14 Hijuela V Los Rulos
15 Lo Ovalle
16 Hijuela IV Los Rulos
■ Area of small property

Figure 7. Landowership in Maria Pinto 1953.

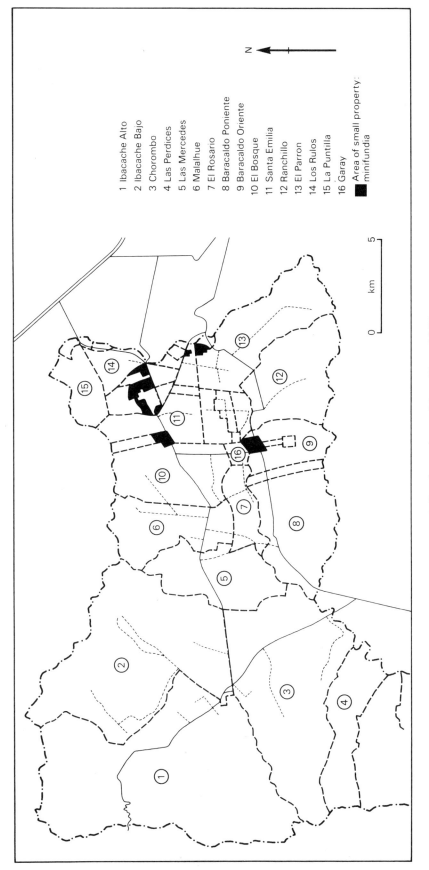

Figure 8. Landowership in Maria Pinto 1965.

Legend:

1 Ibacache Alto
2 Ibacache Bajo
3 Chorombo
4 Las Perdices
5 Las Mercedes
6 Malalhue
7 El Rosario
8 Baracaldo Poniente
9 Baracaldo Oriente
10 El Bosque
11 Santa Emilia
12 Ranchillo
13 El Parron
14 Los Rulos
15 La Puntilla
16 Garay

Area of small property: minifundia

0   km   5

Table 2. Land tenure structure in Maria Pinto commune: 1965

Size of holding (ha)	No. of cases	Area (ha)	% of total area
0.1 - 9.9	90	183	0.4
10 - 19.9	10	154	0.4
20 - 39.9	6	177	0.4
40 - 79.9	11	701	1.6
80 - 149	4	484	1.1
150 - 499	2	486	1.1
500 - 999	7	4787	11.8
1000 - 2499	7	13,792	32.4
2500 - 4999	1	2765	6.5
More than 5000	3	18,766	44.1
	142	42,295	99.8

Source: Internal Revenue Service.

programme. The revenue of the asentamientos was divided up as follows; 65-95% to the peasants, who were organised cooperatively and 5-35% to the Corporation of Agrarian Reform (CORA), which was the government body in charge of the technical aspects of the reform process. Wages of individual peasants were established according to the number of days worked. For about the first 5 yr the property of the asentamientos was to be held collectively by the peasants, but after this period members of the cooperative could obtain the *individual* rights of property over small plots within the production units.

This Christian Democrat policy had important and complex effects on the political consciousness of the peasantry. In one sense, the 'Christian Democrats' could argue that the asentamientos 'liberated' the peasants and represented a more 'advanced' form of social organisation, for under the Latifundia system, not only the peasants' work but also their lives outside work – their socialising and education – were repressively controlled and limited by the latifundia owners. Often the inquilinos had to buy their provisions from the hacienda owner's store. In Chile, in general, the internal social organisation of the latifundia took the form of a patronage system in which the inquilinos would be relatively favoured with rights to private plots and use of pasture, while others would have to do heavier jobs with less in return –

less rights to land and often no house so that they would usually have to live in the houses of inquilinos or in temporary huts. Acquiescence to the system was maintained by the hope of the less-favoured that they could one day join the more privileged inquilinos and by threats of violence where this was not enough. The 'patrón' in return was expected to fulfil certain moral obligations. The structure of social interaction was therefore a peculiarly 'vertical' one in which families remained in the same latifundia for generations and knew each other personally, but had little 'horizontal' contact with peasants in similar positions on neighbouring latifundia.

These social relations began to disintegrate in the 1950's and 1960's as competition between latifundia increased and induced mechanisation which, in turn, reduced the need for permanent workers. They were finally weakened by the pressure – chiefly from permanent workers and backed by the Christian Democrat government's encouragement – to unionise agricultural labour, and by government legislation which forced landlords to pay higher wages, including a minimum in cash, social security benefits and taxes (LEHMANN, 1974). Therefore the establishment of asentamientos also gave the peasants greater individual 'freedom' in the sphere of reproduction.

Although the asentamientos were cooperatively owned, their production was still dominated by the law of value; they were still operating in competition with each other and with other types of production unit. The de-restrictions on the 'private lives' of the peasantry and the promise of more individually-owned plots encouraged the development of bourgeois values — individualism, consumerism, concern with property. In these ways, the capitalist nature of agricultural production was enhanced rather than limited by the Christian Democrat agrarian reform. The promise of individually-owned plots accentuated the pressure from the peasantry on government institutions and political parties to extend the agrarian reform process. This curious combination of bourgeois and anti-capitalist (or anti-big capitalist) political feeling was encapsulated in the ambiguous slogan which characterised the 1970 presidential election campaign — 'the land for those who work it'. And so it was the expectation of *private* ownership of land which both strengthened the peasant organisations' support of new expropriations during the months prior to Allende's election in September 1970 and encouraged the development of individualistic values within sectors of the peasantry and stifled their political radicalisation.

(iv) The U.P. Agrarian reforms, 1970-1973

The U.P. government was torn between bowing to the peasants' demands that the 80 'hectareas basicas' limit should be reduced, and avoiding a major confrontation with bourgeois factions by offering guarantees to the rural middle class that they would not be expropriated, and hence not be tempted to disinvest. In succumbing to the latter pressures the U.P. reluctantly was forced to inhibit the revolutionary transformation of Chilean society. Meanwhile the small, but highly efficient 'reservas' and the small fundos, which could be retained under private ownership according to the 'hectareas basicas' limit, tended to out-compete the poorly equipped and organised asentamientos. In some cases, the non-expropriation of capital equipment led to the absurd situation where asentamientos had to hire machinery from the private sector. The U.P. government recognised that continued expropriations were not enough, and that the asentamientos were

both capitalist and inefficient, and so it tried to introduce new types of production unit in the reformed areas — the CERA (Centro de Reforma Agraria) and the Hacienda Estatal.

It was hoped that these would avoid the following major problems of the asentamientos; firstly, the possibility of individual, private ownership of land by the members of the asentamientos (asentados), and the individualistic values and unplanned production which resulted; secondly, the payment of 'advances' to asentados regardless of actual work done and the resulting complacency regarding collective work that this encouraged; and thirdly, the possibility of contracting labour from outside to do the heaviest jobs on the asentamientos. All these things were considered to inhibit the economic and political mobilisation of the peasantry, although, as we have seen, the historical origins of the lack of political consciousness amongst the peasants can be traced back to the social structure of the latifundia.

The CERAs were intended to be the basic units of organisation of production in the Reformed Area and were created through the combination of two or more expropriated units, with the participation of all the peasants working there at the time of expropriation plus other workers according to the needs of the production plan. Wages of the peasants consisted of a basic rate proportional to time worked plus a bonus or economic incentive which varied with the performance of the production plan. Of the surplus obtained in the operation of the unit, 10% was allocated for the internal needs of the CERA (e.g. administration) and the rest was distributed as a development fund for the whole commune by the Consejos Comunales Campesinos (Communal Peasants Councils). It was hence possible, in principle at least, for the development of backward parts of the commune to be subsidised by more advanced parts. Therefore, although in the sphere of circulation (i.e. distribution and sale, purchase of inputs) the CERAs were still subject to the law of value, in the sphere of capital accumulation the operation of the law of value was limited in that the allocation of the development funds could be governed by use-value as well as exchange-value considerations. Also, insofar as the funds could not be invested outside the commune as and when more profitable investment opportunities might arise – in the way in which the latifundia owners had been able to invest their money-capital – the operation of the law of value was modified further.

The intention was that the land of the CERAs would remain as Government property for a period of up to 5 yr, after which it would either be taken over by a cooperative formed by the peasants of the unit or remain in government hands as an 'Hacienda Estatal'. The latter were only intended to be established in particular technical circumstances, such as where specialised types of agriculture were practised or where the unit was suitable for training of workers. One Hacienda Estatal was established in Maria Pinto and was used as an experimental capital-intensive farm for seed production. Its internal organisation was similar to the CERA, but state ownership gave the government greater control over production. However, it was not until 1973 that the government succeeded in establishing a CERA in the North-West of Maria Pinto commune by combining two large production units. The long and complicated legal procedures of land transfer, and the resistance of a part of the peasantry who feared the loss of their rights to the land, impeded the setting-up of these units (see Table 3).

Tensions had been growing within the peasantry, especially where some workers found

work in the private sector preferable to work under collective organisation (sometimes it paid better). Generally divisions developed between the heavily subsidised workers living within the reformed areas and those outside it not receiving its 'benefits', such as the unemployed in the minifundia areas. The bourgeoisie was not slow in exploiting these tensions; for example, by warning peasants that the U.P. would replace the old 'patrón' by the state so that they would never get ownership of the land. In response to this the Popular Unity government introduced a provisional form of production unit – the 'Comité Campesino', which was similar to the CERAs, but which had a more flexible form of organisation that did not force political confrontations with peasant groups or challenge existing legislation. In the end, the Comité Campesino almost completely replaced the original idea of the CERA.

The U.P. programme also tried to emphasise the collective use and ownership of the means of production by encouraging nucleated settlement where 'horizontal' solidarity and collective responsibility might be fostered, and by encouraging more communal and regional coordination of the socialised area through the Consejos Comunales Campesinos. Unfortunately, as we have seen, it was unable to establish this programme completely and universally in the face of right-wing opposition and against the wishes of those peasant unions

Table 3. Land tenure structure in Maria Pinto: end of 1972

Tenure	Size/Type of production unit	Number of cases	Area (ha)
Private	Less than 4 ha	82	113
	4 - 9.9 ha	11	72
	10 - 19.9 ha	12	173
	20 - 39.9 ha	9	268
	40 - 79.9 ha	16	940
	more than 80 ha	14	4884
Reformed	Asentamientos	7	8455
	Comites Campesinos	10	20,768
	Expropiated land (not transf.)	8	5957
	Hacienda Estatal	1	340
	CERAs	0	0

Source: Internal Revenue Service, Corporation of Agrarian Reform (CORA), and information collected from fieldwork in 1972.

which were controlled by the Christian Democrats.

However, this opposition of many sections of the peasantry was certainly not just a subjective traditionalist obstinacy. On the contrary, their individualistic political consciousness was grounded in objective, material practices and relations with which they had little alternative but to comply. Given the largely *private* control of marketing of agricultural produce, the exhortations embodied in the U.P. programme to develop the collective side of agriculture and build a socialist consciousness inevitably seemed unreal and utopian to most of the peasants. In real terms, their work was small-scale and private, and the primary economic signals – the material incentives – came mainly through the market, not through the regional and communal organisations. The government set up its own marketing structure to compete with the private sector, but this was unsuccessful for a number of reasons. Firstly, the government structure was founded without adequate finance or experience. Secondly, it was ignored by most of the peasants in the reformed sectors because the private organisations, (with the support of right-wing political parties) often succeeded in offering higher prices than those fixed by the government, and so a black market developed. The alternative of controlling the private distribution firms directly was not feasible for two reasons. In the case of the larger firms, most of their capital was held in money form, while fixed capital and raw materials were largely hired or only bought in when required. This meant that expropriation would not have given the government real control. In the case of the numerous small distribution firms run by middle class families, the government did not wish to risk antagonising these people by expropriating their businesses.

The U.P. programme had been based on the dubious assumption (on this occasion) that ownership of land gave only formal and not real control of production, such that it was possible to meet the peasants' demands for land *and* establish a socialist agriculture. Moreover, the programme failed to counteract the tendency – initiated by the Christian Democrats – for a rural middle class to form based chiefly on the asentamientos, as effectively capitalist organisations, and their members, the asentados.

In the Christian Democrat period, these people, who had formerly been inquilinos, first became wage-labourers and then, with the creation of the asentamientos, owners of land, employers of wage-labour and full participants in capitalist production and marketing. The U.P. government did not manage to change this situation in any fundamental way.

However, although the U.P. programme, like its Christian Democrat predecessor, inadvertently accentuated the tendency of peasants to neglect collective work and concentrate on their family plots, certain limited advances were made. With the development of the CERAs and the Comites Campesinos, the organisation of the reformed area became less fragmented as it was now possible to bring in workers from outside the reformed area, and a greater degree of collective control over the surplus through the Consejos Comunales Campesinos became possible. Table 3 and Figure 9 summarise the situation in Maria Pinto at the end of 1972 when the process of expropriation was almost complete.

A comparison of Tables 3 and 4 with Table 2 shows that important changes occurred in the organisation and size-distribution of production units. In particular, the average size of privately-owned units fell. Also, settlement – and hence everyday spatial interaction – became more nucleated, largely as a result of government encouragement. However, the change in spatial structure was limited by the fact that the reformed areas were based upon the old latifundia-minifundia pattern. Nevertheless, the changing form of social and economic organisation of production generated new patterns of spatial interaction within this framework. For instance, the increasing dependence of peasants upon commodities rather than use-values for their reproduction and their correspondingly larger contribution to the production of commodities must have increased spatial interaction between Maria Pinto and other areas in terms of the circulation of goods, although it would be difficult to establish the form of these changes empirically.

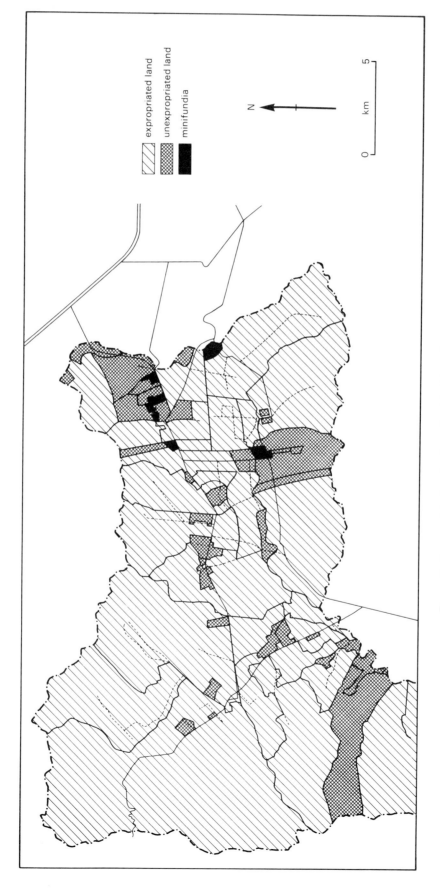

Figure 9. Expropriated and private land in Maria Pinto 1972.

Table 4. Organisation of production units in the reformed area (1973)

Production units	% of the total reformed area
Asentamientos	25.5
CERAs	3.0
Comités Campesinos	61.1
Hacienda Estatal	1.0
Expropriated and not transferred	9.3
	100.0

Source: As Table 3.

It would also seem reasonable to expect that there must have been (and still be) some tension and sub-optimality in the relation between these new types of spatial interaction and the inherited spatial framework of production units.

Although this article is only intended to deal with the period up to the coup in September 1973, we provide a brief description of changes in agriculture after the coup in the Appendix.

IV. Class Analysis

We can now summarise the structure of social classes in Maria Pinto and the changes therein which resulted from the agrarian reform and the development of capitalist agriculture. We would stress that the theoretical analysis presented here is only a first step and that some of the categorisations are provisional. The basis of this outline analysis is a conception of class not of the 'sociological' type, that is, a population group sharing a wide range of similar characteristics, but in terms of social relations of production. On this view, classes are determined through the relations between people in the sphere of production in terms of their ownership or non-ownership and control and non-control of land, means of production, the immediate labour process and the disposal of the product. These relations *define* the classes: classes are not contingently related but presuppose one another. The classes identified in this way certainly form an interlocking structure, but as would be expected in a transitional society combining pre-capitalist, capitalist and post-capitalist social forms, they are less secure

than those of a capitalist social formation. Following Banaji's authoritative discussion of the nature of modes of production (BANAJI, 1977), we do not consider it fruitful to debate whether the latifundia 'really were' pre-capitalist or capitalist — in other words to turn these categories into analytical straitjackets when, properly used, they can denote complex and quite varied sets of circumstances. Data on the sizes of classes are drawn from the 1964-1965 Agricultural Census (see Table 5), the 1970 population census and a survey conducted with the assistance of peasant organisations and government officials in 1972.

The 1970 Population Census shows only a small increase in the total population of the area of 6212 inhabitants, the bulk of which was located in reformed areas and the small rural settlements of the commune. Table 6 shows the approximate distribution of population in relation to production unit structure (cf. Figure 2).

Although it is not possible to draw any precise conclusions regarding class structure from the categories used in Table 6 we can provide a qualitative analysis of the main classes and their relationships in the Maria Pinto area.

Inquilinos (Share-croppers and Tenant-farmers)

These constituted the labour force of the traditional haciendas and fundos, especially in the central zone of Chile. Until the mid-60's, their wages were paid partly in kind and they had the right to use a small plot (maximum size usually 1 ha) which they worked

Table 5. Population working in agriculture: Maria Pinto 1964-1965

Employees; administrators, office workers, others	106
Inquilinos (tenant-farmers or share-croppers)	528
Asalariados permanentes (permanent wage-earners)	441
Asalariados temporales (temporary wage-earners)	
up to 3 months a year	292
3 - 6 months a year	168
Total	1535

Source: Agricultural Census 1964-1965.

Table 6. Distribution of the population in Maria Pinto: 1972

Size of production units	No. of cases	% of land	% of population
Private area: agricultural land			
Less than 4.9 Ha	82	0.2	
5 - 9.9 Ha	11	0.1	7.0
10 - 19.9 Ha	12	0.4	
20 - 39.9 Ha	9	0.6	
40 - 80 Ha	16	2.1	5.0
More than 80 Ha	14	11.0	
Private area:			
Small rural settlements and Maria Pinto town		1.1	31.0
Social Area: Expropriated Land			
Asentamientos	7	10.0	15.0
Comites Campesinos	10	49.0	38.0
Expropriated and not transfered	9	14.7	4.0

Source: 1970 Census and 1972 Survey.

with their family. The Christian Democrat's introduction of a minimum money wage was largely an effort to incorporate the inquilinos into the cash economy and this in itself altered the nature of the inquilino class for their reproduction was increasingly mediated by exchange-value and less and less by personalised reciprocal relations within the hacienda or latifundia. While this made the inquilinos' subsistence vulnerable to price inflation, it also had the (intended) effect of enlarging the national internal market for commodities and was therefore acceptable to the more progressive elements of the bourgeoisie. The inquilinos were therefore incorporated into the capitalist economy at the level of circulation of commodities and reproduction whereas previously their involvement had been almost exclusively in the sphere of production. In short, in Bernstein's terminology, there was a 'commoditization' of the inquilinos (BERNSTEIN, 1977). This contributed to the proletarianisation of the peasantry and weakened the 'vertical' ties of patronage. Some of the latifundia owners tried to resist this process by opposing attempts to nucleate settlement and introduce electricity and telecommunications, which, it was felt, would have a dangerous 'modernising' and radicalising effect.

With the development of the reformed area the inquilinos almost disappeared as a class as they became members of the Asentamientos, Comites Campesinos, CERAs and Haciendas Estatales. As we have seen, by several complex processes, the feared or hoped for radicalisation was over-ridden by the development of individualistic political values.

Asalariados Permanentes (Permanent Wage-earners)

Although no adequate statistics are available, it is certain that this class decreased numerically after the agrarian reform. Some of the asalariados permanentes were incorporated *in situ* into the reformed area. The asentamientos employed only a few asalariados permanentes, but more were incorporated into Comites Campesinos and CERAs. This class, although properly constituting the agrarian proletariat in Maria Pinto, tended to be poorly organised and politically conservative, partly as a result of association with workers in the 'reservas'.

Asalariados Temporales (Temporary Wage-earners)

This group is formed mainly by owners of small plots (< 10 acres) and their dependents. As proprietors, they tended to share the political values and social aspirations of the larger landowners. While in some ways they are similar to the petty bourgeoisie, they live by their own production, using family labour without employing wage-labour. Since their family plot is usually insufficient to support them, they were forced to work temporarily in the fundos and reservas or in the asentamientos. They were also commonly involved in the service sector. As one might expect from their dual class role, this group tended to have mixed political attitudes, and to resort to individualistic responses to their problems.

The Bourgeoisie

Three different fractions of the bourgeoisie were identifiable. The 'petty bourgeoisie' consisted mainly of those working on services connected with agriculture and with commerce. Traditionally, they played the role of intermediary between the peasants and the market for the distribution of inputs and sale of agricultural products. Given the restricted size of their market, and the low productivity characteristic of this kind of production, opportunities for capital accumulation were limited. In terms of output, they were of little economic significance.

The 'grande' bourgeoisie was represented by the proprietors and landowners of the old haciendas and fundos of Maria Pinto. Although most were expropriated, as we have seen, they were able to keep the 'reservas', — normally the best land — plus control of water, machinery and buildings, and hence retain their political and economic power. This situation induced them to intensify and industrialise their agricultural production, and in general to dominate the agricultural sector.

Between these two fractions is the so-called rural middle class, formed mainly by the owners of the medium-size agricultural units of less than the 80 'hectareas basicas' and who were hence able to avoid expropriation. As might be expected they shared the right wing political views of the grande bourgeoisie.

Looking at the class structure in general, it is clear that while the bourgeoisie lost some of its land and political power it retained its economic dominance. Meanwhile, the radicalisation of agricultural workers was weakened and their political struggles diverted into petty-bourgeois channels.

As we have noted, this is no more than an outline of a class analysis. However, it serves to show the kinds of contradictions which can develop in a transitional society in which there is a conscious effort to change social relationships and political consciousness in the context of diverse pre-capitalist and capitalist social forms. In order to develop this analysis it would be necessary to supplement it with specification of circuits of capital and use-values in the rural areas, and with studies of actual levels of wages, profits and transfers of capital within agriculture and between it and the rest of the Chilean economy. For although the form of these relationships is always mediated through class relations and class struggle, they also make up the material structure within which this struggle takes place. Such a class analysis is necessary for understanding the development of the region, whether for academic or political purposes. Indeed, throughout the period of Unidad Popular government, the various political factions in the coalition argued about the complexities and contradictions of this class structure, about the allegedly reformist character of the programme, and about the kind of political support which derived from this class structure.[5]

V Conclusions

The conclusions which we should like to draw chiefly concern the *approach* adopted in this study. First, and most important, there is the impossibility of making sense of the relationships of people to their environment and the spatial structure of society, without examining the types of social organisation of production, the social classes and forms of political power in that society. The human geography of a region is largely a product of these relationships and in turn this socially-produced structure acts as a context for subsequent development.

Political power, political organisations and factions are not normally considered to have significance for understanding spatial organisation and relationships between people and the land. However, it should be clear from this example of agrarian reform and attempted revolutionary change that political relationships depend crucially upon forms of socio-economic organisation – for example, types of production unit in agriculture – and in turn political forces reproduce or modify these forms of organisation. Also, the success of political programmes depends partly upon their adequacy for a wide range of different physical contexts within which people live. Moreoever, far from being a separate sphere of life, political ideas are firmly grounded in everyday social practices. These relationships are transparent in the case of societies undergoing radical change, but they are no less important in shaping the structure of more stable societies: it is just that their stability can easily lead us to overlook them or to take them for granted.

Second, we hope to have demonstrated the importance of treating the problem not only historically, but historically in two senses – objectively and subjectively. That is, it is necessary to show both how the present objective structure developed from pre-existing forms of physical and social structure and how, *subjectively*, the historical *experience* of that development has affected contemporary political consciousness. The last point is often overlooked, but in this study it was

particularly important for understanding the wide range of responses to successive policies among the different social classes.

Third, the necessity of understanding the *complexity* of so-called transitional societies such as this is worthy of note. As BANAJI (1977) has argued, we see no point in forcing Chilean society into a simple mould of a single mode of production or even in arguing, in the abstract, about what modes of production exist and are articulated. While there can be no doubt that capitalism dominates present-day Chilean society, the way in which it does so while incorporating more traditional structures is not to be discovered by high-level, abstract discussions of modes of production, but can only be worked out using lower-level theoretical concepts in empirical investigation. There has not been space here to pursue the latter kind of inquiry fully, but the argument does, we think, point in that direction. Nor do we find it helpful to reduce social classes to a definition based upon social relations of production *and no more*. It is perfectly possible to combine a recognition of the structural importance of the latter in the economy with an examination of the divisions and political groupings which exist within and sometimes cut across these broad classes.

Fourth, there are some points about the treatment of political programmes. It seems to us to be essential to consider a programme such as the Chilean Agrarian Reform, which was intended to change the structure of the society, as an *ongoing political process* and not, as geographers often assume, as the simple implementation of a policy by an internally-homogenous government with respect to an internally-homogenous population. Any evaluation of a programme such as this which takes this latter approach will almost inevitably assess the successes and failures in simple-minded fashion as pertaining to the nature of the policies themselves alone. Evaluation which treats the programme as a political process inevitably goes beyond this and becomes an assessment of political changes in general.

Perhaps the major substantive conclusion concerning the agrarian reform is that as part of a revolutionary programme it cannot be expected to produce a successful restructuring of economic, social and physical organisation on a piecemeal basis, for fundamental contradictions will inevitably arise between different types of economic organisation and political forces. It is easy to say that only total reform can work but much harder to achieve it. Nevertheless, on the basis of the Chilean and other experiences in Latin America, we see no alternative.[6]

Appendix: Changes in Agriculture since the 1973 Coup

The military government has attempted to restructure agriculture in order to orient it towards production for export. This has been in part a response to the rapid reduction in the size of the internal markets produced by drastic cuts in real wages. While wages fell, support for investment in large production units increased so that in 1974 there was a 16.2% growth in value of the gross agricultural product, in 1975 a 3.8% growth in the same, while in 1976 there was a 39% growth in exports [E.C.L.A., (1976) Economic Survey of Latin America 1976; Business Latin America (1977) June 1977, p.204]. Some indication of the enormity of these changes is given by the fact that the internal markets for certain products have almost completely disappeared, for example, the country as a whole has changed from being a net importer of meat to a net exporter.

The changes introduced under the agrarian reform have been stopped and reversed. In the first year after the coup, 1200 farms were returned to their previous owners while 3000 former owners have challenged expropriations which took place under the U.P. (NACLA, 1974). In a tiny number of well-publicised cases, asentados have been granted property rights, but in general, passage of law 208 restricting peasants rights has undermined their political and economic power. This law made it possible for the state to deny title to land to anyone who can be charged with a 'major crime', as defined by the governments' criteria. Interest-free credit for peasants has also been withdrawn. Most peasant organisations have been outlawed and their leaders imprisoned or killed.

Notes

1. Cf. GIDDENS's (1977) concept of 'structuration'. GREGORY (1978) has stressed its importance for geography.

2. In this context, see the debate between STUCKEY (1975) and FRIEDMANN (1975).

3. This research was carried out by a team led by the first author at the Center of Urban and Regional Studies (CIDU) of the Catholic University of Chile.

4. In connection with the evaluation of Agrarian Reform during the U.P. Government, see for example ASTELARRA (1975), BARRACLOUGH and AFFONSO (1973), BARRACLOUGH and FERNANDEZ (1974) and KAY (1974).

5. An analysis of social classes and peasantry in Chile before the Allende Government can be found in PETRAS and ZEITLIN (1970).

6. On this point see FRANK (1969) Varieties of Land Reform, and GARCIA (1970).

Acknowledgement – The authors would like to thank Sue Rowlands for drawing the maps and diagrams.

References

ALALUF, TOMIC and TRUMPER (1972) El Sector Agrario en el Gobierno de la Unidad Popular In: *La Economía Chilena en 1971*, Universidad de Chile, Instituto de Economia, Publicacion No. 141. Santiago, Chile.

ARANDA S. and MARTINEZ, A. (1970) Chile Hoy: Estructura Economica. Algunas caracteristicas fundamentales, In: *Chile Hoy*, Universidad de Chile, Centro de Estudios Socio-Economicos. Editorial Siglo XXI.

ASTELARRA, J. (1975) Land Reform in Chile during Allende's Government, Latin America Studies Program, Dissertation Series, No. 64. Cornell University.

BANAJI, J. (1977) Modes of production in a materialist conception of history, *Capital and Class* 3, 1-44.

BARAN, P.A. and HOBSBAWM, E. (1961) The stages of economic growth, *Kyklos,* **14.**

BARRACLOUGH, S. *et al.* (Ed.). (1973) *Chile: Reforma Agraria y Gobierno Popular*, Ediciones Periferia, Buenos Aires, Argentina.

BARRACLOUGH, S. and AFFONSO, A. (1973) Diagnóstico de la Reforma Agraria Chilena. Nov. 1970-Junio 1972, In: *Chile: Reforma Agraria y Gobierno Popular, et al.* Barraclough S. (Ed.) Ediciones Periferia, Buenos Aires, Argentina.

BARRACLOUGH, S. and FERNANDEZ, J.A. (1974) *Diagnostico de la Reforma Agraria Chilena*, Siglo XXI, Mexico.

BERNSTEIN, H. (1977) Notes on capital and peasantry, *Review of African Political Economy* **10,** 60-73.

BORDE, J. and GONGORA, M. (undated) *Evolucion de la Propiedad Rural en el Valle del Puangue*, Universidad de Chile, Instituto de Sociologia, Santiago.

BUSINESS LATIN AMERICA Weekly report to managers of Latin American operations. Published by Business International Corporation, New York; 29.6.1977, 204; 15.12.1977, 384; 15.3.1978, 86.

FRANK, A. G. (1969) Varieties of Land Reform, in his *Latin America: Underdevelopment or Revolution*, Monthly Review Press, New York.

FRANK, A.G. (1969) Sociology of development and underdevelopment of sociology in his *Latin America: Underdevelopment or Revolution*, Monthly, Review Press, New York.

FRIEDMANN, J. (1975) A comment on: spatial analysis and economic development, In: *Development and Change*, Vol. VI.

GARCIA, A. (1970) *Dominación y Reforma Agraria en America Latina*, Instituto de Estudios Peruanos, America Problema No. 3. Lima, Peru.

GIDDENS, A. (1977) *Studies in Social Theory*, Hutchinson, London.

GREGORY, D. (1978) *Ideology, Science and Geography*, Hutchinson, London.

HERNANDEZ, S. (1972) El desarrollo capitalista del campo chileno, in *Sociedad y Desarrollo*, No. 3 CESO-Universidad de Chile.

JOUVIN, J.-J. (1966) La agricultura en el reciente desarrollo de America Latina In: *Desarrollo Economico*, No. 20, Buenos Aires.

KAY, C. (1974) Chile: an appraisal of Popular Unity's agrarian reform, University of Glasgow, Institute of Latin American Studies, Occasional Papers, No. 13.

LEHMANN, D. (1974) Agrarian Reform in Chile, 1965-72: An Essay in Contradictions In: *Agrarian Reform and Agrarian Reformism. Studies of Peru, Chile, China and India*, LEHMANN, D. (Ed.) Faber & Faber, London.

NORTH AMERICAN CONGRESS ON LATIN AMERICA (NACLA) (1974) NACLA's Latin America and Empire Report. Volume VIII, No. 8.

PETRAS, J. and LA PORTE, R. (1970) United States Policy toward Agrarian Reform, In: *Politics and Social Structure in Latin America* Petras J. Monthly Review Press, New York.

PETRAS, J. and ZEITLIN, M. (1970), Agrarian Radicalism in Chile In: *Agrarian Problems and Peasant movement in Latin America*, STAVENHAGEN R. (Ed.). Anchor Books.

SLATER, D. (1974) Contribution to a critique of development geography, *Canadian Journal of African Studies* 8, 325-354.

STUCKEY, B. (1975) Spatial Analysis and Economic Development, *Development and Change*, Vol. VI.

UNITED NATIONS-ECLA. (1974) Situation and Evolution of Agriculture and Food Supplies in Latin America, *Economic Bulletin of Latin America*.

UNITED NATIONS-FAO-ILO. (1976) *Progress in Land Reform: Sixth* Report. 1976, United Nations, Department of Economic and Social Affairs. New York.

YUDELMAN, M. (1967) *El desarrollo agricola de America Latina*, Banco Inter-Americano de Desarrollo. CEMLA.

Geoforum, Vol. 10, pp.81-108, 1979.
Pergamon Press Ltd. Printed in Great Britain.

Capital Accumulation and Regional Development in France

MICHAEL DUNFORD,* Brighton, U.K.

Abstract: The paper examines the interlinked development of social process and spatial form in the analysis of the changing patterns of production and employment in France. A major hypothesis is that specific phases of capital accumulation are associated with the use and production of specific forms of spatial diferentiation, and that recent changes in the location of employment in France are connected with the transition from one stage of capitalist development to another. Thus the changing spatial pattern of agricultural employment is seen as part of the decay of petty commodity production and the intergration of family farming into a new capitalist agriculture. Similarly, spatial change in manufacturing employment is also a component of industrial restructuring, and the associated development of new infrastrucural and labour requirements. The French state is one element of these processes and the article concludes with a case study of the relationships between capital accumulation and regional policy.

1. Introduction: Capital Accumulation and the Regional Question

The aim of this paper is to outline a theoretical framework for analysing some recent changes in the evolution of the French space economy. It begins by focusing upon several striking features of the recent development of the geographical structure of France connected with the marked changes in the pattern of regional employment growth observed in the period after 1962. From 1954 to 1962 the reduction in agricultural employment contributed to the continued depopulation of rural areas and agricultural regions, while population and employment continued to increase in most industrialised and highly urbanised regions. But in the period after 1962 a new pattern began to emerge largely because of a modification of trends in the location of manufacturing employment. In this period the fastest rates of growth of industrial employment were recorded in rural regions to which industry was being decentralised. At the same time industrial employment de-

clined in traditional industries in the Nord and Lorraine which consequently experienced a net loss of manufacturing jobs. It also declined in more modern industrial centres in the Paris Region and eventually in Rhône-Alpes, but in the last two regions the decline in industrial employment was usually out-weighted by growth in tertiary employment (see Figure 1 for regional divisons).

The main hypothesis that lies behind the interpretation of these trends is that specific phases of accumulation are associated with the use and production of specific forms of spatial differentiation and that these changing trends in the location of employment in France are connected with the transition from one stage of capitalist development to another. It is possible to identify various phases in the development of capitalist economies associated with stages in the development of the productive system and in the organisation of the labour process and division of labour. The structure of the productive system is characterised by the dominance of particular branches of production and specific relations between industry and

*School of Social Sciences, University of Sussex.

Figure 1. The zones d'études et d'aménagement du territoire and the programming regions.

agriculture and this in turn is closely associated with the use of specific kinds of spatial differentiation and specific forms of territorial development. But these phases are also characterised by particular sets of class relations and class alliances and particular forms of integration of local populations with the central state reflected in differentiated local social and political arrangements.

Each phase of accumulation is therefore characterised by distinctive economic and political structures, both of which are reflected in specific forms of territorial development. However, the contradictions of each phase of accumulation including those associated specifically with the geographical form of development eventually lead to their disruption in periods of crisis.

The crises create some of the conditions necessary for the establishment of a new model of accumulation and spatial development and mark turning-points in the evolution of the space economy. (See Appendix for a brief guide to concepts from marxist political economy used in this paper.)

In the case of France there has been a delayed but rapid modernisation of activities dominated by pre-capitalist modes of production, i.e. the decline of petty commodity production in agriculture. For a while this process was associated with an accelerated depopulation of rural areas and a continued concentration of employment in metropolitan centres. But it is argued that the rising costs of labour and infrastructure in developed regions combined with a restructuring of leading industrial sectors subsequently led to a new stage of development and to new forms of use of geographical space. The main features of the process of spatial development in this period are the tertiarisation and deindustrialisation of metropolitan regions, the implantation of modern capitalist enterprises in rural areas and the development of complex units of production. These spatial effects of the transition to a new phase of capitalist development are associated with marked changes in local social and political organisation and the emergence of new political structures establishing a new relation between the state and local societies and new class alliances. The disruption of established social and political structures and changes in the structure of regional and urban economies have led to the emergence of new forms of social protest in metropolitan centres, in traditional industrial regions and in peripheral areas.

However the aim of this paper is not to provide a comprehensive historical account of the recent evolution of the French social formation and space economy. Instead there is an attempt to examine several elements of this evolution mainly on the basis of some recent French work concerned with regional problems. It begins with: (1) a brief account of recent trends in the location of employment in France. The next sections are concerned with: (2) the evolution of agricultural employment in the French regions, and (3) recent changes in the structure of industrial

space including the decentralisation of industry from the Paris Region and the formation of major industrial and port complexes. The conclusion will then include a discussion of: (4) the way in which the interpretation of the economic and social and political aspects of the regional question can be integrated more completely with one another.

2. New Trends in the Location of Employment in France

There have been some marked changes in the location of employment in France in the period after 1962 compared with the period between 1954 and 1962, and some important changes in the structure of regional economies have also occurred in the post-war period.[1]

The period between 1954 and 1962 was broadly characterised by the same trends in aggregate regional employment as had occurred throughout much of the present century in France. The fastest rate of growth of employment was recorded in the Paris Region with an average annual rate of 1.46% compared with 0.14% in the country as a whole, but employment also tended to increase in most of the other highly industrialised and urbanised regions in which the growing industrial and especially tertiary sectors continued to be concentrated. The only exception to this pattern was the industrial region of the Nord where employment fell largely because of modernisation and rationalisation of the coal and textile industries in this period.

The concentration of employment in established industrial poles was thought to be a necessary consequence of economic growth in the immediate post-war period, but it was also associated with a disorganised process of urbanisation and a housing crisis in the Paris agglomeration and other major urban centres. It was these contradictory effects of the growth process which led to the integration of regional and urban planning and the promotion of industrial decentralisation from Paris in the early stages of French planning after 1950. These measures were intended to help plan the development of major urban centres like Paris and to support and reinforce the decentralisation of industries for which access to the metropolitan centre was less important.

Some industrial employment was decentralised from Paris in this period, but it usually only involved the relocation of plant within the Paris Region or in regions in the Paris Basin, reducing congestion in the Paris agglomeration but without reducing regional disparities between Paris and the backward regions in the provinces or establishing new poles of development in these regions. The small number of major investments elsewhere in the provinces was attributed to politically motivated state interference with the decisions of nationalised industries (FREYSSENET, 1974: 172). But what is interesting about this period is that the fastest rates of growth of industrial employment were actually recorded in parts of the Paris Basin, and that above-average rates of growth of industrial employment were also recorded in parts of the Zone d'étude et d'aménagement du territoire (ZEAT) West. These increases contributed to a rise in total employment in some regions in the Paris Basin in which agricultural employment was relatively unimportant. However, the drastic reduction in agricultural employment was generally associated with rapid rates of decline in total employment and continuing depopulation of unindustrialised regions located largely in the Western half of France.[2]

Although trends in the location of industrial employment were beginning to change in this period, a modification in the location of employment and the pattern of migration of labour and population was only observed in the period after 1962. Between 1962 and 1968 the national rate of employment growth was higher than in the preceding intercensal period, but there was a slower rate of employment growth in the Paris Region and a pronounced deindustrialisation of the region with industrial employment declining at −1.30% per year. The level of industrial employment also fell in the traditional industrial areas of the Nord and Alsace and Lorraine, and the rate of growth of industrial employment fell below the national average in Rhône-Alpes. In contrast, there were rapid rates of growth of industrial employment in rural regions. The fastest rates of growth were recorded in the Paris Basin, especially in Basse Normandie (4.34%), Centre (3.52%) and Picardie (2.09%), while the average annual rate of growth of industrial

employment in the ZEAT West was 2.76% compared with the national average of 0.32%. Since these developments were often accompanied by increases in employment in construction and public works, and especially since they were associated with quantitatively smaller reductions in agricultural employment than in the preceding period, total employment increased in almost all these regions sometimes at more than the national average rate and emigration from rural regions became less pronounced. The only region in which total employment actually fell in this period was Limousin (−0.54%).

The evidence collected for the period after 1968 is more fragmentary, but it generally indicates a continuation of these new trends in the location of employment. In the period 1968-1977 the rate of national employment growth fell slightly to 0.73% per year, and the rate of growth in the Paris Region (1.24%) increased while that in the provinces (0.59%) decreased, although both were still closer to the national average than in the earliest period. The slower rate of employment growth in the provinces can be partly attributed to the acceleration in the decline of agricultural employment which fell at 5.23% per year between 1968 and 1976 compared with 3.18% between 1962 and 1968. For example, the very rapid rates of decline and large quantitative reductions in agricultural employment in the ZEATs West (4.94% or 34,000 jobs per year compared to 37,000 in 1954-1962), Paris Basin (5.62% or 34,000 jobs per year compared with 33,000 in 1954-1962) and South-West (6.16% or 29,000 jobs per year compared with 33,000 in 1954-1962) contributed to the slackening of employment growth in parts of these regions. But the trends in the location of industrial employment observed in the earlier period continued with the fastest rates of growth recorded in the ZEATs Paris Basin and West and below-average rates recorded in industrialised regions.

These new trends had important consequences for the development of the French regions, but it must be noted that they have not so far been sufficient to radically alter the regional distribution of employment existing in 1962. Thus, agricultural employment still accounts for a relatively large proportion of total employment in western regions while industrial employment is still strongly concentrated in the area around Paris, in the Rhône-Alpes region and in the traditional industrial areas in the Nord and in the ZEAT East. Tertiary employment is more equally distributed but predominates in the more urbanised regions and especially in the Paris Region and Provence. On the other hand these statistics conceal many qualitative changes in the structure of regional economies and societies. For example, DULONG (1978) has pointed out how the structure of the Breton economy and society has been transformed by its integration with monopoly capitalism. This transformation includes both quantitative and qualitative effects on the peasantry associated with the integration of petty commodity production with capitalist agricultural production and the integration of agricultural units with the food processing industry. It also includes the effects on the operation of local labour markets and the local class structure of the restructuring of local non-monopolistic industries and the decentralisation of industries requiring relatively unskilled labour. The political centralisation which took place during the Fifth Republic, and the establishment of new regional institutions linking the area more closely with monopoly interests, undermined the position of local notables and was associated with the emergence of new local elites, e.g. modern fractions of the peasantry and the medium bourgeoisie in the building industry and tourism. An adequate explanation of recent changes in the structure of the French space economy should be able to account for these qualitative changes as well as for trends in the location of employment.

3. The Displacement of Peasant Agriculture and the Regional Question

Some of the most striking aspects of recent changes in the structure of the French space economy are connected with the restructuring of agricultural production. This section is largely concerned with the delayed but accelerated decline in agricultural employment in France and the regional differences in this process rather than with the emergence of new regional agricultural structures. However, an examination of this process

will entail some general discussion of changes in the organisation of agriculture and in patterns of regional specialisation to the extent that they are connected with employment trends.

It will be necessary to provide an account both of the laws of motion of the basic units of agricultural production and of the connection between the development of agriculture and the evolution of the economy as a whole. For example, there is a close relation between agriculture and industry based on the relative prices of agricultural commodities. The level of prices of agricultural commodities directly influences the value of labour-power and the cost of material inputs into industrial production processes. It is also associated with a certain rate of rural depopulation and formation of a reserve army of labour and hence indirectly with the value of labour-power. This interdependence of agriculture and industry means that changes in agriculture must be partly sought in changes taking place in industry and in the economy as a whole.

It is for this reason that LIPIETZ (1977: 28-53) has attempted to analyse recent national and regional trends in agricultural employment as the result of a process of articulation of modes of production. He suggests that the French social formation is dominated by the capitalist mode of production, but that the latter is articulated with other dominated modes of production. These other modes of production provide a pool of labour, products necessary for the process of economic reproduction and an outlet for commodities produced by capitalist industries. Lipietz focuses upon petty commodity production in agriculture, and he argues that recent changes in French agriculture can be explained largely in terms of the articulation of capitalism with this mode of production. This issue is therefore 'the basis of the regional question in France' (LIPIETZ, 1977: 31). This view is based upon Rey's examination of the transition from feudalism to capitalism.

3.1 Rey's Model of the Transition from Feudalism to Capitalism

Rey attempted to establish a periodisation of this transition, conceptualised as a process of articulation of different modes of production within a social formation in which there is a change in the dominant mode, and he subsequently tried to generalise these conclusions to include the articulation of capitalism with other modes of production. One of his main objectives was to examine the formation of alliances between classes defined by the modes of production during the process of articulation, and indeed it is the evolution of class alliances which plays a central role in explaining the persistence and the subsequent accelerated decline of small-scale agricultural production in France.

Rey distinguished three phases in the penetration of capitalism into modes of production in which agriculture and handicraft production are closely linked (REY, 1973: 69-70; 156-165).

(1) In the first phase the social formation is dominated by the feudal mode of production which is based in agriculture, but it also includes simple forms of commodity production and merchant capital which commissions work from a number of direct producers and subsequently collects and sells their produce. In this phase which precedes a bourgeois revolution there is a partial replacement of peasant agriculture by capitalist farming and handicraft industries by manufacturing. However, rural handicraft production is not destroyed because the mechanism facilitating the emergence of capitalist production is not one of economic competition. In fact, this phase only involves the formal subsumption of labour under capital, i.e. a transformation in the social position of the various agents of production without a revolutionisation of the labour process.

The labourer is separated from the means of production and labour-power becomes a commodity, and the objective and subjective conditions of labour now assume the forms of constant and variable capital, but capital takes over an existing labour process developed under different and more archaic modes of production and produces additional surplus-value by increasing absolute surplus-value (MARX, 1976b: 1019-1023; 1025-1034).

Rey believes that the actual penetration of capitalism into the closed circuit of rural handicraft industry and agriculture involves recourse to extra-economic means, e.g. legal and political measures. When the process of transition proceeds from a social formation dominated by feudalism, the existence of landed property and ground rent within feudal agriculture provides the necessary mechanism. This happened in the case of Britain when with the development of cloth manufacture in Flanders some landowners sought to increase their rents by enclosing their land and by expelling peasants and leasing it to capitalist farmers for wool production. The expulsion of some peasants created a class of wage-labourers for manufacturing industry and commerce. At the same time the payment of money rents by those peasants that remained required them to market a large part of their surplus product providing industry and the towns with necessary raw materials and consumption goods. For these reasons Rey argues that there was an essential complementarity between the interests of the landed classes and the emerging bourgeoisie in this period, and that this formed the basis for a class alliance which was able to secure from an absolutist state measures necessary to promote the process of primitive accumulation.

(2) The second stage is characterised by the dominance of the capitalist mode of production and the production of relative surplus-value in branches which it dominates. This means that this period corresponds to the early stages in the real subsumption of labour under capital which is characterised by the complete and continuous alteration in the nature of the labour process and the establishment of a specifically capitalist form of production (MARX, 1976b: 1023-1025; 1034-1038).

This stage begins with the development of large-scale industry which destroys handicrafts production by increasing substantially the productivity of labour and reducing the prices of production of commodities. With the decline of rural handicraft industry, the peasantry comes to depend completely on the market for supplies of means of production (agricultural tools, etc.) and non-agricultural consumption goods, and so it must continue to supply agricultural products to capitalist industries and urban markets both to pay the rent on its land and to finance these purchases. Rey argues that capital does not yet take over most agricultural branches because of the low level of development of the productive forces and because the development of capitalist agriculture presupposes the development or urban industry to supply inputs to agriculture. This means that agricultural productivity does not increase as rapidly as industrial productivity at this stage.

He also argues that the continued provision of labour still requires extra-economic coercion. This can be accomplished by landed property through the continued clearances of estates as occurred in England and Scotland although this action by landed interests may have been precipitated by measures to which the landed classes were opposed. Where landed property is not able to play this role of collecting land rent and expropriating the peasantry the process must rely on other mechanisms such as the effect of increasing indebtedness stemming from the severe weight of mortgages and taxes incurred by small French peasants. Finally, Rey points out that if the agricultural population is reduced too quickly to be absorbed by industry, emigration can restore some kind of equilibrium.

(3) The third phase can be largely avoided if the expropriation of small peasants and their replacement by capitalist farmers was completed by landed property as occurred in Britain. Otherwise capital is invested in agricultural production at this stage cheapening agricultural commodities and thus destroying peasant agriculture by competition.

Rey suggests that this process has been completed only in the United States, and that it is now taking place in France. In the latter case the process is accelerated by competition from neighbouring capitalist countries in which the peasantry has already been expropriated and in which capitalist agricultural production is more developed. One result of the operation of economic mechanisms is that landed property is now superfluous, and that the continued division of surplus-value between profit on capital and land rent is associated with a contradiction between capital and landed property which according

to Rey is simply a relic of the feudal mode of production.[3]

3.2 *The Application of Rey's Model to the Case of French Agriculture*

This model provides the basis for an interpretation of recent trends in agricultural employment and changes in the structure of agricultural space in France, and it provides a framework for more detailed concrete studies. It is possible to distinguish two types of evolution of agricultural employment in advanced capitalist countries. In countries such as Britain there was a rapid and early reduction in the agricultural population due to the role of large landed interests in the transition to modern capitalism, while in the case of North America there was a slower and more regular reduction in the agricultural population because it stemmed from the articulation of petty commodity production with capitalism.

French agriculture was also dominated by petty commodity production, and the decline in the percentage of the active population employed in agriculture conformed initially with the second pattern. But Lipietz has pointed out that after 1871 the rate of decline slowed down markedly compared with other countries in this group and that agricultural employment remained at a comparatively high level throughout the period of the Third Republic. It was only after the Second World War that the share of agriculture in total employment fell very quickly and approached the share in other advanced capitalist countries (see Figure 2). Lipietz has attempted to explain the distinctiveness of the French experience by examining the way in which Rey's phases of development worked out in the French context.

(1) In the middle of the eighteenth century land was generally owned by aristocratic or feudal interests and agriculture was typically capitalistic in the northern provinces where there was a well-defined class of capitalist farmers while peasant agriculture was the rule in the south. Lipietz focuses upon the small independent peasantry formed after the abolition of the Ancien Regime and not on capitalist agriculture which characterised parts of the Paris Basin or on persisting

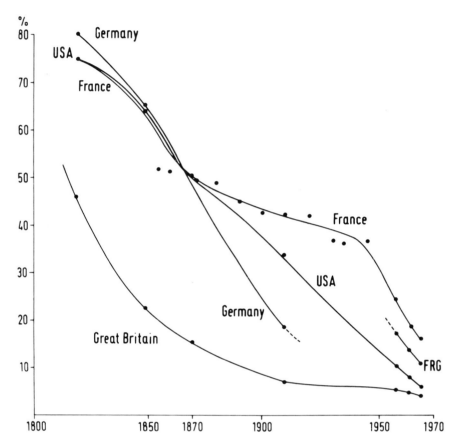

Figure 2. The percentage of the total active population engaged in agriculture.
Source: LIPIETZ (1977).

feudal forms of agricultural production. This layer of the rural population owned its own means of production often including its land and owned its product, and was concerned with the simple reproduction of the unit of production. Geographically this form of production was associated with the location of small family farms around market towns.

Lipietz locates the first phase in the articulation of these petty commodity producers with capitalism in the period between 1789 and 1848. After the first generation of peasant farmers had been replaced there was a progressive increase in peasant indebtedness. This resulted from the acquisition and growth in the size of mortgages and the acquisition of other debts at usurious rates of interest and was accelerated by the ever-increasing burden of taxes and legal costs (MARX, 1973b: 115-117; 241-245). The acquisition of morgages and debts can be attributed to

the purchase of land when some landowners decided to capitalise their rents by selling or leasing their land to peasants, and to the way in which population growth and the fragmentation of holdings led to increasing land prices which often exceeded the capitalisation of the rent and limited improvements in agricultural technique and labour productivity.[4] These forces obliged the peasantry to market part of its surplus product and marginalised many of the smaller peasants forcing some of them out of agriculture.

(2) The second phase took place slowly and unevenly over a period lasting from 1848 to 1945 or later. Lipietz calls this phase one of 'external articulation' and argues that the most important process is the exchange of commodities between petty commodity producers and the capitalist mode of production. In this phase the existence of money payments combined with the decline of rural handicraft industries and increased use of

capitalistically produced commodities led to an increase in the marketed surplus. Lipietz argues that these exchanges are unequal and result in the appropriation of much of the surplus product of petty commodity producers by capitalist branches in the sphere of circulation. This is because the prices of agricultural commodities are only set equal to cost price, allowing the direct producers to replace their means of production, to support themselves and their families and to pay the rent on their land, whereas the prices of commodities purchased by the peasant from capitalist industries are equal to their price of production, i.e. cost price plus the average profit on the capital advanced. Thus, in this period petty commodity producers supplied commodities at low prices to the capitalist sphere. Lipietz argues that these low prices eventually resulted in a reduction in the standard of living of the peasantry and a lengthening of their working day, and that this relative devalorisation of their labour-power led to unequal exchange in the narrow sense (EMMANUEL, 1972).[5] This process contributed to the decomposition of petty commodity production and a differentiation within the peasantry with the bankruptcy of some small peasants and their employment as wage-labourers either by the owners of larger holdings or in capitalist industries.

Lipietz argues that the process of external articulation proceeded quite quickly during the Second Empire with a reduction in marginal arable land and the development of regional specialisation, but was slowed down after 1871 with the formation of a political alliance between the bourgeoisie and the peasantry, landed interests and the aristocracy. This alliance was formed because the bourgeoisie feared that the peasantry might be pushed into an alliance with the working-class and precipitate a socialist revolution (REY, 1973: 12-13 and 87), and it was cemented by the introduction of protectionist measures which slowed down the expropriation of the peasantry (DULONG, 1978: 67-68) and stablised the numbers of non-mechanised agricultural units engaged in mixed farming and stock-rearing. However, this strategy increased the prices of agricultural commodities and restricted the development of large-scale industry by limiting the supply of labour (MARX, 1976b: 1075-1076). This accounts partly for the recourse to immigrant labour in periods of economic expansion. But at the end of the war the demographic explosion in France and the need for post-war reconstruction required an intensive process of investment. On this occasion labour shortages and the need to raise agricultural productivity led to a reduction in the degree of protection of agriculture and an acceleration of the second phase of articulation.

(3) Since the third phase only began in the post-war period in France, it is hardly surprising that the process of 'integration' of petty commodity production sometimes assumed a different form from the one posited in Rey's schema (REY, 1973: 87).

Within the peasantry a process of competition between small producers led to the mechanisation of agriculture and the modernisation of methods of production and hence to the strengthening of links with capitalist branches supplying agricultural inputs and finance for investment. At the same time direct capitalist control over the labour process and the nature of the product increased with the rationalisation of methods of distribution and the establishment of contracts with the food processing industries. These changes are associated with the production of relative surplus-value as farmers attempt to reduce the individual value of their product beneath its social value to obtain an additional surplus-value. Moreover, since the decisions of individual capitalists are based on the requirement that they obtain at least the average rate of profit, the price of the product will now include profit on capital advanced by the food-processing industry and interest on capital borrowed to finance investment, so that prices tend to be set equal to prices of production.

This process of competition is connected with the decomposition of petty commodity production and leads to a differentiation within the peasantry. This differentiation is based upon differences in the conditions of production between agricultural units. In some cases it involves the emergence of some layers of the peasantry with relatively large holdings as capitalist farmers employing some wage-labourers while the small and part of the medium peasantry becomes bankrupt and is expropriated. The result is an accelerated expulsion of labour from agriculture, especially day-labourers and family helpers.

In other cases the process of integration is not associated with the emergence of capitalist farms in which the owner advances and valorises his own capital but with the integration of family farms into the circuits of capitalist food processing industries. In this case the male head of the household does not become a wage-labourer and maintains a limited degree of freedom of action, but his control over the labour process and his product is reduced. The result is a qualitative change in the nature of family farms which tend to form an element in a geographically dispersed agricultural enterprise combining these farms with a distribution system and processing plants for agricultural products.

3.3 Regional Differences in the Decline in Agricultural Employment

This model provides a general account of the delayed but accelerated decline in agricultural employment in France and of some of the recent changes in the class structure of agricultural regions. However, the rate of decline of agricultural employment has varied markedly between French regions. GERVAIS, SERVOLIN and WEIL (1965) have shown that at least in the period 1954-1962 the rate of decrease of male agricultural employment was greatest in départements in the north and east of France dominated by large-scale agriculture and was lowest in regions of small-scale agriculture in the south and west of the country in which the share of male employment in agriculture was larger and in which rural areas were less depopulated (see Figures 3 and 4). They attribute these differences to the greater availability of indus-

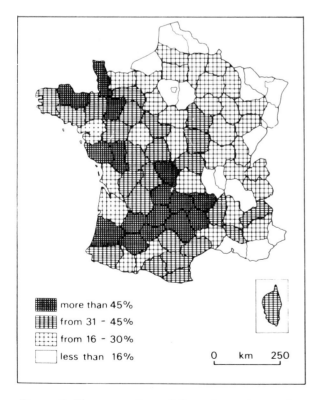

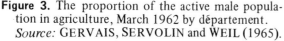

Figure 3. The proportion of the active male population in agriculture, March 1962 by département.
Source: GERVAIS, SERVOLIN and WEIL (1965).

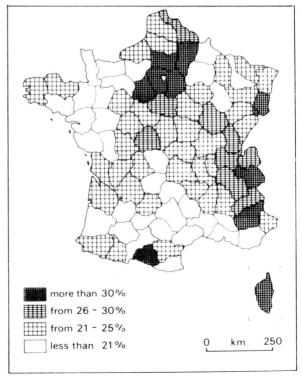

Figure 4. Percentage decline in the active male agricultural population, 1954-1962 by département.

trial employment in the northern and eastern regions. Lipietz criticises this view and suggests that these differences simply reflect the greater resistance of petty commodity production illustrated by the differences between the two main models of agricultural development. It seems more sensible to suggest that these differences are the product of both external and internal forces. The decline in agricultural employment in the mountainous area in the south east of France must partly be attributed to the marginality of much agriculture in this area and not simply to the availability of industrial employment in this part of the country. But these internal forces are also connected with the uneven development of techniques between branches of agricultural production and the emergence of new forms of regional specialisation. There has been a tendency for large farms in the Paris Basin to become specialised in arable farming and for smaller, more labour-intensive units in parts of the west of France to concentrate on milk production (REBOUL, 1977). This process of regional specialisation in different kinds of agricultural production with different labour requirements accounts for part of the differences in the rates of agricultural employment decline between regions, and it indicates the importance of a much more careful analysis of the comparative profitability of different kinds of agricultural activity in different regions and of the role of differential rents in structuring agricultural land use.

The rationalisation of agriculture therefore released a large regionally differentiated supply of labour on which the process of reconstruction and accumulation after the Second World War depended since there was an excess demand for labour in this period. At first employment continued to be concentrated in industrial and highly urbanised regions and especially in the Paris Region where the largest pools of available labour were to be found, while labour released from agriculture and young people unable to find local employment in rural areas tended to migrate via local towns to these more developed regions. This pattern of industrial development was encouraged by the Monnet Plan which concentrated investment in established industrial centres in order to increase industrial production as

quickly as possible in the immediate post-war period. However, the rates of growth of industrial employment in highly urbanised regions subsequently began to decline, and industrialisation began to take place in some rural regions. With this decentralisation of plants requiring relatively unskilled labour the supplies of labour available in some rural areas were increasingly employed locally and emigration was checked. Industrial decentralisation took place first in the Paris Region which was dominated by large-scale capitalist agriculture but in which the rates of decline of agricultural employment were very rapid. It then occurred in regions like the west dominated by petty commodity production and where the new industrial enterprises could employ some of the labour released by the integration of this mode of production. However, it has not been very marked in remote and mountainous areas which continue to be depopulated as agricultural employment declines. But while the availability and cost of labour has had a profound influence on the development of the French space economy in the post-war period, an account of trends in regional employment must also include a consideration of other elements. In particular the decentralisation of industry to rural regions is also a reflection of the rising costs of development in congested regions and the recent restructuring of French industry.

4. Industrial Restructuring and the Regional Problem

The most striking changes in the structure of industrial space in France in recent years have been (1) the tertiarisation of metropolitan centres like Paris and Lyon and the decline in manufacturing employment in these areas with the rationalisation and decentralisation of industry[6] and (2) the decline of industrial employment in traditional industrial areas like the Nord and Lorraine with the reorganisation of basic industries on which these regions depended and the establishment of new complex units of production.[7]

These changes reflect the restructuring of French industry and the evolution of state policy, but both of these are conditioned by the spatial form of development. This means that new trends in the location of industry are based upon certain changes in the actual organisation of the mode of production and in the relevant locational requirements of units of production as well as upon changes in geographical conditions and in the pattern of production costs. Moreover, these spatial forms influence not only the location of units of production but they also condition the evolution of the economy. This makes it necessary to study:

(1) The evolution of the industrial structure of the French economy and changes in the branches in which it specialises, i.e. the position of France in the international division of labour. This is important because different branches have different locational requirements, and will therefore use geographical space in different ways. Thus, one reason for the deindustrialisation of Paris is the specialisation of French capital in consumption good industries which can be reorganised and located outside urban regions and basic industries located in new coastal industrial complexes rather than technologically-advanced capital goods industries which are more likely to be located in major industrial regions.[8]

(2) The changes in the financial structure and in the production processes of individual branches which give rise to new locational needs and new locational patterns. This level of analysis has been emphasised by MASSEY (1978), who has concentrated on concrete studies of specific branches of production. For example, a study of the electronics and electrical engineering sectors in the United Kingdom focused upon the way in which economic processes at a national and international level combined with specific conditions of production and exchange to produce specific forms of financial restructuring and of reorganisation of labour processes. It then showed how these changes have spatial implications such as closures resulting from reductions in capacity, relocation of plant, the establishment of locational hierarchies, etc. (MASSEY and MEEGAN, 1979).

These changes in the relative importance of different industrial branches and the restructuring of individual branches produced by the historical process of accumulation are thus associated with the emergence of new necessary conditions for accumulation e.g. new infrastructural and labour requirements. Since the relevant conditions of accumulation have changed and since they are unequally distributed in geographical space, these changes in the structure of the productive system are associated with the appropriation of new kinds of spatial differentiation and new forms of use of geographical space. These new forms of spatial development are superimposed upon and articulated with the pre-existing structure of space to produce new forms of regional and urban development and new forms of regional inequality. However, it is also necessary to examine two other elements:

(3) The production of the spatial forms which constrain the current phase of development. It is for this reason that is was necessary to provide a historical account of the decline in agricultural employment and the creation of a reserve army of labour which can be employed by industry.

(4) The way in which the spatial form of development conditions the process of social reproduction. For example, the concentration of labour in a small number of rapidly growing urban centres was associated with rising labour and infrastructural costs which slowed up the process of accumulation.

In short, it is necessary to examine the historical process of production of spatial forms and their reciprocal influence on the course of social reproduction, i.e. the determination of spatial forms by social processes and social processes by spatial forms.

4.1 *Industrial Decentralisation from Metropolitan Regions*

The growth and subsequent decline in manufacturing employment in metropolitan areas and especially in the Paris Region exemplifies the role of both the evolution of the structure of the economy in changes in the structure of industrial space and the spatial form of development in the evolution of the economy and space economy.

The continued concentration of employment in metropolitan areas was ultimately limited by the increasing costs associated with this process, and these played an important role in promoting the subsequent deindustrialisation of these zones. These costs included increasing costs of production and circulation for private capitals, increasing costs of state provision of productive infrastructure and increasing costs of provision of private and collective means of consumption necessary for the reproduction of labour-power, and they were reflected in rising wages and increasing state expenditures which both limited the continued accumulation of capital.

These problems largely account for the main characteristics of regional planning when it was first established in France in 1950. It was mainly concerned with the integration of regional and urban planning and with industrial decentralisation from the Paris Region. The state sought to encourage decentralisation through measures designed to restrict industrial development in the Paris Region, through financial aid from the state and local authorities for development in the provinces and through policies relating to the provision of infrastructure and the process of urbanisation. These policies were designed to encourage the decentralisation of industries which did not need central locations and to convert the major agglomerations into centres of financial and research activities. Infrastructural policies played an important role in promoting the decentralisation of industry. Thus, the state developed a transport and communications network adapted to an extension of the spatial division of labour, and it provided productive infrastructure and means of training and reproduction of labour-power required by the new autonomised functions of capital both in major provincial cities and in smaller growth centres. At the same time the internal structure of the main metropolitan centres was reorganised so that it corresponded more closely with the needs of financial and commercial activities and of technically advanced industries which required access to the key advantages of metropolitan areas. These changes in the structure of metropolitan areas were also encouraged by market forces especially increasing land costs and land speculation, which encouraged firms to realise the value of their sites by decentralising manufacturing activities. At the

same time closures in metropolitan areas also helped firms to rationalise production, to modernise plant and equipment and to reduce labour costs.

These early developments in French regional planning illustrate a number of general features of state intervention in advanced capitalist societies. They show how the state reacts albeit imperfectly to contradictions in the process of accumulation. In this case the increasing costs of spatial concentration stemming from the anarchy of capitalist competition led to measures designed to regulate the spatial organisation of capital. But they also show that the provision of infrastructure plays a central role in growth policies pursued by the state to safeguard the process of accumulation. The state seeks to lay the foundations of renewed accumulation by reorganising the general conditions of production and the means of collective consumption, i.e. use values provided by the state such as transport and communications facilities, research and information services, industrial zones, new towns and social, educational and medical facilities (HIRSCH, 1978). Since these infrastructural policies form a central element in regional planning, it is clear that regional planning itself plays an important role in policies designed to promote national economic growth.

However, the decentralisation of industry also reflects some important changes in the organisation of industry which were supported and encouraged by the state. An adequate analysis of these changes and their spatial implications must ultimately be based upon detailed studies of individual branches (MASSEY, 1978), but in the absence of these concrete studies it is only possible to trace broad connections between changes in the structure of industry and trends in the location of employment in France. The general changes in the structure of industry have been discussed by a number of authors including FREYSSENET (1974: 171-216) and LIPIETZ (1977: 82-83),[9] but we shall focus upon the account presented by PALLOIX (1975: 101-120).

Palloix has pointed out how the need to restore the rate of profit during the historical course of the process of accumulation has led to the concentration and centralisation of capital and to the development of finance capital with the fusion of industrial and banking capital. The development of finance capital is associated with important modifications in the structure of industry. It entails the integration of the relatively autonomous spheres of production, circulation and realization under a single decision-making centre combining industrial, commercial and banking capital. This results in the recovery of surplus-value which used to be distributed to these capitals and weakens market regulation. It also entails the restructuring and rationalization of these activities, increasing the speed of circulation of capital and commodities and increasing labour productivity by re-organising the labour process in accordance with the knowledge produced by scientific and technical research. Palloix suggests that the principal characteristic of this stage of industrial development is the autonomisation of intellectual labour and the development of methods of creating, circulating and processing information, but there are also important changes in the direct production process. Finally, there are other changes in the hierarchical structure of these multi-regional companies with a centralisation of major strategic decisions and decentralisation or rather delegation of management and administration not connected with the company's basic strategy. The result is a new sub-division of the functions of capital into four activities:

(1) The highest level is concerned with medium- and long-term planning and decision-making.

(2) The second level is concerned with the creation, circulation and processing of information including basic research, development research, studies connected with the organisation of the labour process and the marketing of products, etc. This work is undertaken by a layer of skilled technicians and engineers directly subordinated to the interests of the financial owners to the company, but it may also lead to the development of separate design engineering firms and service firms.

(3) The third level is concerned with planning and decision-making in connection with the day-to-day activities of the firm. It includes the application and implementation of decisions about new projects, the setting-up of production facilities, the co-ordination of plants and enterprises at a regional, national and international level and the regulation of the actual flow of production operations. This level is growing rapidly.

(4) The last level is concerned with the production activities themselves. These are subdivided in their turn into various stages of manufacture and assembly, as the continual reorganisation of the direct labour process tends to fragment skills into separate and repetitive tasks. These changes combined with the tendency to introduce flow processes and automation into production have repercussions for both the quantity and quality of labour required in the direct production process.

The multi-regional company is a complex combination of these productive and unproductive activities, and it now plays a central role in advanced capitalist economies. In the case of France multi-regional enterprises employed more than 60% of industrial employees, produced about 65% of industrial value-added and accounted for more than 78% of industrial investment in 1970 according to regional accounts which admittedly excluded firms with less than five employees (BRIQUEL, 1975: 41).

These levels and activities can be separated from one another and, given an adequate development of transport and telecommunications, located in different places where their different infrastructural and labour requirements can be met, increasing the rate of surplus-value. It is these structural changes and these possibilities which enable these companies to make use of the spatial differentiation in the value of labour-power, in the levels of skill and in the degree of organisation of the labour movement which all stem from the differentiated conditions of formation of the class of free wage-labourers and of reproduction of labour-power in different localities. LOJKINE (1977b: 141-159) argues that each of these separable levels or types of activities corresponds with a specific social and spatial organisation of the general conditions of production necessary for the realisation of each of these functions, and that these differentiated forms of the social division of labour give rise to the specific features of the urban system under state monopoly capitalism. The latter appears as a network of medium towns and provincial, national and international metropolises with appropriate types of infrastructure.

The development of these separable levels and the ways in which these activities use the prevailing forms of spatial differentiation in France leads to a new spatial division of labour (HYMER, 1972; LIPIETZ, 1977; MASSEY, 1978) and especially to the tertiarisation of metropolitan areas and the decentralisation of industrial employment. Broadly speaking capitals characterised by these tendencies use space in the following way:

(1) Levels 1 and 2, i.e. the central managerial control functions and the activities connected with research, design and development, are located in central metropolitan regions which have close links with business centres, centres of design engineering and research and centres of technological and scientific education and where there are high proportions of managerial and skilled technical strata. These regions become the centres of control of the valorisation process of finance capital and ultimately of the labour process. In France the main centre of this kind is the Paris Region, but to reduce congestion some of these activities possessing a certain degree of financial autonomy and technological control are located in provincial metropolises, e.g. Lyon or even Nantes and Rennes in the case of electronics, and Toulouse in the case of aeronautical engineering.

(2) Skilled manufacture, which forms one part of level 4, is typically located in regions with a high proportion of skilled labour and an average level of wages. These conditions presuppose an industrial tradition corresponding at least to the stage large-scale industry.

Indeed these regions are frequently old centres of nineteenth-century industry. However, most of them have not been able to maintain their former dominance with the emergence of a new division of labour because of the lack of a diversified industrial structure, the rigidity of ownership of capital

and, according to Lipietz, the displacement of profits by unequal exchange. With the continued decline and rationalisation of traditional industries and with standardisation and automation releasing capital from its old ties to skilled labour, skilled manufacture is likely to become less important, and these regions face continuing industrial decline. However in some of these regions the decline in industrial employment is associated with the growth of level 1 and level 2 activities. In this case the major cities may become sub-centres managing the local valorisation process and labour process of finance capital. At the same time other parts of these regions may become locations for new externally-controlled plants engaged in manufacture and assembly.

(3) Mobile plants requiring semi-skilled or unskilled labour and needing few links with other local units of production tend to be located in regions with available supplies of relatively unskilled, cheap and non-militant labour provided their basic infrastructural needs are met. These plants include both small- and medium-sized assembly plants which are relatively labour-intensive (e.g. electronics and electrical goods) but which can be set up in small- and medium-sized towns, and plants requiring relatively large amounts of unskilled labour even in relatively capital-intensive plants (e.g. heavy engineering and the car industry) which are located in larger towns and whose labour may be drawn from large catchment areas. These investments take place in rural areas where the rationalisation of agriculture or the dissolution of non-capitalist modes of production have created pools of relatively cheap labour, e.g. by releasing female family helpers from small-scale agriculture. But they also take place in traditional industrial regions which were dominated by a small number of industrial branches in the period of large-scale industry but where these industries have now collapsed resulting in a devaluation of the skills and reduction in the status of the existing labour force. Some local labour and especially female labour is subsequently incorporated into externally dominated circuits of capital in the process of reconversion of these regions. However, to the extent that industrial traditions and industrial processes that have not yet been deskilled are preserved

this set of regions also falls into the second group.

It is with this schematic account of the use of space by monopoly capital that we can begin to explain the deindustrialisation of metropolitan regions like the Paris Region, the industrialisation of rural regions observed in the first section of this essay, and also the location of some new employment in old industrial zones. This does not mean that the role of state intervention is underestimated but merely that it alone cannot be seen as altering the course of development of industrial space in France and that it should be situated in the context of these developments in the structure of industry and its locational requirements. State intervention facilitates these changes in the structure of industry, and the effectiveness of regional planning depends largely upon the extent to which it is compatible with the new spatial division of labour stemming from this reorganisation of industry.

These new investments in both former rural areas and old industrial centres have a number of important effects on the economic and social structures of these regions. The relocation of plant in these areas and the decline of traditional employment modifies the operation of local labour markets. The implantation of new factories is associated with a deskilling of direct labour, a reduction in the wage and often a replacement of male by female labour. In fact there has been an acceleration in the rate of growth of female activity rates since 1962 despite the rapid decline in the number of family helpers in agriculture. This has been especially marked in some areas of recent industrialisation such as the West and Basse Normandie, Centre and Bourgogne in the Paris Basin where the number of female employees has grown rapidly and where women account for a relatively high proportion of industrial employees.

The restructuring of these regional economies is also associated with an increase in unemployment which cannot be simply attributed to the recent recession in advanced capitalist countries since it also reflects changing local labour-market conditions. LIPIETZ (1977: 88-89) suggests that this is usually due to the fact that the creation of employment transforms a 'latent reserve army' into a 'floating reserve army' (MARX, 1976a: 794-802 and HOLLAND, 1976: 41-43). In rural areas there was substantial under-employment or disguised unemployment. As soon as new firms locating in these areas sought local wage-labour, this large potential demand for employment was revealed but always exceeded the available number of jobs. However its conversion into a floating reserve army and dependence on wage-labour is irreversible, especially with the reorganisation of agricultural production (CARRERE, CATIN and LAMANDE, 1978: 48-50). In the case of the old industrial centres their reconversion is associated both with redundancies and the devaluation of labour in traditional industries and the appearance of new strata of women and young people seeking employment both of which increase regional unemployment.

The relation between these new plants and the local economy is usually fairly limited, since these investments do not usually depend upon the interpenetration of their production processes with the production processes of other branches forming part of the regional economy. Nor do they create these interdependencies since they continue to operate inter-regionally maintaining links with centres of supply of raw materials and semi-finished goods and with downstream production processes or markets outside the region. LOJKINE (1977a: 145) cites a study by Boussard of the effects of the location of a plant belonging to a large electronics company, AOIP, in a small industrial town in Brittany. Having pointed out that the head office, administration and skilled manufacturing jobs were located in Paris and that the local assembly plant employed mainly unskilled workers, Boussard states that:

"AOIP was to be a propulsive industry with catalytic effects on the other units with which it had transactions. *In fact, it has no multiplier effects:* none of its purchases are made within the region. *It has no polarisation effect:* no local factory does subcontracting work for it. *It has no accelerator effect:* its presence is not bringing about investments in local firms. Finally, it has no complementation effect: *it is content with the infrastructural investment made by the local authorities*" (quoted in LOJKINE, *ibid.*).

Finally these changes in the structure of industrial space are also connected with recent changes in the pattern of migration and urban growth in France. There has been a decline in the rate of population growth in urban areas. The most pronounced declines were recorded for larger urban areas and especially for the Paris agglomeration. In the intercensal period 1968-1975 the fastest rates of growth were recorded for urban settlements with between 100 and 200 thousand inhabitants. On the other hand the rate of population growth increased in larger rural settlements and the rate of decline became less pronounced in medium-sized rural communes (INSEE, 1977: 28-29). These changes cannot simply be attributed to a process of suburbanisation since they also reflect changes in the location of employment and especially the decentralisation of plants employing local labour and requiring few links with other local enterprises.

The argument developed in this section provides a preliminary account of some new trends in the location of employment which are having a marked effect on the geography of France, although the continued weakness of regional economies whose industrialisation depends on the location of plants requiring few links with other local enterprises and attracted by the availability of cheap unskilled labour should not be underestimated. The argument itself can only be elaborated by the completion of concrete studies of specific branches of production. These studies would also show that the development of multi-regional companies and their forms of appropriation of geographical space do not follow a simple economic logic. Instead the whole process is one of class struggles in which the reorganisation of the structure of industry and the recomposition of the working class will be resisted by the dominated classes and in which the development of mobile forms of capital will be restricted by for example connections with fixed capital and landed interests. There will also be conflicts over the locational strategies of mobile enterprises. For example, there are likely to be conflicts between small and medium local capitals and even large regional capitals based in a single branch and national or international capitals which will usually, have different infrastructural needs and do not have to take account of the political interests of dominant regional classes. These kinds of contradiction often crystallize around questions connected with land policies, infrastructural policies or policies about industrial location.[10] It is for this reason that it is frequently necessary for the relation between the state and local societies to be reconstituted to facilitate the reorganisation of industrial space. In short, the analysis of changes in the structure of industrial branches and their use of geographical space must encompass the social and political aspects of these processes and their effects.

4.2 The Formation of 'Complex Units of Production'

So far we have focused upon trends in regional employment and especially in regional industrial employment. The regional distribution of industrial value-added and investment reveals a rather different picture, and ultimately draws attention to the importance of some large-scale investments in basic industries in changing the structure of geographical space in France.

In 1970 industrial value-added and aggregate industrial investment were strongly concentrated in the industrial regions in the north and east of France, i.e. the Paris Region, Rhône-Alpes, the Nord and Lorraine, and were under-represented in the relatively under-industrialised regions in the south and west of the country including those with rapid rates of growth of manufacturing employment. On the other hand, value-added per employee exceeded the national average in the Paris Region and Lorraine and in Haute Normandie, Provence and Aquitaine reflecting the relative importance of highly capital-intensive industries in the last three regions. But it is the geographical distribution of industrial investment per employee in 1970 which reflects most clearly the significance of major investments in capital-intensive industries in recent years. It was highest in Provence (12,408 francs per employee), Haute Normandie (11,245 francs) and Languedoc (10,135 francs).[11] The high level of investment per employee on the Mediterranean coast reflects the effect of investments in oil and petrochemical industries and in the iron and steel industry, while Haute Norman-die includes the Lower Seine with its complex of oil and chemical industries. Another major industrial pole has been established on the coast in the Nord. In other words, an exam-ination of the geographical distribution of value-added and industrial investment per employee brings out more clearly than that of manufacturing employment the quest-ion of the development of major coastal industrial poles at Le Havre, Dunkirk and Fos-sur-Mer since the 1960s.

These projects have played an important role in reshaping the geography of France. Two of them have been the object of specific studies. The formation of the port and industrial complex at Dunkirk has been examined by CASTELLS and GODARD (1974) while the one at Fos-sur-Mer has been studied by BLEITRACH and CHENU (1975), ROBERT (1974) and CULTIAUX (1975). The complex at Dunkirk is composed of an iron and steel plant and productive units connected with metallurgical industries, shipbuilding and oil refining. The central element in the complex at Fos-sur-Mer is also an integrated shore-based iron and steel plant. In addition, it includes plants producing metal products, an Esso oil refinery established in 1965 and plants connected with the chemical industry. The development of an oil port and oil storage area and the construction of an oil pipeline system have also been associated with an expansion of the capacity of refineries belonging to Shell, BP and CFR at Berre and Martigues and the development of petro-chemical plants in the region.

The development of these new coastal indus-trial zones indicates the way in which the evolution of the economy and the establish-ment of new conditions of production and exchange have led to a revaluation of some of the qualities of coastal sites. In particular, the increased use of imported supplies of energy and raw materials, the developments in maritime transport and the creation of large production units in basic industries to obtain scale economies have increased the import-ance of coastal sites with deep-water access and large supplies of available land as long as they are provided with appropriate infras-tructures. It follows that an account of the structure and development of these projects

must include an examination of the restruc-turing of basic industries in France since the 1960s and their new locational requirements and an account of the more recent evolution of government policy. This section of the paper therefore outlines the recent develop-ment of French regional policy and its inte-gration with policies designed to increase the international competitiveness of French in-dustry. Then it seeks to show how the im-plantation of a new steel plant in the new industrial pole at Fos resulted from the joint strategy of the iron and steel industry and the French government and from the specific forms of restructuring imposed on this branch by the exigencies of international competition rather than from the elaboration of a project compatible with the proclaimed objectives of regional planning.

It has already been pointed out that the early stages of regional planning in France were concerned with the regulation of urban de-velopment and industrial decentralisation from the Paris Region. BLEITRACH and CHENU (1975) have pointed out that after 1955 and especially after 1962 regional planning was integrated with and subordin-ated to the medium-term plans for national economic expansion. This was associated with major changes in the institutional and administrative framework of regional planning and the introduction of more selective forms of intervention. They argue that the main regional planning policies developed in the period between 1962 and 1965 were con-cerned with the development of internationally competitive industrial poles combining large-scale modern industry and appropriate in-frastructure and the promotion of *métropoles d'équilibre*. The industrial poles were to be

established in the Paris and Lyon agglomera-tions and on the coast at Le Havre, Dunkirk and Fos. In the rest of France industrial development would only involve the implan-tation of average-sized plants in accordance with the size of the labour force available in each urban centre and the surrounding rural area. The *métropoles d'équilibre* were in-troduced to reduce congestion in Paris and to promote development in the provinces by re-equilibrating the urban system. They were intended to be regional metropolises with improved transport and communications and services which could become centres of high-level tertiary activities.

Bleitrach and Chenu point out that this concentration of state intervention on a limited number of zones of intensive investment was presented as a correction of previous state policies which had not secured balanced regional development. However, a geographical concentration of investment is not strictly speaking compatible with the social objective of promoting equal regional development while it is implied by the pursuit of international competitiveness in some industrial branches. It therefore seems reasonable to suggest that these changes in regional policy were based upon a recognition of some of the limitations on regional planning in France in this period, and that these new forms of selective intervention also facilitated the use of regional policy to promote increased international competitiveness. Indeed regional planning was explicitly related to this objective in the Fifth Plan (1966-1970) and in the Sixth Plan (1971-1975).

This integration of national and regional planning also stems from the complementarity of some of the activities involved in planning at these levels. Regional planning includes a number of forms of state intervention connected with the reproduction of fixed capital, e.g. land acquisition, the provision of productive infrastructure such as port facilities, transport and communications facilities and public utilities, and the provision of loans and grants to industry. But it also entails the provision of infrastructure required for the reproduction of labour-power. The state is involved in planning the process of urbanisation and in providing, with the help of local authorities, housing and other collective facilities necessary for the local labour force. Regional planning is therefore one important area in which devalorised capital is advanced, i.e. capital which received less than the average rate of profit and whose central role is to contribute to a growth strategy by redistributing surplus-value between private capitals and providing privileged conditions for accumulation in leading industries, although it may also be diverted to meet certain social objectives including balanced regional development. The integration of national and regional planning therefore stems in part

from the use in regional planning of devalorised capital and from its connection with infrastructural policies. In this period it facilitated the subordination of regional planning to the need to promote the international competitiveness of French industry especially because it made it possible to plan differentiated and selective forms of provision of devalorised capital in favour of leading industrial and financial groups. Consequently, the change in regional planning from a relatively undifferentiated to a selective form of intervention enabled it to form part of a policy of mobilising resources largely in favour of the dominant monopolistic fraction of the power *bloc*.

This change in the nature and priorities of regional planning partly reflected conjunctural political and economic conditions in France during this period. CASTELLS (1976: 192-195) has pointed out that during the Fifth Republic (1958-1969) the power of the executive was reinforced and the administration obtained increased autonomy and that this led to an expansion of the technocracy. When it sought to promote the political and economic power of France in a period of European economic integration, the technocracy was then in a position to pursue a policy of promoting monopolistic accumulation. The contradictions of this process and the economic crisis subsequently led to changes in the structure and role of the state and to changes in regional and urban policies. However, the point is that specific political and economic conditions played a central role in explaining how specific industrial projects forming part of a strategy for national economic growth could become the starting-point and rationale of large-scale planning operations presented as regional development projects.[1][2]

In the case of the industrial pole at Fos the implantation of an iron and steel plant owned by the *Société lorraine et méridionale de laminage continu* (SOLMER) stemmed from an agreement between the state and the Lorraine-based Wendel-Sidelor company, the main steel producer in France. SOLMER was initially controlled by the *Société lorraine de laminage continu* (SOLLAC) in which 65% of the capital was owned in 1970 by Wendel-Sidelor. The decision to locate at Fos was officially announced in 1969.

The location of an iron and steel plant at Fos had been envisaged as early as 1955, and the local bourgeoisie and local authorities began to purchase land from 1962. From 1964 the project was increasingly managed by the central state. The law on autonomous maritime ports passed in 1965 removed the development of the port and industrial zone from local control, and central control over the process of urbanisation was increased by the establishment of the *Organisation pour les études d'aménagement de l'aire métropolitaine* (OREAM) for Marseille in 1966 to plan the development of the metropolitan area. A whole series of other missions by-passing local political structures were also established, although the state subsequently sought to re-establish links with the local population via consultative bodies.

At the same time joint planning between the state and the iron and steel industry was proceeding. During the early part of the period covered by the Fifth Plan (1966-1970) the government lent 2.7 thousand million francs from the *Fonds de développement économique et sociale* (FDES) to the iron and steel industry in the framework of the '*Plan professionnel*' mainly for the modernisation of the industry in Lorraine. But towards the end of this period Lorraine was increasingly considered not to be a viable location for the steel industry despite the loans and infrastructure provided by the state for the industry's development in this region. This led to further financial restructuring of the industry and a reorganisation of production in Lorraine and resulted in more redundancies. For example, the reorganisation announced at the end of 1971 was to lead to 12,350 redundancies and an effective loss of 10,650 jobs (FREYSSENET and IMBERT, 1975: 52-53). These redundancies occurred in addition to job losses in the mines and in the textile industry in this region.

The development of a new integrated shore-based plant had been contemplated by de Wendel since 1963. In the existing technical and economic conditions this kind of plant had the lowest costs of production, partly because access to a deep-water port would allow provisioning with high-grade foreign minerals by large tonnage ore-carriers and access to cheap supplies of American coking-

coal, and because it would afford a good position for seaborne exports. Such a new plant could have been located in a number of places, but it was obvious that the new plant would represent a new stage in the restructuring of the French industry and a major change in the location of steel production in France.

The choice of Fos rather than Le Havre or even a location on the Atlantic coast is frequently attributed to the influence of the government rather than the company. It is of course true that location at Le Havre would have reinforced the disequilibrium between northern and eastern France and the rest of the country, but it is probable that Wendel-Sidelor also opted for location at Fos in the under-industrialised south because it was thought at the time to offer the best conditions for a new strategy designed to restore the rate of profit (ROBERT, 1974).

The availability of loans and grants was obviously one attraction of the site. The state lent 1850 million francs on very favourable terms from the FDES for the construction of the first stage of the project. With additional loans from banks and financial institutions SOLMER had to advance only 2000 million francs of the 6000 million originally thought to be necessary for this stage of the project. When the project faced financial difficulties in Autumn 1972 and Wendel-Sidelor sought further help from the government, the state provided an additional cheap loan of 800 million francs on the condition that a regrouping take place between SOLLAC and the *Union sidérurgique du Nord* (USINOR) which already owned the shore-based plant at Dunkirk. This agreement was concluded in 1973. With the subsequent participation of the German company Thyssen which took a 5% share in SOLMER, the two main steel producers in France each held 47.5% of the capital. The new loan from the state and additional private loans meant that SOLMER had to provide only 1000 million francs of the 7700 million necessary for the construction of the first stage of the project.

It has also been pointed out that the choice of this location formed part of an offensive commercial strategy orientated towards new export markets in the Mediterranean and

Middle East which were thought to have more growth potential than those in North and North-West Europe. However, the success of this strategy would depend upon the competitiveness of French steel products in these markets and hence on the competititiveness of the output produced by the new plant. This was expected to be enhanced by a number of features of the site at Fos including the relatively low construction costs and the availability of local raw materials but it depended mainly on the organisation of the labour process and the composition of the labour force.

The port and industrial zone at Fos possessed the advantage that it afforded a large expanse of flat land and the companies locating there were able to obtain very large sites for their own use at very low prices. The original site amounted to 5520 ha. Out of the 2935 ha allocated by the *Port Autonome de Marseille* (PAM) at the beginning of 1974, 1560 had been sold to SOLMER of which it was using only about 400, and 275 had been sold to Ugine-Aciers, although it was using only 15 ha. Similarly, ICI was using only 12 out of 132 ha allocated to it. The allocation of a large proportion of the available land for industrial development limited the possible implantation of other enterprises on the site and led the PAM to attempt to extend the industrial zone to the north-west. The value of these large industrial sites was of course enhanced by the provision by the state of appropriate infrastructure such as port facilities and public utilities, e.g. power stations and water supplies. A second advantage lay in the fact that the area was relatively unpopulated enabling the companies to make relatively low initial investments in antipollution measures. This had unfortunate consequences for the local landscape, local ecological balances and the quality of the lives of the inhabitants of the region, but reduced the costs of the new investments in the industrial and port zone.

However, the main advantages for the steel company stemmed from the reorganisation of the labour process and the recomposition of the labour force. A whole series of conditions at Fos allowed a form of organisation of the labour force which was more advantageous than those prevailing in Lorraine. First, the company was able to limit direct employment to management and production activities and to use sub-contractors or temporary workers for other tasks such as maintenance and repairs, distribution, transport of personnel and so on. This not only enabled SOLMER to realise a number of economies but it also contributed to the disorganisation of sections of the labour force. Secondly, a large proportion of the labour force employed not only in the construction of the plant but also in production activities was composed of workers from other parts of France and foreign workers. Workers brought from Lorraine accounted for 2200 out of 3400 employees in the steel plant at the end of 1973. The recruitment of workers from Lorraine eased the rationalisation of the industry in that region and the early stages of production at Fos especially by providing skilled labour which was not available locally. But at the end of 1975 only about 2600 out of almost 6500 employees in the SOLMER plant came from the local départements of Gard, Vaucluse and Bouches-du-Rhone. Employees from these départements filled 29.8% of skilled jobs and only 58.3% of unskilled jobs. Many of the other unskilled jobs were filled by immigrant workers. This kind of recruiting strategy which created divisions in the labour force combined with the geographical isolation of the zone could be expected to limit trade-union militancy.

One result of this strategy is that the project has not resolved the problems of local unemployment and underemployment. This has occurred partly because the project has not provided jobs adapted to the employment needs of the region and its local industrial traditions, but it also reflects the limited opportunities for the local labour force to adapt to the needs of the new enterprises because of the inadequate development of training programmes. Investment in the area has also created very little female employment despite the very marked levels of female under-employment in the region. Moreover, the new plants are unlikely to encourage the development of other related industries in the region. Instead they will tend to remain 'cathedrals in the desert' with limited multiplier effects on the local economy. Indeed, the firms located in the region would probably not wish to encourage the proliferation of other plants in the zone lest it increase competition between firms over employment and wages and reduce their ability to select their own employees on the local labour market. Finally the restructuring of the regional economy which is partly related to the local impact of the new project has contributed to the deindustrialisation of Marseille and the rationalisation of local industry.

With these changes in the local economy the local bourgeoisie had become orientated towards land speculation and property development, and the process of urbanisation which has accompanied the development of the industrial zone has posed many problems. The central state was meant to plan the process of urban development in the metropolitan region through the medium of various institutions and to provide with the help of local authorities housing and other collective facilities necessary for the local labour force. However, investment in housing has been inadequate contributing to an escalation in house and land prices, while there have been delays in the provision of necessary collective facilities and marked increases in the degree of social segregation.

Thus the location of steel production and the development of an industrial and port zone at Fos did not conform with the declared social objectives of regional and urban planning. This occurred because this project did not provide a means for resolving the problems of employment in the region and because it was associated with some negative effects such as pollution problems which gave rise to belated and limited measures of control and a chaotic process of urbanisation. Both BLEITRACH and CHENU (1975), and ROBERT (1974) attribute these discrepancies not to failures in the application of otherwise satisfactory planning principles but to the logic of the project and to the gap between the real objectives and the official planning objectives which merely had an ideological role. The main objective was to develop an internationally competitive port and industrial complex centred on the production of steel with a key position in the international division of labour. This is indicated by the fact that a number of circumstances prevailing at the time made Fos a good loca-

tion for a new iron and steel plant and that the relocation of steel production was part of an attempt by the steel industry and the state to promote the international competitiveness of the French industry. In this period regional policy was one of the forms of state intervention which could be used to attain this end.

Subsequent events have cast some doubt upon the viability of the project. There was to be a second stage in the development of the iron and steel plant expanding capacity from 3.5 million tonnes per year in 1974 to 7.0 million tonnes in 1978. The second stage of the project has now been postponed partly because of the recent recession in the steel industry. However, there are also increasing doubts about the long-term future of the whole project because of the possibility of changes in the French productive system with the decentralisation of basic industries and the establishment of a new international division of labour. This illustrates some of the problems of planning in capitalist societies. The priority granted to production for profit means that the possibility and nature of investments depends upon their profitability and not upon their ability to meet human needs. But if the conditions of profitable production should subsequently change it is possible even for massive infrastructural investments to be under-utilised.

5. Conclusion

The main aim of this paper has been to illustrate a method of analysing regional problems in capitalist countries. It began by focusing upon some recent changes in the structure of the French space economy which are frequently discussed in the geographical literature. But these changes were explained by certain aspects of the evolution of the French social formation rather than by purely spatial processes, although it was also pointed out that the development of the social formation and the forms of spatial development have in their turn been conditioned by the structure of geographical space.

Thus it was argued that the need to provide cheaper agricultural products and a supply of labour necessary for the process of accumulation at the end of the Second World War led to the accelerated decline of petty commodity production. Combined with the rationalisation of capitalist agriculture this led to a marked but regionally differentiated decline in agricultural employment. Initially this new labour force tended to be employed in established industrial and urban areas. But under the impact of increasing infrastructural and labour costs and with a restructuring of some industrial branches some relatively unskilled manufacturing employment was decentralised to rural regions. The decline in agricultural employment and the reorganisation of agriculture combined with the implantation of modern capitalist enterprises in rural regions have in their turn modified local social structures and have necessitated a reconstruction of the relation between the central state and local societies through the formation of new class alliances, the establishment of new political and administrative structures and the elaboration of new regional plans.

The decentralisation of manufacturing employment to rural regions was closely related to the deindustrialisation and tertiarisation of metropolitan regions which stemmed not only from the movement of capital but also from the effects of state regional and urban policies. At the same time there has been a decline and rationalisation of traditional industries which has contributed to the decline of major centres of nineteenth-century industrialisation in areas such as the Nord and Lorraine. The restructuring of basic industries encouraged and supported by the French state has in fact led to their decentralisation with the establishment of large coastal industrial complexes since the 1960s. However, the outcome of both of these processes obviously depended and still depends upon social and political forces as well as economic ones, and these changes in the structure of the space-economy have important social and political dimensions. Thus, it has been pointed out that the formation of new industrial complexes requires the establishment of new political institutions to plan the provision of productive infrastructure and leads to changes in the class structure of the receiving regions. Similarly, the concentration of certain kinds of non-production activities in metropolitan areas leads to marked changes in the composition of local employment. In this case there is likely to be an increase in the proportion of higher social strata which has important consequences for the structure of local political power and the provision of housing and other collective facilities in metropolitan areas.

These changes in the structure of the French space economy have been interpreted as aspects of the establishment of a new spatial division of labour connected with the transition to a new phase of capitalist development. The earlier decline of rural areas resulted from changing relations between agriculture and industry, but the marked redirection in the evolution of the space economy stemmed from a subsequent restructuring of French industry under the impact of the law of international value and intervention in the economic sphere by the French state. These changes in the development of the economy and the space economy are connected with the worst economic crisis since the 1930s. It has been suggested that this crisis stems from the contradictions of the previous phase of accumulation including the geographical concentration of economic development, and that it is helping to create the conditions necessary for renewed accumulation although the outcome of the present crisis has still not been settled.

But it has also been pointed out that this transition to a new phase of capitalist development has at the same time important social and political dimensions. It has been associated with the disruption of established local social and political structures, it has modified the class structure of the various regions and it has led to the formation of new class alliances and the establishment of new political institutions to plan the new spatial division of labour. Indeed it is because there have been changes in the nature of employment and because these social and political changes are so inextricably bound up with the economic development of the regions that attention was drawn in the introduction to the need to broaden our conception of spatial development to include the qualitative and superstructural changes in regional economies and societies as well as quantitative trends in the location of employment.

The method advocated in this paper therefore begins to examine some of the phenomena discussed by DULONG (1976; 1978). In his work on the regional problem in France he has emphasized the disruption of the relation between the state and local societies where this relation is considered to exist largely at a superstructural level. France was composed of a mosaic of local societies integrated politically and ideologically with the central state through the medium of local relay institutions dominated by local notables. The role of these mechanisms of integration was to organise and maintain the consent of the local dominated classes to bourgeois hegemony in France by concealing class divisions and limiting the possibilities of mobilisation of the dominated classes. But the transition to a new phase of capitalist development modified the class structure of the regions and disrupted these mechanisms of integration producing a crisis in the relation between the state and local societies. These superstructural processes are reflected in the emergence of new forms of regionally-based social protest and in the reorganisation of state apparatuses and state policies to establish a new mode of class domination and direction reintegrating local societies with the state and maintaining bourgeois hegemony.

This account of the regional question in France is constructed by generalising from studies of a number of regionally-based social movements. In analysing this object it advances well beyond studies which allude to the process of uneven economic development under capitalism and then focus upon the contradictions between this process and the existence of distinctive cultural traditions, and it poses the central question of the relationship between regionally-based social movements and class relations in capitalist societies. But the analysis still tends to take the process of economic development as a basis to which a sociological analysis of superstructural forms is simply added. It therefore tends to remain a sociology based upon an impoverished technical conception of the economy and employing a mode of analysis which does not sufficiently allow political and cultural determinations to influence the course of the process of economic reproduction.

A political economy of regional development

must combine the analysis of superstructural processes with the analysis of the process of uneven economic development. This means that it must develop formulations based upon a historical conception of the relation between the state and society in which the economic sphere is understood as embracing both material production and the production of social relations and which includes concrete analysis of the political processes through which the requirements of capital are translated into specific kinds of state action and specific forms of organisation of the state. But to reproduce in thought the concrete forms of spatial development it must also combine economic analysis of the reciprocal relations between spatial forms on the one hand and the reorganisation of industrial branches and the economic aspects of state intervention on the other hand with regionally-based studies of the social and political structure of localities. This may seem to be a rather ambitious project, but it is the only way in which geographers can develop an adequate account of their object of analysis.

Acknowledgements — I would like to thank Peter Cromar, Simon Duncan and Diane Perrons for their comments on an earlier version of this paper, and Susan Rowland for drawing the figures.

Notes

1. The statistical evidence cited in this section was calculated from statistics published by the *Institut national de la statistique et des études économiques* especially in the annual publications entitled *Statistiques et indicateurs des régions françaises.*

   The average annual rates of growth of employment for the intercensal periods were computed by solving for r in the equation:
   $X_t/X_s = (1 + r)^{t-s}$, where X_t denotes employment in year t and where $t-s$ was set equal to 7.825 for the period 1954-1962, 5.985 for the period 1962-1968 and 6.975 for the period 1968-1975 (INSEE, 1977: 16).

2. The fastest average annual rates of decline of total employment were recorded in Limousin (-1.51%), Auvergne (-1.06%), Brittany (-1.00%), Aquitaine (-0.76%) and Poitou-Charentes (-0.70%). In these regions agriculture accounted for between 35.1 and 51.4% of regional employment in 1954.

3. This model has been introduced because it provides a number of general hypotheses about the evolution of agricultural employment in advanced capitalist countries. It obviously needs to be developed in a way which can account for the specific forms of development in different countries and this may necessitate some modification of the argument. For a discussion of these processes as they operated in Ireland see PERRONS (1978).

4. It is necessary to explain more fully the reasons for population growth and the fragmentation of holdings. In the Irish case fragmentation occurred in the period between 1780 and 1820 when some pasture was converted to more intensive arable production, when there were rising prices for the marketed surplus and when the introduction of the potato as a subsistence crop made it possible to produce subsistence goods from a smaller amount of land. It was these developments which encouraged landlords to subdivide land and encouraged population growth, and it was only subsequently that these holdings became less viable and surplus population appeared. Population growth is a dependent and not an independent variable. See PERRONS (1978).

5. The fact that agricultural producers provided part of their own subsistence needs may have lowered their reproduction costs. But this thesis can only be elaborated by developing an account of the formation of prices of agricultural commodities. These prices were presumably determined partly by conditions in the international market and not by the costs of the marginal French producer. With above-average costs these producers could only survive by accepting a low standard of living.

6. In the Paris region there has been an accelerated closure of small- and medium-sized firms and a decentralisation of some kinds of manufacturing employment. More recently some tertiary employment has also been decentralised.

7. This concept was introduced by Bettelheim and was subsequently used to refer to major industrial and port complexes by CASTELLS and GODARD (1974).

8. MICHON-SAVARIT (1975) shows how two contrasting political scenarios involving the emergence of a world dominated by two or five major political blocs will have different implications for the position of France in the international division of labour. This in turn has implications for the development of the French regions which are studied by examining the way in which the evolution of different industrial branches and their use of geographical space will determine the position of the regions in the international division of labour and by examining the probable evolution of regional economies according to their sectoral structures. Broadly she points out that:

(a) in a bipolar world composed of two blocs (USA and USSR) there will be a concentration of research and advanced industries in the USA and French development will be based on traditional industries with little change in the pattern of regional imbalance, whereas

(b) in a multipolar world composed of five blocs there will be some development in France of research and advanced industries and a decentralisation of some traditional industries leading to a relative decline in the Paris Region, more serious problems of reconversion for regions whose economies were based on traditional industries and the growth of some regions in the south of France with the development of economies in the Mediterranean Basin.

9. FREYSSENET (1974: 171-216) emphasises the way in which the possibility and indeed the necessity of undertaking an increasing part of production with unskilled labour has contributed to the decentralisation of industry from the Paris Region.

LIPIETZ (1977: 82-83) focuses upon the analysis of individual branches. He argues that a new division of labour is emerging within the branches dominated by monopoly capital. This gives rise to different stages of production within a single branch circuit (e.g. conception, manufacture, assembly) which can be located in different, unequally developed regions with different values of labour-power.

This process results in the establishment of a new interregional division of labour with different areas specialising in activities corresponding to different stages in the process of producing commodities.

10. This problem is discussed in the study of local politics in Roanne where medium local capitals adopted opposing attitudes to the development of a new industrial estate (PICKVANCE, 1977: 233-235).

11. Briquel points out that in 1970 national industrial value-added was concentrated in the Paris Region (28.8%) Rhône-Alpes (11.5%), the Nord (9.0%) and Lorraine (6.1%), and it was low in Basse Normandie, Brittany, Poitou-Charentes, Limousin and Languedoc which each accounted for less than 2% (BRIQUEL, 1975: 17). Regional industrial investment can obviously fluctuate

from year to year with changing economic conditions and because of the quantitative importance of some individual investment projects. However, in 1970 the geographical distribution of aggregate industrial investment closely resembled that of industrial value-added. It was concentrated in the Paris Region (22.6%), Rhône-Alpes (10.5%), the Nord (9.3%) and Lorraine (8.6%), and it was low in Basse Normandie, Brittany, Poitou-Charentes, Limousin, Auvergne and Languedoc which each accounted for less than 2% (IBID, pp. 33-34).

12. BLEITRACH and CHENU (1975) make a number of important points about the nature of planning in contemporary France. They argue that the Plan is an instrument of general planning between fractions of the dominant class which results in an effective programming of certain activities and an agreement on the broad aspects of government policy. They also point out that in the formulation of the Plan it is changes in the nature of private interests which give rise to new forms of state intervention and not vice-versa. State intervention involves a subordination of public to private interests and not private to public interests (pp. 379-380). But they also argue that regional planning in contemporary France is characterised by a contradiction between:
(1) its role as an element of state economic policy which promotes the interests of the dominant classes and hence creates unequal regional development; and
(2) its role in maintaining social cohesion by ideological and more importantly material means which implies a diversion of resources from accumulation and hence constitutes action against the immediate interests of the dominant classes (pp. 367-375).
The problem with this statement is that it is only true at a high level of generality, and that the formulation of this position in their paper appears to be an unhistorical generalisation from one period in the development of French regional policy.

Appendix: Some Concepts taken from Marxist Political Economy

This paper employs a number of concepts from Marxist political economy. One of the central ideas is that the evolution of the space economy depends upon the laws governing the development of various forms of capital of which the most important is industrial capital advanced in the spheres of agricultural and industrial production. In the *circuit of industrial capital* a sum of money M is advanced to purchase commodity inputs C comprising means of production MP and labour-power LP bought respectively on the commodity and labour markets with the constant and variable parts of capital. It is initially assumed that these commodity inputs are bought at their values, i.e. the amounts of socially necessary labour-time required for their production. Thus, labour-power is purchased with an amount of money equal to the value of the consumption goods necessary for the reproduction of the labourer.

The purchase of these inputs presupposes their availability as *commodities* and the existence of *particular social relations of production*, i.e. the existence of a class of free wage-labourers separated from the means of production and of a class of capitalists holding a minimum amount of money wealth. These preconditions are initially established during the process of *primitive accumulation*. This process is incompletely examined in this paper as a process of articulation of modes of production. In the next stage these commodity inputs leave the sphere of circulation and enter the sphere of production as the elements of productive capital P. They are then used in the capitalist process of *production* to produce new commodities C'. The value of these new commodities exceeds the value of the commodity inputs. In the production process the value of the means of production used up is passed on to the new commodities, but the value of labour-power is less than the value added by labour in production, i.e. the use-value of labour-power or the quantity of labour supplied in return for the wage. It is this difference between the value of labour-power and the value added by labour that gives rise to the increment in value. At the end of the production process the produced commodities enter the sphere of circulation and are converted into money form $M' = M + m$ by their sale on the market or *realisation*. Thus the capitalist receives back the original sum advanced plus an increment or excess over the original value, This increment produced because the labourer works for a longer period than is necessary to replace the value of labour-power is called *surplus value*.

The circuit of an individual industrial capital can be represented by a circular flow diagram:

This process whereby industrial capital increases its own value through the addition of surplus-value is called the process of *valorisation of capital*. The rate of surplus-value, i.e. the ratio of surplus-value and variable capital or the ratio of surplus labour and necessary labour, can be increased in two ways when real wages are held constant:

(i) by increasing absolute surplus-value, i.e. by increasing surplus labour time by extending the length of the working-day or by intensifying the labour process to reduce the amount of time the worker is idle, or

(ii) by increasing relative surplus-value, i.e. by reducing the labour-time necessary to reproduce the value of labour-power by increasing labour productivity in the wage-good sector of production.

As the circuit is repeated there is a continual renewal of the production and realisation of surplus-value. If m is consumed unproductively there is a process of *simple reproduction* of commodities, surplus-value and the social relations of production. But if the value of the capital advanced is increased through the transformation of part of surplus-value into additional capital the circuit grows in an outward spiral movement in a process of *extended reproduction* or accummulation of capital. The employment of surplus-value as capital is called *accumulation of capital.*

References

BLEITRACH D. and CHENU A. (1975) L'aménagement: régulation ou approfondissement des contradictions sociales? Un example: Fos-sur-Mer et l'aire métropolitaine Marseillaise, *Environment and Planning A* **7** 367-391.

BRIQUEL V. (1975) Les comptes regionaux des branches industrielles en 1970, *Les Collections de l'Insee*, series R, 21.

CASTELLS M. (1976) Crise de l'Etat, consommation collective et contradictions urbaines In: *La Crise de l'Etat*, N. POULANTZAS (Ed.). Presses Universitaires de France, Paris.

CASTELLS M. and GODARD F. (1974) *Monopolville. L'Entreprise, l'Etat, L'Urbain*, Mouton, Paris.

CARRERE P., CATIN M. and LAMANDE J. (1978) Evolution de la situation économique des régions françaises de 1972à 1977, *Economie et Statistique* **100**, May 39-50.

CULTIAUX D. (1975) L'amenagement de la region Fos-Etang de Berre, *Notes et Etudes Documentaires*, nos. 4 164-4 166, 19 February.

DULONG R. (1976) La crise du rapport Etat/societe locale vue au travers de la politique regionale, In:

La Crise de l'Etat, N. POULANTZAS (Ed.). Presses Universitaires de France, Paris.

DULONG R. (1978) *Les Régions, l'Etat et la Société Locale*, Presses Universitaires de France, Paris.

EMMANUEL A. (1972) *Unequal Exchange. A Study of the Imperialism of Trade*, New Left Books, London.

FREYSSENET M. (1974) *Le Processus de Déqualification - Surqualification de la Force de Travail*, Centre de Sociologie Urbaine, Paris.

FREYSSENET M. and IMBERT F. (1975) *La Centralisation du Capital dans la Sidérurgie 1945-1975*, Centre de Sociologie Urbaine, Paris.

GERVAIS M. SERVOLIN C. and WEIL J. (1965) *Une France sans Paysans*, Editions du Seuil, Paris.

HANNOUN M. and TEMPLE P. (1975) Les facteurs de creation et de localisation des nouvelles unités de production, *Economie et Statistique*, 68, June, 59-70.

HIRSCH J. (1978) The state apparatus and social reproduction: Elements of a theory of the bourgeois State, In: *State and Capital. A Marxist Debate*, J. Holloway S. Picciotto (Eds.). E. Arnold, London.

HOLLAND S. (1976) *Capital versus the Regions*, Macmillan, London.

HYMER S. (1972) The multinational corporation, and the law of uneven development, In: *Economics and World Order from the 1970's to the 1990's*, J. Bhagwati (Ed.). Collier-Macmillan.

INSEE (Institut national de la statistique et des études économiques) (1973), Statistiques et indicateurs des régions francaises, édition 1972, *Les Collections de l'Insee*, series R, 9.

INSEE (1977) Principaux résultats du recensement de 1975, *Les Collections de l'Insee*, series D, 52.

INSEE (1978) Enquête sur l'emploi de mars 1977. Resultats détaillés, *Les Collections de l'Insee*, series D, 53.

LIPIETZ A. (1975) Structuration de l'espace, probleme foncier et aménagement du territoire, *Environment and Planning A* **7** 415-425.

LIPIETZ A. (1977) *Le Capital et son Espace*, F. Maspero, Paris.

LOJKINE J. (1977a) 'Big firms' strategies, urban policy and urban social movements In: *Captive Cities. Studies in the Political Economy of Cities and Regions*, M. Harloe (Ed.). J. Wiley & Sons, London.

LOJKINE J. (1977b) *Le Marxisme, L'Etat et la Question Urbaine*, Presses Universitaires de France, Paris.

MARX K. (1973a) The class struggle in France: 1848-1850, In: *Surveys from Exile*, Penguin Books, Harmondsworth.

MARX K. (1973b) The eighteenth Brumaire of Louis Bonaparte, In: *Surveys from Exile*, Penguin Books, Harmondsworth.

MARX K. (1976a) *Capital. A Critique of Political*

Economy, Vol. 1, Penguin Books, Harmondsworth.

MARX K. (1976b) Results of the immediate process of production, in *Capital,* Vol. 1, Penguin Books, Harmondsworth.

MASSEY D. (1978) Regionalism: some current issues, *Capital and Class, 6.*

MASSEY D. and MEEGAN R. (1979) The geography of industrial reorganisation: the spatial effects of the restructuring of the electrical engineering sector under the Industrial Reorganisation Corporation, *Progress in Planning,* **10** (3).

MICHON-SAVARIT C. (1975) La place des regions françaises dans la division internationale du travail: deux scénarios contrastés *Environment and Planning A* 7 449-454.

MUET P. and BOLTON P. (1970) Evolution de l'emploi dans les régions d'après les recensements de 1954, 1962 et 1968, *Les Collections l'Insee,* series R, 4.

PALLOIX C. (1975) *L'Economie Mondiale Capitaliste et les Firmes Multinationales,* Vol. 11, F. Maspero, Paris.

PERRONS D. (1978) The dialectic of region and class in Ireland, Urban and Regional Studies Working Paper 9, University of Sussex, 1978.

PICKVANCE C. (1977) Marxist approaches to the study of urban politics. Divergences among some recent French studies, *International Journal of Urban and Regional Research,* **1**, (2), 219-255.

REBOUL C. (1977) Déterminants sociaux de la fertilité des sols, *Actes de la Recherche en Sciences Sociales,* 17-18, 85-112.

ROBERT G. (1974) L'opération Fos. Un test de l'aménagement capitaliste du territoire, *Urbanisme* **145**, 63-76.

REY P.-P. (1973) *Les Alliances de Classes,* F. Maspero, Paris.

SEYS B. and LAULHE P. (1976) Enquête sur l'emploi de 1976 (Résultats provisoires), *Les Collections de l'Insee,* series D, 48.

Geoforum, Vol. 10, pp.109-116, 1979.
Pergamon Press Ltd. Printed in Great Britain.

The Inner City: In Search of the Problem

RAY FORREST, JOHN LLOYD, * NICK ROGERS
and PETER WILLIAMS, † Birmingham U.K.

Abstract: This paper explores the theoretical content of the inner-city debate in Britain and seeks to examine the extent to which the 'problem' is either new or primarily economic. It is argued that the inner-city issue, while subject to specific political and ideological forces, is associated with the general processes of uneven capitalist development. In this sense, metropolitan decline is a further manifestation of the relationship between the built environment, the transience of economic activity and social change. More specifically the decline of the inner city relates to the incipient role of Britain in the development of capitalism and its current position in the world economy. The emergence of this as a 'problem' for the British state is combined with a convenient spatial determinism, which isolates the inner city as an anomaly even as the search for palliatives is erected to the status of a major social task.

Introduction

The flood of comment related to the inner city is such that it might almost be assumed that everyone who reads this article has a familiarity with the 'inner-city problem'.[1] We do not disagree with much of the comment made about the inner city though much of it deals with symptoms rather than causes and the term itself has become a convenient shorthand for a whole variety of the malaises affecting British society in the 1970s. Explanations of the inner city range from notions of personal failure, the cycle of deprivation, mismanagement and the inadequacy of planning to much more deep seated explanations based upon analyses of a capitalist economy.[2] Often elements of a number of explanations are incorporated into an analysis of the problem and certainly structural explanations are not unique to radical analysts (see, for example, THE TIMES, 12.10.78). However, there is a strong tendency to see the inner city as a new problem and primarily as an economic one. The purpose of the article is to challenge both of these views. We do so broadly within

the framework of marxist political economy thus implying, to use Boddy's recent definition, 'the centrality of marxian conceptualisations of the process of production and circulation of commodities, class structure, ideology and the State' (BODDY, 1976). The article begins with a brief consideration of uneven development within capitalist economies. This is followed by a discussion of the British economy and the emerging inner-city problem. These two elements are set into the social and political context surrounding uneven economic growth and decline and particular stress is given to the associated ideologies that are so crucial in creating the public image of a problem. Throughout we seek to demonstrate the underlying continuity of problems and solutions associated with the process of uneven development.

Combined and Uneven Development

The two main classes of capitalist societies interact in a number of different though related ways, i.e. economically, politically, ideologically. It is the changes in these relationships that constitutes development, or underdevelopment, the central dynamic being that of capital accumulation.[3] Due to the transfers of value within capitalist economic relationships the accumulation of capital is uneven;

*University of Sussex.

†Centre for Urban and Regional Studies, University of Birmingham.

value is created in production. The process of transfer occurs. through the medium of commodity and capital circulation, so that development is directly linked to under-development (see KAY, 1975; MANDEL, 1975; ROGERS, 1978). Thus 'problems', political structures and ideas associated with 'under-development' can be interpreted in the light of this basic process.

Differential accumulation takes place in the context of competition; the struggle for increased productivity and the concentration and centralisation of capital. The inherent expansion of this process produces new spatial scales for production and circulation, and thence for the process of development. This is the economic root of uneven development implicit in the development of the capital relation. However, there are no 'purely econo-mic terms' to this process, the process is political in the widest sense of inter-class relationships. Consequently resistance to the tendency is expressed in many different forms, as is state activity to counter the tensions generated by this process.

Differentials in the production and accum-ulation process, therefore, give rise to changes in the relative importance of centres of deve-lopment and their spatial structures. Areas once central to the accumulation processes are superceded by more advanced centres whilst other areas once largely ignored are drawn into the accumulation process. Such changes generate tensions within society and the management of these is central to state activity. The differentials in development between town and country produced large-scale migration in the 18th century. These in turn were superceded in the 19th century by regional and national variations on a much larger scale whilst in the 20th century geo-graphical and political boundaries even at a national level have become irrelevant as the spatial manifestation of uneven development are increasingly to be seen and considered at the global level (FRIEDMAN, 1977).

The British economy in the 20th century had to adapt to a loss of world dominance and empire, with the result that erstwhile major centres became backwaters of the world economy. Hitherto 'traditional' industries declined rapidly, even though more enterpris-ing capitalists moved into new lines, e.g. motor cars. The result was a restructuring of the space economy giving rise to uneven development within the national boundary on a new scale. This was particularly evident in advanced areas of the imperial economy such as Clyde-side and Merseyside.

In the post-1945 period there has been a marked trend towards the internationalisa-tion of capital and the integration of the capital circulation process on a world-wide scale. Associated with this has been an increase in competition and the pressure for restructur-ing of the production system, and therefore also for restructuring the space economy (MASSEY and MEAGAN, 1978). This is in part evidenced by the collapse or migration of small enterprises, particularly those in older urban areas (CDP, 1977a). The inter-national movement of capital has also been matched by the movement of labour with migration now occurring on a global scale (STUCKEY, 1977 and CARNEY, 1976).

Uneven development has been a necessary feature of the capitalist mode of production throughout its history and the effects are manifested within cities, regions and nations, and even continents. At any point in time uneven development will be more apparent in certain locations than in others reflecting the competitiveness (or lack of it) of the economic units in these locations relative to the wider economy. The extent to which the effects of these basic forces manifest them-selves and become part of the 'natural' situation of an area will depend, in part, upon the extent to which those groups affected generate political activity and how the state responds in the form of preventative or amel-iorative policies. The State's attempted management must be set against a backcloth of change, i.e. the evolving national and inter-national economy. Interventions may provide temporary solutions but cannot in any sense resolve problems finally since the problems are always changing. In Britain, economic decline continues despite continuous state intervention since the 1st World War. Problems bring solutions which do not resolve the under-lying economic issues referred to earlier. They do however provide solutions to the political and ideological crises which economic collapse brings sharply into focus.

The Inner City: Economic and Political Dimensions

In post-war Britain, it has been the regional dimension of uneven development which has been the subject of most political concern. Recently this concern was focussed on the concept of urban decay. Previously, the economic problems of the city were more positive in nature, i.e. the need to decentralise and control the growth of urban centres. Planning was primarily concerned with servicing the expansion of cities and restricting capital's excesses. Planning in a period of non-growth and non-development is a situation for which planners are poorly trained. The title of Hall's seminal work (HALL, 1973) on British planning, *The Containment of Urban England,* underlines the primary role of the planning profession. Wherever planners have been called upon to create rather than service and control development there have been few successes. By and large, the problem regions of the thirties remain problem regions despite a plethora of legislation and policies. More specifically, in relation to housing, PARIS, BLACKABY and LAMBERT (1976) have shown that local state housing policies are ultimately dependent on broader economic processes and particularly the capacity of the housebuilding industry. The point is that almost without exception it is the movement and investment of capital in the economy which determines the success or failure of state policy. The inner city is the latest in a long line of 'problems' for which planners are expected to bear responsibility and which they are expected to solve.

Blaming local state mismanagement or the incompetence of the planning profession serves to obscure the real basis of the inner-city issue and begs questions on the position and actual power of managers and planners. Similarly, attributing social problems to the presence of particular groups in areas, defined as problematic, or indeed to the areas themselves either ignores the social structures and processes that create such groups, or alternatively posits the crudest form of physical determinism. Implicit in terms such as 'regional' or 'inner city' is the notion that the problems (however defined) are somehow self-contained. This approach is of course paralleled in literature on international development.[4]

The term, inner-city problem, has already entered the popular consciousness as appropriate shorthand for a combination of bad housing conditions, vandalism, racial conflict, a declining economic base, decaying infrastructure, high unemployment, and vacant and high priced land. To that extent state policy initiatives are less isolated and compartmentalised than previously. The problem is no longer low educational attainment (Educational Priority Areas 1968-1971), transmitted deprivation through the family (Cycle of Deprivation Studies, 1972-1974) or environmental improvement (GIA and HAA policies) and quality of life (Quality of Life Studies, 1973-1977). As the parts multiply, the whole becomes increasingly vague and undefined. Nevertheless, the problem remains. It is somewhere in the inner city. To admit that deprivation is transmitted from elsewhere threatens an epidemic.

In physical terms, it is not the *actual* centres of cities which concern planners and politicians. It is not for example, the Central Business District of London or Birmingham. More specifically, it is those parts of the urban centres most closely associated with working class housing built before the turn of the century. It is also those parts of the city cleared of working-class housing and not as yet redeveloped. It is the decaying industrial infrastructure of the imperial age. To that extent, it can be argued that 'inner-city' decay is most obvious in cities which developed during Britain's imperial dominance, the 'workshops' of the world.

Through sheer physical decay much of the housing built in the centre of cities is crumbling. Much of this housing was built quickly and cheaply. Because this housing is adjacent to high-rent areas in the CBD, the contradiction between high land values and the low exchange values of the dwellings themselves both hasten their decay and inhibits further development of derelict and cleared areas. This has been particularly associated with the recent expansion of loan capital into the property market (JEFFERY, 1978).

The inner city is therefore a concentrated expression of these different components of the two clearly contrasted sides of the development process. It is where high land values, high rents and an affluent commercial and financial sector co-exist with decaying infrastructure, high unemployment and poverty. It is precisely this concentration of the contradictions of capitalism which poses such an ideological threat. It is one thing to have underdeveloped regions and declining villages, it is quite another when the cities, centres of culture and civilisation, and thus the epitomes of human advance, are seen to be subject to similar processes, e.g. London. Material reality is then seriously out of line with ideology.

The commercial and industrial areas of the imperial age have experienced decline through the general processes of increased concentration and centralisation of the capital and through Britain's decline within the world capitalist economy. In this sense it is a dual decline of 19th century housing and 19th century workplace. Add to this a new lumpen-proletariat of immigrant workers and we have the three main strands of the inner-city debate. The other side of the coin is the tendency for manufacturing to be an increasingly non-urban activity. Particularly in relation to multinational firms seeking a cheap, weakly organised labour force in often sparsely populated areas. This trend has been encouraged by post-war renewal of the retailing sector of cities, the growth of consumerism and suburbia and the need for adjacent warehousing rather than antisocial non-conforming uses.

What constitutes the inner-city debate must therefore be set within a wider economic context. That is, amidst a context of Britain as a declining economic power with an important imperial heritage, with obsolete branches of the imperial economy; where there is increased concentration and centralisation of capital on a world scale with capital intensive multi-nationals seeking peripheral locations and labour intensive industries seeking cheap peripheral labour; Britain with high unemployment, cuts in state social expenditure and sectoral decay. Part of the inner-city issue revolves around the fact that the focus of production is now elsewhere both internationally and intranationally.

If parallels were possible, the inner city would be most appropriately viewed as a contemporary type of 'depressed' area. Areas previously subject to intense capital exploitation, where the constant tension between the mobility of capital and the fixed nature of the built environment is most manifest. These are areas where capital has moved on leaving labour and infrastructure in its wake, e.g. London Docks. The difficulties are compounded by the declining rates base of the large urban centres further restricting the state's ability to intervene. This specific manifestation of fiscal crisis is of course set within a general crisis affecting state intervention in capitalist social formations. (O'CONNOR, 1973; CHILD-HILL, 1976).

The inner-city debate is thus a specific manifestation of uneven development in the U.K., part of a general process currently affecting different areas in different ways. On the one hand there is productive decentralisation and more intense exploitation of the periphery; on the other, the increased marginalisation of the urban proletariat (MINGIONE, 1978). At this level, the more fervent nationalism of the peripheral areas in recent years and the increasing political concern over urban social conflict are different symptoms of the same process. This political concern is intensified by the threat of racial conflict and the concentration of Labour voters in the large urban areas. Thus, while the processes affecting the British city of the 1970s are not new, they coalesce uniquely with the specific form of the contemporary British city and are in turn subject to and acted upon by specific ideological and political forces.

The Inner City as Ideology

Whilst in no sense disputing the significance of an economical and political analysis of the inner city we are concerned here to explore some of the less obvious but in our view equally important ideological aspects of the inner-city crisis. We are not alone in this interest. In all of the Inner Area Studies it was made clear that the existence of such large and obvious areas of poverty and stress put not only economic strategies in doubt but also threatened the legitimacy of central and local government and even the total social order. To quote the Liverpool Inner Area Study:

'By degrees the credibility of the local authority is put in jeopardy... the insensitivity and remoteness of government; the failure to recognise, let alone tolerate different values; the uncertainty, fear and anger and the deep-seated and growing alienation from government on the part of many residents of the inner areas; the failure of elected representatives to more than speak for a few individuals across the barrier between governors and the governed' (DEPARTMENT OF THE ENVIRONMENT, Change or Decay, 1977, p. 204).

The collapse of the political order which such 'alienation' threatens, amounts if one likes to a localised 'crisis in hegemony' and inevitably calls into question the role of the State. We have argued elsewhere that because much of the work on 'the State' is at an early stage of development it is at a level of abstraction that makes it difficult to use in an analysis of specific policies or government actions (FORREST and LLOYD, 1978). Whilst such criticisms remain generally true, the problem of abstraction is less evident when discussing a general notion like the 'inner-city problem'. This is precisely because the inner-city problem is seen and experienced even though the image developed as a result is a highly mystified view of the processes of capitalism.

Following HALL et al. (1978) we may state that such a 'public image' is a cluster of impressions, themes and quasi-explanations gathered or fused together. As such, a 'public image' is used to resolve or to cut short the analysis of difficult social and economic problems 'tending to appear in the place of analysis—or analysis seems to collapse into the image'. The inner city is arguably a 'public image' *par excellence* for it is both new and old, abstract and concrete, one problem and many problems. Essentially the term inner city has become a form of ideological descriptive shorthand, a conjurer of images, a black and white snapshot of physical and racial decline. As such, it is an image with a history and draws on its antecedents.

Thus there are similarities between the current entanglement of political and ideological dimensions regarding the inner city and the debates of the 19th and early 20th centuries. The view that inner-city decline was linked to immigration, was an entrenched view not only amongst the established residents of declining inner-city areas but also the social scientists who added their knowledge to this assessment.

But once again image has triumphed over reality for as Dyos demonstrates in his analysis of the slums of Victorian London, as the 'sluminess' of areas intensified so the proportion of London-born residents increased and he comments 'the slums of Victorian London are more properly thought of as settlement tanks for submerged Londoners' (DYOS, 1967:30). Those who escaped the pit, the inner city, by dint of hard labour and good fortune were in Victorian eyes 'the respectable' working class. All around 'the edge of this incomprehensible region were the homes of those who have crawled out of it; the residents of the villas, the clerks who are sustained in their long hours of unhealthy toil by the one triumphant thought that they have not fallen back into the abyss below' (STEDMAN-JONES, 1971:326).

However, as striking as the parallels are, one should not be deceived into thinking that today's inner-city 'problem' is simply a repeat of the 19th-century experience. The capitalist mode of production , as we have argued, does not stand still. Monopoly capitalism, i.e. post great Victorian Depression of 1873-1896, is qualitatively and quantitatively a different animal to early industrial capitalism. However, the uneven nature of capitalist development at the economic level, coupled with the 'uneven' correspondence between the different levels of the social formation, may well mean that in appearance, there are certain similarities. In this sense, one can argue that many of the notions associated with the inner city have their ideological roots in the 19th century. As PEARSON (1975) has suggested in the more general context of deviance:

"The earliest form in fact in which the space of 'deviance' announced itself was that of the 'city mob'. To put that another way: the forms, categories and images which are brought to bear in the modern social thought and practice which fixes its gaze on 'deviance' were born out of the confrontation with the dangerous energies of King Mob... These categories have not changed, although they have rearranged themselves across history in different points of emphasis."

The rediscovery of the inner city during the 1970s was of course not a sudden event, heralded by a new ministerial initiative. The inner city as 'slum', as a real housing problem, has never been absent, bar perhaps a short period during the 1950s in the age of consensus and 'having it good'. What is new about the 1970s version of the inner city is the range of problems the term now encompasses. The two words Inner City take in all the problems that surfaced in the 1960s through the consensual haze of the 1950s — race, crime, youth, permissiveness, 'urban deprivation' plus the most apparent manifestation of the 1970s economic crisis — unemployment.

The inner city then as an image is a powerful ideological tool in the hands of the media and party politicians, and a 'godsend' to academics who are asked in ever increasing numbers to describe in ever more detail the nature of the symptoms. The hypnotic power of the 'abyss' has been with us ever since the enormous expansion of urban populations concomitant with the development of capitalism and in consequence has created a complex set of beliefs, a jumble of mythology and fact, that now lies deeply embedded in 'British' culture(s). Each successive rediscovery of the inner city produces a new ideological constellation that builds upon past values whilst meshing with the current set of economic and political factors.

The inner-city problem of the 1970s is primarily about managing unemployment and race relations.[5] but at the same time all the other things the image brings to mind cannot be ignored.

Present day notions of the inner city would then seem to be an amalgam of what can be regarded as a number of analytically separate but entrenched cultural myths; the mob, the slum, the 1930s depressed area, youth cultures and crime as evidence of the undermining of traditional values and racism. The term inner city in a sense binds all these together, allowing politicians and media to focus on one particular aspect, without ever really distinguishing foreground from background:

"What is more worrying is the unbalanced nature of the migration, with a disproportionately high number of skilled workers and young people moving out, leaving the inner areas with a disproportionate share of unskilled and semi-skilled workers, of unemploy-

ment, of one-parent families, of concentrations of immigrant communities and over-crowded and inadequate housing" (P. SHORE, Secretary of State for the Environment, in a speech in Manchester, 17.9.76).

"I personally inspected many such places, and I have been appalled that such conditions can exist in a civilised country such as ours. Every generation has a dominating social task, and so let our age, our generation be remembered as the one in which we swept away this blot that disgraces our national life" (The Prince of Wales 18.5.33, quoted in BRANSON and HEINEMANN, 1973).

"Handsworth... a blot on any country that claims to be civilised" (Daily Express, quoted in HALL et al. 1978).

The inner city has, for the last 100 yr at least, presented a problem for the State in terms of maintaining political and ideological legitimacy. For most of this century such areas have been traditional Labour Party strongholds. Lack of action when in power, the incorporation and embourgeoisification of the Labour Party at national level, paralleled by a demise of working-class party politics at local level (HINDNESS, 1971) created a political vacuum within the inner areas.[6] As such there was no official machine to mediate the challenges from below, and instead a varied collection of community action groups grew in their place. (Within the factories of course a similar process occurred with the growth of a shop stewards movement but here the Unions were invoked to put their house in order.)

The growth of the various community action groups in the 1960s was perhaps the most visible manifestation of the increasing inability of local government to maintain a 'legitimate' profile in the eyes of the public, particularly in inner-city areas. Local government reorganisation and a further shift towards an increase in executive power plus more visible actions such as talk of increased public participation, municipal newsletters and vigorous action against squatters can all be interpreted as ways in which the State sought to resolve the dilemma of declining legitimacy. Despite it all, the underlying malady refused to go away and in particular, unemployment grew worse. Increasingly, the inner city was submerged within, and identified with, 'the national interest'.

"Cities serve and sustain the whole region around them in cultural, social and economic terms. If cities fail so to a large extent does our society. That is the urgency of tackling the problem and why it has to be of concern to everyone in this land" (P. SHORE, *op. cit*.)

The increased attention which resulted carries with it the implication that because it is now a matter of national concern the problems can and will be resolved. This promotion of the problem tends to result in its depoliticisation and diminution as an important issue likely to challenge the effectiveness and relevance of local and central government control. For the inner city now transcends government and can be classed in the ideological category of Dunkirk, success depending on the combined action of the nation.

Concluding Remarks

In summary, our argument has been that inherent in capitalist social relations is an unevenness of spatial, political and economic development. Constant political intervention is necessary to try and resolve the tensions produced by this unevenness. The problems identified, the solutions offered and the ideological constellations that form around them cannot be viewed statistically. They are all undergoing constant change. The emergence of the inner-city problem should be seen in this light. It is not, as such, a new problem in that uneven development has always existed, its novelty lies rather in its promotion to the status of a problem, a matter of national concern and state action. This is not a cynical view but rather a recognition of the relationships between economic processes and social and political action and the ways in which problems, in the sense used here, emerge. It is in this process of problem discovery and promotion that academics occupy an important position. The research programmes initiated are seen as a necessary part of the action to solve the problem. However, their findings are used selectively within the changing political and economic environment as the fate of earlier research demonstrates, for example the CDP's.

New problems will emerge to displace the current discussions. Immediate possibilities would seem to be the family and the economic integration of Europe. What is certain is that the old problems remain. If one considers a map of Britain identifying 'distressed' or underdeveloped areas, only the Midlands, East Anglia and the South (with the exception of Cornwall and Devon) are not identified as requiring assistance. Even then within this area parts of London, Birmingham, Sandwell, Wolverhampton, Leicester and Nottingham have been designated as requiring special assistance. All of this illustrates the progressive relegation of Britain as a capitalist economy to the status of underdeveloped within the development relationship. The inner-city problem is firmly located within this context and should be interpreted as such.[7]

Acknowledgements — We would like to thank Martin Boddy and Simon Duncan for their comments.

Notes

1. An extensive literature now exists as can be seen in the Inner City Bulletin published by Birmingham City Library. See also KIRBY, A. (1978).

2. See, for instance the final reports of the LIVERPOOL INNER AREA STUDY (1977), NATIONAL COMMUNITY DEVELOPMENT PROJECTS (1977a and b) and PARIS, C. (1978).

3. Capital Accumulation is the addition of money capital to that originally advanced for production, through the realisation of surplus value in the form of profit, rent or interest.

4. For review of literature see BROOKFIELD, H. (1975).

5. These issues are further discussed by COCKBURN, C. (1977).

6. This vacuum being itself partly a result of this depopulation produced by clearance and redevelopment and general decay.

7. An explicit recognition of this relationship is amply demonstrated in suggestions in America that the inner city should be abandoned. A similar suggestion regarding Regions was made in the FINANCIAL TIMES, 1976.

References

BODDY, M. (1976), Urban Political Economy: Introduction, *Antipode* **8**, (1).

BRANSON, N. and HEINEMANN, M. (1973), *Britain in the Nineteen Thirties*, Panther, London.

BROOKFIELD, H. (1975), *Interdependent Development*, Methuen, London.

CARNEY, J. (1976), Notes on migrant labour, *Antipode* **8**, (1).

CHILD-HILL, R. (1976), Fiscal crisis and political struggle in the decaying US central city, *Kapitalistate*, Nos. 4-5.

COCKBURN, C. (1977), *The Local State*, Pluto Press, London.

COMMUNITY DEVELOPMENT PROJECT (1977a) *The costs of Industrial Change* Benwell CDP, Newcastle-upon-Tyne.

COMMUNITY DEVELOPMENT PROJECT (1977b) *Gilding the Ghetto*, Benwell CDP, Newcastle-upon-Tyne.

DEPARTMENT OF THE ENVIRONMENT (1977), Change or decay. Final report of the Liverpool Inner Area Study, H.M.S.O.; Inner London, policies for disposal and balance: Final report of the Lambeth Inner Area Study, H.M.S.O., London.

DYOS, H.J. (1968), *The Study of Urban History*, Arnold, London.

FINANCIAL TIMES (1976), Lombard, June 29th.

FORREST, R. and LLOYD, J. (1978), Recent state theory — the implications for policy research, in Papers in Urban and Regional Studies, Vol. 2, Centre for Urban and Regional Studies, University of Birmingham.

FRIEDMAN, A. (1977), *Industry and Labour: Class Struggle at Work and Monopoly Capitalism*, Macmillan, London.

HALL, P. *et al.* (1973), *The Containment of Urban England*, Allen & Unwin, London.

HALL, S. *et al.* (1978), *Policing the Crisis, Mugging, the State, and Law and Order*, Macmillan, London.

HINDESS, B. (1971), *Decline of Working Class Politics*, MacGibbon & Kee.

JEFFERY, N. (1978), Relationships between 'Urban Crisis' and the crisis of British Capitalism: recent 'inner-city' industrial closures. Paper to Conference of Socialist Economists Annual Conference.

KAY, G. (1975), *Development and Underdevelopment, a Marxist Analysis*, Macmillan, London.

KIRBY, A. (1978), *The Inner City: Causes and Effects*, Retailing and Planning Associates.

MANDEL, E. (1975), *Late Capitalism*, New Left Books, London.

MASSEY, D. and MEAGAN (1978), Industrial restructuring versus the cities, *Urban Studies* **15**, 3.

MINGIONE, E. (1978), Capitalist crisis, neo-dualism and marginalisation. *International Journal of Urban and Regional Research*, **2**, (1).

O'CONNOR, J. (1978), *The Fiscal Crisis of the State*, St. James Press, London.

PARIS, C. (1978), The parallels are striking ... crisis in the inner city, GB 1977, *International Journal of Urban and Regional Research* **2**, (1).

PARIS, C. BLACKABY, B. and LAMBERT, J. (1976), State urban policy and the housing problem, *Antipode* **8**, (1).

PEARSON, G. (1975), *The Deviant Imagination*, Macmillan, London.

ROGERS, N. (1978), An enquiry into the political economy of combined and uneven development and its significance for regional analysis. *Papers in Urban and Regional Studies*, Vol. 2, Centre for Urban and Regional Studies, University of Birmingham.

SHORE, P. (1976), Inner Urban Policy, a speech at Manchester Town Hall, 17.9.76., Department of the Environment Press Notice 835.

STEDMAN-JONES, G. (1971), *Outcast London*, Clarendon, Oxford.

STUCKEY, B. (1977), The Spatial distribution of the Industrial reserve army, Zone Werk Kongress, Amsterdam, May.

THE TIMES (1978), Housing: a special report, Tuesday, September 12th.

Geoforum, Vol. 10, pp.117-127, 1979.
Pergamon Press Ltd. Printed in Great Britain.

The Origins and Use of Theory in Urban Geography: Household Mobility and Filtering Theory

FRED GRAY, *Brighton, U.K.
MARTIN BODDY, † Bristol, U.K.

Abstract: The paper looks in detail at one particular interpenetration of academic theory and state policy making – filtering theory in urban geography. While household mobility and turnover are important processes in the housing system, they are extended in filtering theory to form a universal explanatory model embracing the entire housing system. In this model idealised concepts of the operation of the housing market—valid only under conditions that do not occur in practice – are used to legitimate a *laissez-faire* natural-market view of how the housing system *should* operate. Translated into government policy, used to justify the dominant private interests in housing, and supported by academic explanation, the theory then comes to legitimate the persistence of gross inequalities in housing provision and to maintain the allocation of resources away from those most in need. This paper reviews this use of filtering theory both in Britain and the United States, and makes a variety of empirical and theoretical criticism of its validity.

The paradox of modern geographical enquiry is that despite major errors and inadequacies in explanation and method, the mainstream of the discipline continues to maintain and sustain itself. This paper examines a set of linked ideological and theoretical reasons for this state of affairs in one branch of the discipline, urban geography. We provide a detailed critique of a particular family of models of the housing market – those which may be grouped generically under the term 'filtering theory' – to draw out the ideological bases for the preservation of inadequate methodology.

Perhaps the most concise but comprehensive recent critique of geography is the essay by

*Centre for Continuing Education, Sussex University.

†School for Advanced Urban Studies, Bristol University.

SLATER (1975) on the nature of modern geographical enquiry. Slater lists seven 'salient weaknesses' general to the discipline: inverted methodology; accumulation of data out of all proportion to the development of theoretical explanation; mechanistic abstractions from socio-economic reality; concentration on the description of measurement of forms rather than an explanation of underlying processes; failure to grasp the vitally important inter-connections between spatial structure and political economy; and, capitalist ideology concealing the fact that the organisation of space in any given social formation is directly related to the internal class structure of that formation and its external connections and development.

How then, given these weaknesses, is ortho-dox geography maintained and sustained? Slater himself suggests the dominance of capitalist ideology in our construction of reality and hence in aiding the survival of orthodox geography. He adds that institutional factors, such as the compartmentalisation of knowledge and research, act to support the status quo.

Capitalist ideology and institutional factors may indeed be of paramount importance, yet at the level of particular branches of the discipline we still have little rigorous understanding as to how they operate in practice. At this detailed level it is apparent that orthodox geography has the ability — indeed need — to by-pass or ignore seemingly obvious contradictions in research and understanding. It is here that the role of theory and explanation in mainstream geography assumes a position of fundamental importance.

However lop-sided and biased research is towards, for example, data collection and spatial fetishism, some explanation of processes and causes (albeit sometimes implicit or nebulous) must exist and be generally accepted for orthodox geography to survive. In effect explanation and theory act as key-stones, supporting existing schools of thought, sustaining current geographical practices, and acting to relate the discipline to wider society. To radical geography they assume considerable significance. If they remain unchallenged there is little reason for other geographers to abandon them. If they are challenged, and proved inadequate, there is some hope that qualitative change in geography will be hastened.

Filtering Theory and Geography

Turning to urban geography, GRAY (1975) suggests that work on urban residential patterns and processes suffers many of the shortcomings pointed to by Slater. Yet over a long period, and particularly the last decade, research in this area has been extensive and enjoyed considerable popularity (HERBERT and JOHNSTON, 1976). In turn, the filtering concept has been one prominent explanatory concept sustaining the development of such work.

To develop this argument it is necessary to examine some of the features of geographical work in this area. One basic premise is that residential mobility is of considerable, indeed

ultimate, significance as a causal process leading to the socio-spatial pattern in cities. Thus Moore in an early paper suggests that:

"The importance of residential mobility as the proximal cause of changes in the social structure of cities has become widely appreciated" (MOORE, 1966).

Similarly, Simmons in his influential review paper asserts that:

"The spatial differentiation of residential attributes is largely the result of the cumulation of intra-urban moves..." (SIMMONS, 1968).

More recently Pritchard has conformed to this view:

"Residential mobility can ... be identified as a process of paramount importance in the spatial evolution of the city" (PRITCHARD, 1976).

Household movement is, however, usually seen as an essentially individual and disaggregated act, perhaps most obviously so in behavioural approaches with their stress on household decision making. As MASSEY (1975) indicates explanation and research couched in terms of the individual leaves much to be desired. Indeed one problem immediately apparent in arguing that household mobility creates the socio-spatial structure of the city is to demonstrate precisely how, or through which mechanism, the micro-movement process relates to and produces the macro-structures and forms described by geographers.

It is here that the filtering concept has often been of crucial significance, for it provides one explanation of the relationship between process and form. Unless some such lynch-pin existed, the study of household movement in isolation would be without wider justification, and similarly the forms described would be without explanation. Pritchard himself recognises this; when reviewing the literature dealing with housing and the spatial structure of the city, he writes:

"That there is some association between movement and changes in the environment of urban areas lies at the heart of much of what has been discussed in this introductory section. The whole argument about the role of external economies and the relationship of these to the progress of changes in the relative value of properties in the housing stock implied by the 'filtering' model assumes such a relationship " (PRITCHARD, 1976).

Bourne also appears to subscribe to this view in arguing that:

"... It is basically through one form or another of the filtering process that most changes in neighbourhood status and housing quality occur" (BOURNE, 1976).

The argument, then, is that filtering theory provides a justification for and rationalization of orthodox geographical study of urban residential patterns and processes. As a reading of the literature makes clear, filtering has been used to *explain* city growth, urban residential change, the operation of the housing system, and the spatial concentration and segregation of social classes. Moreover, the filtering concept has long proved influential outside the academic world, for its evolution is closely related to governmental and private institutional analysis and explanation of the housing market both in Britain and the United States. As later sections of this paper suggest, the ideological nature of filtering theory, both in urban geography and wider society, is quite clear. Superficially detached academic notions are intricately bound up with status quo views concerning the operation and nature of society. The academic use of filtering theory has not been somehow conjured up in a theoretical vacuum, but has a lineage dating back to attempts to legitimate housing inequality and a *laissez-faire* view of the economic system.

Academically the theory of filtering has been subject to a variety of contradictory definitions in a literature which reveals an often heated argument over the correct way to view and (more particularly) measure the process (MAHER, 1974; BOURNE, 1976); MURIE, NINER *et al.* 1976; MURIE, HILLYARD *et al.* 1976; KIRBY, 1979). Nevertheless, in its basic attributes, filtering is widely accepted to refer to the downward movement of dwellings in value and status over time and/or the upward movement of households from lower to higher-quality dwellings. Johnston neatly summarizes filtering as a mechanism:

"... by which the higher-income groups periodically demand new housing and their former homes are brought by lower-income groups, for whom they represent an improvement in living standards. Thus homes slowly filter down the social scale and individuals filter up the housing scale" (JOHNSTON, 1971).

Smith goes a little further, and defines filtering as:

"... an indirect process of meeting housing demands of a lower-income group. When new quality housing is produced for higher-income households, houses given up by those households become available to the lower-income group" (SMITH, 1964).

Filtering theory, then, is not merely a description of housing market processes, but also an explanation of how change occurs — or should occur. Acceptance of the general notion of filtering implies acceptance of a number of related ideas about the nature of society, the operation of the housing market and the function of housing policy; these include, for example, the notion first, that the housing market is an essentially autonomous phenomenon operating in a relatively neutral manner according to a particular set of rules, and, second, that the process of the sifting of urban populations into distinct spatial clusters and housing situations is an independent mechanism, which once set in motion follows a prescribed course without need of regulation of intervention.

At the aggregate level, the development of filtering theory has been closely linked with the field of 'human ecology' and the conceptualisation of urban growth and neighbourhood change derived from this field. The 'human ecologists' translated the ideas of competition and dominance invasion and succession into theories of urban sociospatial structure and change (PARK and BURGESS, 1967). In turn, these theories were simplified as general spatial patterns. Thus BURGESS (1967) conceptualised the city as an idealised series of concentric rings centred on a Central Business District. Around this lay a 'zone of transition' and rings of successively higher-status residential use as one moves outwards. With growth and expansion of the city the zone of transition is invaded at its inner edge by business and light-manufacturing and there is a general tendency for 'each inner zone to extend its area by invasion of the next outer zone. This aspect of expansion may be called succession ...' (BURGESS, 1967). Hoyt later developed a 'sector model' or urban residential structure and change, using an empirical study of land values in Chicago.

In the context of this paper it is highly relevant to note that Hoyt's research was commissioned by the US government, used data supplied by the Real Property Inventories of the Civil Works Administration, and was designed to 'guide the development of housing and the creation of a sound mortgage market' (HOYT, 1939) by attempting to predict the location and change of areas of different land value and residential status. Hoyt stressed the economic mechanisms of changing residential values rather than the socio-ecological mechanisms of Burgess. But, as with Burgess' model, his theory implied a succession of occupancy in dwellings originally built for higher-income families. Thus filtering at the individual level is seen to be the dynamic element in these aggregate models of city growth and neighbourhood change which still prove influential in urban geography. Following Hoyt's work filtering has received considerable attention from academics in the field of urban studies. GRIGSBY (1963) indeed, has argued that it is '... the principal dynamic feature of the housing market'. Nevertheless, the academic success and popularity of filtering theory over a sustained period of time has to be viewed against, and understood in terms of, its wider societal background, and in particular its use as a legitimatory device. It is to this we now turn.

Filtering as a Legitimatory Device

The early use of the filtering concept in 19th century Britain can be related to the contemporary view of society held by those responsible for 'philanthropic' and early State intervention, which stressed ideas of 'self-help', moral improvement and upward mobility. These interventions took place in the context of a pressing 'inner-city' crisis, especially in London, the collapse of working class housing provision by private enterprise, and ideological and political proscription of any direct redistribution of resources to the poor (STEDMAN-JONES, 1971;

BENWELL COMMUNITY PROJECT, 1978). The '5% philanthropy' movement in the latter half of the 19th century met the needs of only a small proportion of the working class since the rents charged excluded all but the skilled and other high-income strata. Ironically, those households displaced by the construction of the new model dwellings rarely occupied this housing. Sydney Waterlow, founder of the Improved Industrial Dwelling Company in 1863, justified the failure of such schemes to house those in the most inadequate housing as follows:

"The lowest of all, those comprising what may emphatically be called the lower orders, and who are least likely to appreciate the comforts of a decent home, will surely, receive their share of benefits enjoyed proportionately by those above them" (TARN, 1973).

"We must take the class as of various degrees; the upper, middle and lower of the labouring classes; it would not have been right to build down to the lowest class, because you must have built a class of tenement which I hope none of them would be satisfied with at the end of 50 years; we have rather tried to build for the first class, and by lifting them up leave more room for the second and third who are below them" (GAULDIE, 1974).

In similar vein James Hole argued in his famous work *The Homes of the Working Classes* (1886) that:

"... By increasing the number of first class houses for mechanics, the vacated tenements increase the supply for the second and third classes and thus all classes are benefitted" (WATSON, 1973).

Finally, a witness the 1885 Royal Commission on the Housing of the Working Classes in Scotland added a spatial dimension in arguing by analogy that the effect of building new houses was:

"... just the same as if you threw a stone into a pool of water, you have a radius of people getting out and out, each one driving his neighbour out. The better class people went further away and got better houses; the people next in grade to them took possession of their houses and so on. The bad houses were totally destroyed, and the people who lived in those bad houses took the next worse houses ... the whole effect of the operation was to compel almost the whole community to provide themselves with better accommodation" (TARN, 1969).

Such views implied that the poor and inadequately housed were unlikely to be helped through direct aid and that such action was unlikely, in fact, to be effective owing to the characteristics of the 'lower orders'. They implied that the slum-problem was best attacked by building for 'better-class' households rather than contributing new dwellings for slum dwellers themselves. Significantly, also, the 'working class' was seen not in monolithic terms but as an amalgam of sub-groups, to be treated differently. Recent studies by BYRNE (1978) and NORTH TYNESIDE CDP (1977) detail the nature of the residential divisions created within the working class in the late 19th/early 20th century by differences in work position, and by the operation of the housing market — in which the concept of filtering played a significant role in both initiating and legitimating the divisions. Filtering theory in this early period served to legitimate existing inequalities and divisions by treating as 'natural' the continuing slum problem and the appalling housing conditions experienced particularly by the unskilled and casual labouring groups within the working class.

The concept of filtering remained important in inter-war public housing policy. One report, *A Policy for the Slums*, by the National Housing and Town Planning Council in 1929 noted that:

> "When post-war building began, it was hoped that there might be a gradual movement of the working-class population of the slums into better houses. This might occur in two ways, either the slum dweller might go direct into a new house or a process of 'filtering up' might occur under which the slum dweller would move from the slum into a better pre-war house, the tenant of which would, in turn, move into a new house" (SMITH, 1964).

The report went on to observe that although both processes had occurred the scale was disappointingly small. Public housing policy after the first war was formulated with ideas of filtering at least implicitly in mind in that a large proportion of the housing, particularly under the 1924 (Wheatley) Housing Act, was built to high standards. With, consequently, high rents the aim was to house the higher-income groups in the working class and allow the vacated property to filter down to poorer families. Referring to Birmingham, Schifferes has observed that:

> "In 1914 Chamberlain advocated municipal development of land on the City's outskirts on a properly planned scale ... Chamberlain had no illusions that this was an immediate remedy for the thousands living in back-to-backs in central Birmingham: "ecological processes" (i.e. filtering up) might ensure that in a generation the slums would die a natural death" (SCHIFFERES, 1975).

In retrospect, however, it is clear that the 'natural' solution to the slum problem was ineffectual. Marshall, writing in 1933, makes the following comment on Government policy in the preceeding decade: "We found that, in effect, we shall have to rely upon the filtering-up process if the poorest class of tenants are to benefit ..." He adds that in consequence: "The poorest will still be clamouring for houses, and the upshot of it all is that the problem of the slums, with all its implications, has not yet been faced" (MARSHALL, 1933).

There has been relatively little overt incorporation of filtering concepts into official post-war housing policy or analysis of the British housing system. While the recent *Housing Policy* Green Paper (DEPARTMENT OF THE ENVIRONMENT, 1977a) emphasises the importance of household mobility and maintains established policies of encouraging the growth of owner-occupation, there is no specific reference to the concept, as one might have expected, say, in an equivalent document in the USA. However, there has been some use of filtering in recent analysis of the British inner city problem. For example, the Final Report of the Lambeth Inner Area Study asserts:

> "It can, of course, be argued that those who move from outer London create space which can be taken up by people from Inner London. Such 'filtering', as it is called, has undoubtedly taken place in the private sector" (DEPARTMENT OF THE ENVIRONMENT, 1977b).

In Britain, significantly, it is the influential Building Societies Association which has made greatest use of the filtering concept — significant in view of the strong support of building societies for, and vested interest in, the maintenance and expansion of the private market in housing, and their opposition to government intervention (BODDY and GRAY, 1979). Giving evidence to the government Housing Finance Review the BSA asserted that:

> "The housing market must be seen as a ladder. People join at the bottom end; they move gradually upwards until they reach old age when they may move down again. Eventually they die and leave the ladder completely. The important point is that there is no room for people to come in at the bottom of the market unless people already there are moving upwards" (BUILDING SOCITIES ASSOCIATION, 1976).

This assertion has been repeatedly used by the BSA to justify concentrating scarce financial resources on the already well-off and well housed (for example in opposing reducing subsidy to better-off house buyers by cutting tax relief on mortgage interest at higher than basic rates).

The BSA's view derives from a strong free-market approach to housing. Having presented the 'ladder theory' the BSA maintains that "Any measures aimed at people at the bottom of the market or in the council sector at the expense of those further up-market seem likely to be counter-productive" and "The conclusion that must be drawn from this analysis is that policy measures which, directly or indirectly, are aimed at particular sectors of housing are likely to create distortions in the market" (BUILDING SOCIETIES ASSOCIATION, 1976).

Turning to use of the filtering concept as a legitimatory device in the USA, the debate over housing policy is frequently polarised into public intervention versus free-market, a polarisation reflected, in turn, in the relationship of filtering theory to housing policy. Lowry for example, summarised the argument as follows:

> "A general improvement of housing standards can be achieved within a framework of the private housing market by a process described as "filtering". Direct government programmes which provide subsidised new housing for lower- or middle-income families interfere with an orderly market process that would otherwise provide second-hand — but socially adequate — housing for the same

families at prices within their means" (LOWRY, 1970).

Daniel's view is similar to that of the BSA quoted above:

> "What may not be immediately obvious is that the filtering process results from competitive market forces. By establishing prices for the services of the existing stock of dwellings, the housing market allocates the stock in such a way as to maximise its aggregate value, hence minimising requirements of new capital expenditure" (DANIELS, 1974).

Having compared direct housing provision for low-income households with indirect reliance on filtering he concludes that:

> "Public housing and subsidies that enable low-income families to purchase new housing are questionable solutions to the problem of improving housing conditions" (DANIELS, 1974).

More generally a review of American Urban Housing published in 1968 observed that, with few exceptions:

> "All major housing subsidy programs have been used primarily to promote new construction and, to a lesser extent, substantial rehabilitation. The basic rationale for this emphasis on new construction is that new projects on vacant sites increase the total housing stock. So long as there is some interplay between different sectors of the market, an addition to the stock of housing tends to relieve prices for everyone. Thus the construction of moderate-income projects in the suburbs may indirectly help to lessen shortages in central city slums" (PRESIDENT'S COMMITTEE ON URBAN HOUSING, 1968).

It is no accident, given the basis of filtering theory in *laizzez-faire* economics that it is in the USA that the concept of filtering has been most firmly and overtly incorporated into both academic work and housing policy. The development of direct intervention through public housing in the USA was initially identified with mitigating the effects of the depression and was subsequently linked to the war effort and the associated need for workers' housing. From the early 1950's, however, the development of public housing explicitly to meet the housing needs of lower-income households, was strongly opposed by those interests committed to the free market. To quote FUERST (1974):

"Public housing has existed in the United States since 1937, but through the efforts of the real estate lobby, segments of the business community and the press, its growth has been successfully stunted since its inception."

Criticism of Filtering Theory

Household mobility and turnover, and exchanges of existing dwellings are obviously of considerable importance in a restricted sense in meeting the housing needs of households with different characteristics and of particular households at different stages in the life cycle (ROBSON, 1973). But, as suggested earlier, the more important question is that of the theoretical and empirical validity of filtering as an explanation of the operation of the housing system and the formation of urban socio-spatial forms.

First, the volume of housing available to filter down to lower-income households is likely to be insufficient. Since the distribution of households incomes tends towards a pyramidal shape, building new houses for those high up the pyramid will simply not release enough houses for those further down where the pyramid is wider. There are too few high-price and high-quality houses to meet the needs of lower-income households [FISHER and RATCLIFF, 1936 (summarised in SMITH, 1964)]. Building enough highest-quality dwellings to enable the lowest income households radically to improve their housing situation would be uneconomic for builders, since prices would be depressed below construction costs, unless there were massive subsidy of high-cost housing units.

Similarly, although filtering may occur in an economic sense (as defined by Ratcliff) this does not mean any necessary increase in the *quality* of housing occupied by lower-income households. For falling prices as a result of increased supply higher up the scale may lead to a more rapid deterioration in house condition. As LOWRY (1970) pointed out, falling rental returns are likely to lead to undermaintenance by landlords and, ultimately, abandonment by landlord and tenant alike. The problem is most relevant where the proportion of privately rented property is high — particularly in older urban areas with a large proportion of houses at risk. The

effect of value-depreciation on owner-occupiers would be a reduction in imputed rental income rather than any 'real' loss. However, an analogous situation occurs in the British situation when lower-income households are forced to filter upwards into inner-city owner-occupation by inability to obtain accommodation in the public or private rented sectors. A significant proportion of such households, having bought cheaper, older property, are unable to afford repairs and maintenance necessary to maintain the value of the property and are, in effect, disinvesting as the property deteriorates (GREEN and WILLIAMS, 1977; BENWELL COMMUNITY PROJECT, 1978). Filtering theory 'ignores evidence suggesting that accelerated filtering, unaccompanied by market support mechanisms for the inner city, accelerates decay' (GRIGSBY and ROSENBURG, 1975). It assumes that dwellings vacated at the bottom of the scale would be vacated and demolished. The evidence of low-income households in unfit houses demonstrates the assumption to be false. Thus, according to Ratcliff:

"The end product of filtering, at the bottom of the chain reaction, is substandard housing; thus filtering produces the very blight which we seek to remedy" (RATCLIFF, 1949).

Turning to recent empirical approaches to filtering, most relevant here have been a series of empirical housing vacancy chain studies in the USA and UK, which have generally sought to establish the average number of moves or vacancies created by different forms of new housing provision — high-cost un-subsidised versus low-cost subsidised, public sector versus private sector etc.

American studies have tended to focus on chain length. LANSING, CLIFTON and MORGAN (1969), in a study of 1100 chains of moves in the USA in the 1960s, found the average chain length (number of households moving as a result of a single new dwelling being occupied) resulting from building houses costing under $15 thousand was 2.2 compared with 3.8 for those costing $25 thousand to $35 thousand; the prices of houses was also found to decline at successively lower places in individual chains. The authors concluded that 'the poor are indirectly affected by the construction of new housing, even if they do not occupy new dwellings.' White, on the basis of this study, concluded that:

> "Subsidised new housing will not, in general, be the most effective path to a national housing policy goal of improving the overall match of families' needs with available houses ... Subsidized housing will not have as large a multiplier effect as new housing built for middle and higher income groups" (WHITE, 1971).

Studies in the UK and a number of later American studies have laid greater emphasis on who benefits from chains of moves rather than simply focussing on chain length. Thus MURIE, HILLYARD *et al.*, commenting on Lansing, Clifton and Morgan's conclusions regarding benefits to poorer households, suggest that:

> "A closer examination of their findings suggests not only that this is not true of all poor people (poor blacks are less well represented) but that poor people in general are not well represented in proportion to their numbers in the whole population" (MURIE, HILLYARD, *et al.* 1976).

A study by Sands in New York State indicated:

> "No clear advantage to either direct (subsidised) or indirect (high cost) construction strategies. Both approaches were about equally effective in the creation of turnover vacancies" (SANDS, 1976).

It was found that most chains initiated by subsidised family housing were frequently terminated by demolition or abandonment of a vacant unit. Sands concluded that:

> "The vacancy chains generated by the most expensive new housing had little effect on the housing need of low income families"

and that:

> "Subsidised central city housing was generally the most effective in creating housing opportunities for low income households."

In a study of housing chains in West Central Scotland, WATSON (1973) found that the average chain length resulting from building for owner-occupation was 2.09 compared with 1.64 in the public sector. The difference, however, was largely due to the proportion of chains initiated in the public sector which ended in the demolition or closure of a vacant

dwelling, as a result of the local authorities' slum clearance activities — 48% compared with 7% of owner-occupier chains. Thus although private-sector chains were longer, public policy did more to meet the housing needs of lower-income households through direct housing provision and slum clearance coupled with rehousing.

Finally, a study by MURIE, HILLYARD *et al.* in Northern Ireland found that new housing was disproportionately used by new households, particularly in the private sector; 26% of new dwellings were occupied directly by new households without further moves being generated. This obviously contradicts the assumption (made by the BSA for example) that new households enter the housing market at the bottom and move gradually upwards. A large proportion of new houses are occupied by new households with the financial resources, and financial status in the eyes of building societies or other credit sources, to buy their way in half-way up the housing 'ladder'. Households in chains initiated in the public sector generally had lower incomes and were more likely to be living in older housing and in overcrowded conditions. Public-sector chains were again found to be shorter due to local authorities' impact on the slum problem. The authors concluded that:

> "Public sector sequences made more impact on those in inadequate circumstances. In this way public control over allocation is more effective in meeting need than the 'trickle down' effect of private development" (MURIE, HILLYARD *et al.*, 1976).

The empirical studies indicate that while *turnover* on a limited scale is important as a way of meeting housing need and matching the available stock to households with different characteristics, they do not demonstrate the general validity of filtering theory. Instead, direct aid in the form of subsidised or public housing is the most effective and efficient strategy for improving the housing conditions of low-income households and the physical fabric of the inner city (WATSON, 1973; NATIONAL COMMISSION ON URBAN PROBLEMS, 1968).

'Filtering theory' is derived from a *laissez-*

faire market economy view of how the housing system operates — or how it should. The continued existence of the slums and inadequate housing in the USA and the UK; the persistence of high-status residential areas and of unequal housing provision; contradictory processes such as 'gentrification'; the numerical insignificance of high-quality dwellings compared with the number of households in poor housing conditions; the effects of racial discrimination; subsidies such as tax relief on mortgage interest which favours the better-off, and untaxed capital gains for owner occupiers; disinvestment by landlords and low-income owners, all indicate the inadequacies of filtering theory in both theoretical and policy terms. The concept is theoretically unsound and hence of only limited empirical validity. To quote MURIE, HILLYARD *et al.* again:

> "...Filtering is an idealised conception of the operation of the housing market under certain conditions. As those conditions do not obtain in practice filtering ceases to be a representation of what happens in the housing market. The implication that filtering does or can occur becomes an untestable assertion which is inseparable from the political associations of the idea. In other words, it becomes an assertion used to justify a reliance on the market process and the capacity of that process to meet policy ends. It is an assertion which is difficult to sustain in theoretical or empirical debate" (MURIE, HILLYARD *et al.*, 1973).

Conclusions

Filtering theory derives from a clear political and ideological position grounded in the processes and structures of capitalist society. It legitimates the status quo, the persistence of gross inequalities in housing provision and the existence of substandard housing, and justifies allocation of resources and subsidies to those already well-off and well-housed, directing support away from those in greatest need. The use of filtering within geography is an at least implicit acceptance of this situation, and has hindered fundamental qualitative change in the discipline. Household turnover and mobility are indeed important processes in the housing system. But to generalise from those processes, observed on a limited scale, to a universal model of filtering embracing the entire housing system and the

socio-spatial structure of cities, is, we believe, illegitimate.

Implicit in our critique of filtering theory has been an alternative view of residential mobility and the operation of the housing system in Britain and America. Some indication of the nature of an alternative perspective will have already been gained during the course of the paper, and there exists a growing literature which provides both theoretical guidelines and detailed case studies (POLITICAL ECONOMY OF HOUSING WORKSHOP, 1975 and 1976; NATIONAL CDP, 1976; HARVEY, 1974 and 1975). In summary, this perspective suggests that the access to housing resources for households of differing financial status and other characteristics, and mobility within the housing system, are structured by a set of financial and governmental institutions situated within the broader economic, political and ideological structure of society. These institutions define the opportunities and constraints within which individual households are able to exercise varying degrees of preference and choice. In Britain, for example, local housing authority allocation procedures (GRAY, 1976) and building society lending criteria (BODDY, 1976) are major factors determining the housing resources available to households with different characteristics. To explain the structuring of access and mobility and the distribution of housing resources, attention must be directed to these institutions in the first instance. This is not sufficient in itself, however. It is also necessary to show how institutions and their operations are located within the broader social structure, and to demonstrate the way in which these institutions continually reproduce the central contradiction between wages and housing costs which underlies the housing 'problem' (BENWELL COMMUNITY PROJECT, 1978).

Acknowledgement — The authors wish to thank Simon Duncan, Tony Fielding, John Holmes, and Alan Murie for their comments and suggestions.

References

BENWELL COMMUNITY PROJECT (1978) *Private Housing and the Working Class*, Benwell Community Project.

BODDY, M. (1976) Building societies and owner-occupation, In: *Housing and Class in Britain*,

Political Economy of Housing Workshop, London.

BODDY, M. and GRAY, F. (1979) Filtering theory, housing policy, and the legitimation of inequality, *Policy and Politics* **7**, 39-54.

BOURNE, L.S. (1976) Housing supply and market behaviour in residential development, In: *Spatial Processes and Form*, D.T. Herbert, R.J. Johnston, (Ed.). Wiley, London.

BUILDING SOCIETIES ASSOCIATION (1976) *Evidence Submitted by the BSA to the Housing Finance Review*, BSA, London.

BURGESS, E.W. (1967) The growth of the city: introduction to a research project, In: *The City*, R.E. PARK, and E.W. Burgess, Chicago University Press, Chicago (first published 1924).

BYRNE, D.S. (1978) Urban consciousness: a longer look at the politics of reproduction. Paper presented to the Institute of British Geographers Annual Conference, Hull, January.

DANIELS, C. (1974) The filtering process and its implications for housing policy, *Human Ecology Forum* 18-20.

DEPARTMENT OF THE ENVIRONMENT (1977a) Housing Policy: a Consultative Document (with a Technical Volume in Three Parts). HMSO, London.

DEPARTMENT OF THE ENVIRONMENT (1977b) Inner London: Policies for Dispersal and Balance Final Report of the Lambeth Inner Area Study. HMSO, London.

FISHER, E.M. and RATCLIFF, R.V. (1936) *European Housing Policy and Practice*, Federal Housing Administration, Washington DC.

FUERST, J.S. (1974) (Ed.). *Public Housing in Europe and America*, Croom Helm, London.

GAULDIE, E. (1974) *Cruel Habitations*, George Allen & Unwin, London.

GRAY, F. (1975) Non-explanation in urban geography, *Area* **7** (4), 228-235.

GRAY, F. (1976) The management of local authority housing, In: *Housing and Class in Britain*, Political Economy of Housing Workshop, London.

GREEN, G. and WILLIAMS, P.R. (1977) Some aspects of building society finance. Paper presented to the Political Economy of Housing Workshop.

GRIGSBY, W.G. (1963) *Housing Markets and Public Policy*, Philadelphia University Press, Philadelphia.

GRIGSBY, W.G. and ROSENBURG, L. (1975) *Urban Housing Policy*, APS Publications, New York.

HARVEY, D. (1974) Class monopoly rent, finance capital and the urban revolution, *Reg. Studies* **8**, 239-255.

HARVEY, D. (1975) The political economy of urbanization in advanced capitalist societies: the case of the United States, In: *The Social Economy of Cities*, G. Gappert, H.M. Rose (Ed.). Sage, London.

HERBERT, D.T. and JOHNSTON, R.J. (1976) (Ed.). *Spatial Processes and Form*, Wiley, London.

HOYT, H. (1939) *The Structure and Growth of Residential Neighbourhoods in American Cities*, Federal Housing Administration, Washington DC.

JOHNSTON, R.J. (1971) *Urban Residential Patterns*, Bell, London.

KIRBY, D.A. (1979) *Slum Housing and Residential Renewal: the Case of Urban Britain*, Longman, London.

LANSING, J.B., CLIFTON, C.V. and MORGAN, J.N. (1969) *New Homes and Poor People*, University of Michigan Institute for Social Research, Ann Arbor, Michigan.

LOWRY, I.S. (1970) Filtering and housing standards: a conceptual analysis, In: *Urban Analysis*, A.N. Page, W.R. Seyfried (Ed.). Scott, Foreman, New York.

MAHER, C.A. (1974) Spatial patterns in urban housing markets: filtering in Toronto, 1953-71. *Can. Geogr.* **18** (2), 108-124.

MARSHALL, H. (1933) *Slum*, Heinemann, London.

MASSEY, D. (1975) Behavioural research, *Area* **7** (3), 201-203.

MOORE, E.G. (1966) Models of migration and the intra-urban case, *Aust. N. Z. J. Sociol.* **2** (1), 16-37.

MURIE, A., HILLYARD, P., BIRRELL, D. and ROCHE, D. (1976) New building and housing needs, In: *Progress in Planning* Vol. 6, No. 2, Pergamon Press, Oxford.

MURIE, A. NINER, P. and WATSON, C. (1976) *Housing Policy and the Housing System*, George Allen & Unwin, London.

NATIONAL COMMISSION ON URBAN PROBLEMS (1968) *More Than Shelter: Social Needs in Low and Moderate Income Housing*, Prepared by George Scherner Associates. Washington DC.

NATIONAL COMMUNITY DEVELOPMENT PROJECT (1976) *Profits Against Houses*, London.

NORTH TYNESIDE COMMUNITY DEVELOPMENT PROJECT (1978) North Shields: working class politics and housing 1900-1977, Final Report Volume 1, North Tyneside.

PARK, R.E. and BURGESS, E.W. (1967) *The City*, Chicago University Press, Chicago (first published 1924).

POLITICAL ECONOMY OF HOUSING WORKSHOP (1975) *Political Economy and the Housing Question*, London.

POLITICAL ECONOMY OF HOUSING WORKSHOP (1976) *Housing and Class in Britain*, London.

PRESIDENT'S COMMITTEE ON URBAN HOUSING (1968) *A Decent Home*, Washington DC.

PRITCHARD, R.M. (1976) *Housing and the Spatial Structure of the City*, Cambridge, London.

RATCLIFF, R.U. (1949) *Urban Land Economics*, McGraw-Hill, New York.

ROBSON, B.T. (1973) A view on the urban scene, In: *Studies in Human Geography*, M. Chisholm, B. Rodgers (Ed.). Heinemann, London.

SANDS, G. (1976) Housing turnover: assessing its relevance to public policy, *Am. Inst. Plann. J.* October, 419-426.

SCHIFFERES, S. (1975) Council housing in the inter-war years. Paper presented to the Political Economy of Housing Workshop.

SIMMONS, J.W. (1968) Changing residence in the city. A review of intra-urban mobility, *Geogr Rev.* **58**, 622-651.

SLATER, D. (1975) The poverty of modern geographical enquiry, *Pacif. Viewpoint* **16**, 159-176.

SMITH, W.F. (1964) Filtering and neighbourhood change, University of California, Centre for Real Estate and Urban Economics, Research Report, 24.

STEDMAN-JONES, G. (1971) *Outcast London: A Study of the Relationship Between Classes in Victorian Society,* Penguin Books, Harmondsworth.

TARN, J.N. (1969) *Working-Class Housing in 19th Century Britain,* Lund Humphries for the Architectural Association, London.

TARN, J.N. (1973) *Five Per Cent Philanthropy,* Cambridge, London.

WATSON, C.J. (1973) Household movement in West Central Scotland: a study of housing chains and filtering, University of Birmingham, Centre for Urban and Regional Studies, Occasional Paper, 26.

WHITE, H.C. (1971) Multipliers, Vacancy chains, and filtering in housing, *Am. Inst. Plann. J.* 88-94

Index